	M			
	1936	1937		
	B	C	LIN
26 CLUBS			1
	£222	£362	2
	105	117	3
	63	12	4
	282	431	5
		4	6
	52	104	7
ANTEEN, ETC.	24	12	8
	30	53	9
	17	116	10
	11	31	11
	8	32	12
	16	149	13
	3	3	14
	9	63	15
	15	25	16

THE MOUNT STREET CLUB

First published in 2014 by
Foxrock Media Limited
2 Duncairn Terrace
Bray
County Wicklow
Ireland

General Editor: Dominic Perrem
Project Editor: Henry Dieterich
Designer: Sam Chelton

Cataloguing in Publication Data: a catalogue record
for this book is available from the British Library.

ISBN 978-1-78117-172-1

Printed in Ireland

THE MOUNT STREET CLUB

DUBLIN'S UNIQUE RESPONSE TO UNEMPLOYMENT
1934-PRESENT

Peter Somerville-Large * Mary E. Daly * Colin Murphy

LIST OF ABBREVIATIONS

CCDBI	Commissioners of Charitable Donations and Bequests for Ireland
CnG	Cuman na nGaedheal
Co.	County
DCLA	Dublin City Library & Archive, Pearse Street, Dublin 2
Dáil Éireann deb.	*Dáil Éireann, diosbóireachtai páirliaminte (parliamentary debates)*; *tuairisg oifigiúil (official report)*, (Dublin, Stationery Office)
MSC	Mount Street Club
NAI	National Archives of Ireland
Seanad Éireann deb.	*Dáil Éireann, diosbóireachtai páirliaminte (parliamentary debates)*; *tuairisg oifigiúil (official report)*, (Dublin, Stationery Office)
SVP	Society of St Vincent de Paul

ACKNOWLEDGEMENTS

The trustees of the Mount Street Club Trust would like to thank all the Mount Street Club members, governors, former trustees, managers, and those who served the club in an honorary capacity. The success and impact of the Mount Street Club was due to the hard work, enthusiasm, and generosity of all who became involved over the past eighty years.

The trustees would like to especially thank all those who have helped create this book: the contributors Peter Somerville-Large, Sarah Campbell, Colin Murphy, Prof. Mary E. Daly, and Sarah Perrem; Dominic Perrem, the editor who managed and oversaw the project; Henry Dieterich for his painstaking editing work; and Sam Chelton for designing the finished product, as well as all those who gave their time and support in providing information, memories, images, and other content which made this book possible.

The trustees would like to extend their appreciation to Oisín Quinn, Lord Mayor of Dublin, for his support.

The editor is most grateful to Dr Mary Clark and Deirdre O'Connell, archivists, Pearse Street Library, Dublin, for their generous help and support; Ms Orla Barry Murphy, Commissioners of Charitable Donations and Bequests for Ireland; the staff of Irish National Organisation of the Unemployed (INOU), One Parent Exchange & Network (OPEN), and Pobal; Mick Creedon, Ballymun Job Centre; Ciarán Walsh, Grow It Yourself (GIY); Dr Carmel Duggan, Work Research Centre (WRC); and the Mount Street Club Trust trustees for their kind assistance with collecting material and refreshing authors' memories.

The editor extends a special thanks to those who kindly responded by post, email, or telephone with personal or family stories about the activities of the club through the years.

The editor would like to extend his thanks to all those who kindly gave permission for images to be used in this history: Dublin City Libraries, Pearse Library Archive, The Irish Times, Mrs Faith Frankland, Helen Mountaine, and Mrs Anne Brew.

CONTENTS

TIMELINE FOR THE MOUNT STREET CLUB TRUST

November 1934	The Mount Street Club is established and a 25-year lease is taken on 81-82 Mount Street.
November 1935	Club is officially opened by Lord Mayor of Dublin Alfred Byrne and has 60 members.
1935	Dublin Corporation donates allotments in Sydney Parade and Merrion to the club.
July 1936	First annual day trip to Gormanston for 400 members, with train and refreshments provided.
1937	Legal aid bureau, sight testing and provision of glasses, and dental clinic provided to members.
1938	Membership of the club stands at 550.
1938	6,800 meals served in the club annually.
1938	Mount Street Club boxing club member wins Six Stone National Juvenile Championship of Éire. Boxing club has 37 members.
1938	Members build a handball court for their own use.
1933-1939	In 1933, 72,000 on weekly live register. By 1939 this number is 105,000.
January 1939	200,000th tally earned by member Jim Gallagher.
February 1939	Larkfield, Clondalkin is purchased to establish the Mount Street Club Farm.
December 1939	37 men reside and work full-time in the Mount Street Club Farm.
May 1939	First issue of *The Mount Street Club Journal* named *Tally-Ho*.
1940	297,049 tallies issued to members. Membership at an all-time peak.
1940	Similar club opens in Waterford.
1941	31 farm workers join the Irish Army during the Emergency.
1941	Club members cut turf in Lullymore, Co. Kildare, which is sold in the farm shop at 1 tally a bag.
1941	War shortages lead to difficulties in farm and club workshops with textiles and leather becoming unavailable.

1943	Club has 653 members.
1944	Governor Dr Piel establishes golf tournament and donates silver cup as trophy, later named the Piel Cup.
1950	Membership numbers dropping.
1958	146,729 tallies issued to members. Half the number issued in 1940.
1959	Lack of funds threatens Club's ability to function.
1960s	Mount Street Club Farm now a hostel housing older men who complete small farm jobs. Production is very low.
1960s	Mount Street Club premises now used as a day centre for elderly men and women in addition to running an informal casual labour exchange.
1970	18 remaining farm residents leave farm. Some are housed in city hostels at the club's expense. Their average age is 60.
1971	81-82 Mount Street premises is sold.
1972	Mount Street Club moves to 62-64 Fenian Street. Club membership and the gaining of casual work for members continues. Mount Street Club Farm is purchased by Dublin Corporation for housing development by means of a compulsory purchase order.
1973	Mount Street Club Farm finally closes.
1974	Plans for a hostel at 62-64 Fenian street are shelved.
1977	Women's Aid is contacted and offered a shelter for victims of domestic violence ('battered wives and their children') but finds alternative accommodation.
1979	Day Centre for physically disabled people is established in Fenian Street and supported by the Mount Street Club.
1980	Club is renamed the Mount Street Centre and considers changing its charitable objects. Name reverts to Mount Street Club in 1982.
1984	Casual work is no longer found for unemployed men. Club membership ceases completely.
1987	Supports the establishment of the Dublin Nautical Trust, later renamed the Irish Nautical Trust.

1991	Offices in 62-64 Fenian Street let to startup business and charities.
1990s	Plans to redevelop the Fenian Street premises into a hostel and community centre are scrapped due to planning issues and high costs.
2001-2004	The Club and Focus Ireland draw up plans to convert the Fenian Street premises into a Foyer style hostel. Loss of funding ends project planning.
2006	62-64 Fenian Street is sold.
2007	The Mount Street Club Trust is established. Its trustees are the existing trustees and governors.
2009-2013	MSCT funds a variety of innovative projects to benefit people who are unemployed and young children in disadvantaged families in the Greater Dublin area.

INTRODUCTION

Oisín Quinn, Lord Mayor of Dublin

I was delighted to be asked by the Board of the Mount Street Club Trust to prepare an Introduction to this important collection of essays. This book tells us the story of the men who had the philanthropic vision to establish the original Mount Street Club—a vision to empower unemployed men to make their own opportunities. More than that, it gives historic recognition to those men and their families who had the courage and fortitude to work together and build new lives by taking advantage of the opportunities presented. Importantly, the essays also bring forward lessons relevant to the challenges we face today, and I have no doubt that this publication will advance the cause of helping communities facing the challenge of unemployment and shed light on many of the innovative initiatives taking place in Dublin today, such as the community garden and allotment projects that will play a vital part on building the sustainable Dublin of the future. It is also interesting to have learned that a previous Lord Mayor and the Mansion House were able to play a role in launching the club.

This excellent collection of essays by five authors, Peter Somerville-Large, Sarah Campbell, Colin Murphy, Mary E. Daly, and Sarah Perrem, tells the story of the Mount Street Club Trust ('the club'), a Dublin-based charity, how it originated, and how it has evolved to the present day. The story is interwoven with historical context told in an insightful and enjoyable way.

Dublin in the 1930s was scarred by extreme poverty, unemployment, and housing decay. The initiative for the club began with the vision of two Dubliners, Jim Waller and Paddy Somerville-Large, of providing a social, recreational, and occupational club for unemployed men. A dilapidated old hotel at 81 and 82 Lower Mount Street was found and refurbished in 1934 so as to provide warm, cheerful rooms where members could eat, read, and write.

Its stables and outbuildings were converted to workshops and premises from which work and physical exercise could take place.

The club was founded upon an ideal of self-sufficiency and personal advancement through the opportunity to work for assistance rather than to be given a hand-out. Its founders aimed to create an enterprise in which a man's hours of service were accorded worth in the form of tallies. These could be exchanged for food, clothing, furniture, and fuel through the Mount Street Club Shop.

Of its nature, membership was intended to be temporary, as the objective was that those who participated would be strengthened in their abilities to secure paid employment. During their period of unemployment, members were empowered through the club to raise the standard of living for themselves and their dependants by their co-operative efforts.

The club was opened by my distinguished predecessor, Alfie Byrne, TD, on 5 November 1935 and in the following years the Mansion House was used for its annual meetings.

In its first decade the club thrived and rapidly expanded its activities beyond the precinct of Mount Street. Starting from a membership of 60 and rising quickly to 550, its members transformed wastelands at Sydney Parade and Merrion to lush and highly productive vegetable gardens. Such was the uptake and interest generated during its first four years that the Club was emboldened to acquire its own farm, Larkfield House, situated on 120 acres in what was then leafy countryside just outside Clondalkin Village.

In 1941 club members operated a highly efficient turf cutting enterprise at Lullymore, Co. Kildare, producing the fuel needs of its members, their families, and members of the public at a time of acute fuel shortages.

In later decades the club experienced a changed environment including that of the improved economic outlook in other countries which led to significant emigration and also changes in the social welfare provision in Ireland. By the early 1970s the Mount Street Club Farm at Larkfield House had been compulsorily purchased and the old club premises at Mount Street were no longer in significant use. The club acquired a new premises in Fenian Street from which a day activity centre was operated by the Eastern Health Board and provided a valuable day resource for people with disabilities for more than twenty years.

The club diversified its activities in the mid-1980s and was instrumental in many community initiatives aimed at revitalising that part of Dublin located around the Grand Canal Basin and particularly through its work in funding the establishment of the Irish Nautical Trust in 1987. The Irish Nautical Trust has been a significant driver of regeneration in the Grand Canal Basin, helping to revive traditional seafaring skills in the Ringsend area. It converted a retired Aran Islands passenger ferry, the *Naomh Éanna*, to a microenterprise centre. It built a replica of one of the first ever catamarans, the 'Simon and Jude,' and ultimately the trust acquired the *Mary Stanford*, a lifeboat from Ballycotton, Co. Cork, which had been involved in an extraordinary rescue. The restoration of the *Mary Stanford* remains an unfulfilled objective.

In 2006 the club sold its property in Fenian Street at the height of the property bubble. Its newfound relative wealth and earlier cessation of its core activity prompted the club to evolve and rewrite its objects and thus embark on a new phase in its civic contribution.

With the approval of the Commissioners of Charitable Donations and Bequests for Ireland, the Mount Street Club Trust was established in 2007.

Over the past six years the club has provided significant financial help to a broad range of organisations that are involved in combating unemployment and the effects of poverty. The initiatives that it is supporting demonstrate the evolution of interventions which are considered to be effective in the relief of poverty. At the core of the Club's ethos is the empowerment of people through collective effort. Three of its most significant projects are:

• The National Early Years Access Initiative, which focuses on children in the free pre-school years and is attempting to identify the factors that can improve the skills and capacity of childcare staff, and how this, in turn, influences each child's development outcomes. The trust is co-funding this initiative in partnership with Atlantic Philanthropies, the Department of Education and Skills, and the Department of Children and Youth Affairs. The initiative is administered by Pobal.

• The Mount Street Trust Employment Initiative, in which three voluntary organisations have developed and implemented specially designed innovative measures to support the labour market integration of specific vulnerable groups among the long-term unemployed. The initiative is administered by WRC–Social and Economic Consultants Limited, on behalf of the trust.

• The Community Growers Fund, which has supported community groups involving unemployed people in a community garden or allotment project. This project, together with First Step, an initiative to support the development of start-up entrepreneurs in the South Inner City of Dublin, is administered on behalf of the trust by the Community Foundation for Ireland.

The Mount Street Club Trust is an early example of social entrepreneurship brought about by philanthropic-minded people. Its evolution, enabled through the realisation of its capital resources, has involved recognition that its philanthropic endeavours are best carried out now, at one remove. This is being done through investment in organisations that have the skills and knowhow to challenge the complex impediments to equality of opportunity in access to education and employment for all who live in the greater Dublin area.

I congratulate the authors and the board on this immensely valuable collection and thank them for their contribution to the city, and I commend the endeavours of the club and all involved in the realisation of its objectives.

Oisín Quinn
Lord Mayor of Dublin
13 November 2013

THE GENESIS OF AN IDEAL

I

Peter Somerville-Large

The Mount Street Club, launched at the end of 1934, and officially opened by the Lord Mayor of Dublin a year later, aimed at easing unemployment in Dublin.

Nineteen thirty-two had seen a change in government, with Fianna Fáil, under the leadership of Éamon de Valera, defeating Cumann na nGaedheal which had ruled Ireland since the initiation of the Irish Free State a decade previously. Cumann na nGaedheal's fiscal policies had been prudent to a degree that its social programmes had proved inadequate. Its richer supporters were protected, while it had done little to protect the poor; on the contrary old age pensions had been reduced by a shilling a week, while means testing among the unemployed had been made more difficult.

Fianna Fáil had been elected largely because of a commitment to social reform; the new government rapidly put into law a number of measures aimed at easing poverty. When the Unemployment Assistance Act of 1933 was passed, almost a quarter of a million people applied for assistance during its first year. In the same year the National Health Insurance Act created a single insurance society on which all members could draw. Old age pensions were increased and pensions for widows and orphans introduced in 1935. Fianna Fáil built twelve thousand local authority houses a year compared with Cumann na nGaedheal's two thousand.

In November 1934, the same month in which the Mount Street Club was conceived, 108,742 men in Ireland out of a population of just under three million were out of work. Because of the world depression, the unemployed were unable to take advantage of emigration, the usual escape from poverty. Since there was so little opportunity abroad, particularly in the United Kingdom, over seven thousand people returned in 1932 to a country where virtually no work was on offer. For the fortunate, the civil service, breweries, or railways might still be reliable employers, but a casual day's work was the best that many city dwellers could hope for.

Poverty was so widespread that throughout the state 43,000 families, amounting to 125,000 people, were living in one-roomed dwellings. In Dublin, in the overcrowded tenements, the rent of a room in a battered Georgian house averaged between three and six shillings a week. Conditions in these 'coffin boxes' were spartan. Furniture might consist of a few chairs, stools or wooden boxes.

A serious problem of tenement life was huge families. Many children slept together in a bed, if they had a bed, but often they lay on straw mattresses on the floor. Nearly all tenements had one lavatory in the yard for a building that often housed more than eighty people. Those who lived upstairs used a slop bucket hidden in the corner or out in a hallway. There would be the one tap for bathing or for the nightmare weekly laundry when water had to be hauled up by buckets and heated over the open fire. Women worked heroically at cleanliness, scrubbing the stairs outside and fighting the smells seeping up from below. Lighting was from candles or paraffin oil lamps, while cooking was done over an open fire. Those who were unfortunate to live in basement rooms lived in semi-darkness, even at midday.[1]

Inadequate diet contributed to a high mortality rate resulting from overcrowding, lack of sanitation, rats, cockroaches, and general filth. The diet of the poor included, in addition to the obligatory bread, porridge, and tea, ham parings, bacon pieces, whiting, herring, mackerel, pigs' tails, and elder or cow's udder.[2]

In 1932 it was noticed by the child and maternity welfare section of Dublin Corporation that many babies were dying in the first month of life, because of ignorance about health and the general conditions in which expectant mothers

1. Kevin C. Kearns, *Dublin tenement life: an oral history* (Dublin, 1994), pp. 27-29.

2. Ibid., pp. 30-34.

were living. The infant mortality rate of 7 percent was high by European standards. Children tended to be undersized and suffering from rickets; they were threatened with diphtheria, whooping cough, pneumonia, and diarrhoea. In summer more babies and young children died from diseases spread by flies thriving on horse dung. Tuberculosis would remain a killer up until the 1950s.

The struggle for economic survival was aided by moneylenders and pawnshops—there were nearly fifty pawnshops in Dublin throughout the 1930s. The great day was Monday, when suits worn for Sunday Mass went back into pawn. Unsurprisingly, many men drank.

Dr Robert Collis, who would found the Marrowbone Lane Club during the early years of the Second World War, or, as it was known in Ireland, the Emergency, wrote to the *Irish Press* in October 1936: 'Dubliners are wont to describe their city affectionately as "an old lady" when visitors admire her outer garment—the broad streets, the 18th century houses…they…feel proud. Lift the hem of her outer silken garments, however, and you will find suppurating ulcers covered by stinking rags, for Dublin has the foulest slums of any town in Europe.'[3]

Of course there were many charities that struggled to relieve poverty, like the long-established Sisters of Charity or the Herald Boot Fund formed by Dublin businessmen which donated boots and socks to barefooted children.[4] (A danger for the barefooted was gangrene from an open wound contacting infected horse dung.)

The largest and best known charitable organisation was the Society of St Vincent de Paul, founded in Paris in 1833, and named after a sixteenth century saint. St Vincent's was introduced into Ireland in 1844, and for almost a century had done sterling work to help the poor by immediate monetary assistance, or by such means as dockets for a daily loaf of bread.[5]

The Mount Street Club came into being at a time when there was a new spirit striving for social improvement. However, its members never considered their creation a charity. When the idea of the club was first proposed, the organisers stated that 'if we are to avoid the mental and physical deterioration of large numbers of our people through unemployment (as we understand the term), they must be given work. Put in the simplest terms our proposals are… that it should be made possible for the unemployed to employ themselves in the production of their own necessities.'[6]

Unfortunately, the original memoranda of the Mount Street Club are now lost, but its creation was remembered in detail by the founders. The initial plan was simply to create a place where unemployed men 'could go in out of the rain, sit down and have a read of the daily paper.'[7] But soon a philosophy evolved 'based on the assumption that decent men wanted to work.' The basic idea developed to a far more elaborate concept, advocating self-help co-operative principles and Utopian ideas reaching back to those advocated by Robert Owen at his Scottish mills at New Lanark in the early nineteenth century.

The founders of the club

The group that started the club in 1934 was dominated by two personalities with strong ideas and opinions, who became the initial trustees. They were both engineers encumbered with lengthy Anglo-Irish names: Major James Hardress de Warrenne Waller, known to many as 'Jim,' and Philip Townsend Somerville-Large, referred to by colleagues and friends as 'Paddy.'

James Waller was a brilliant and innovative engineer who has been described by the architectural historian Jeremy Williams as a neglected Irish genius.[8] He was born on a farm in Tasmania in 1884, the eleventh and youngest son of George Waller, heir to Prior Park, an Irish Palladian mansion near Nenagh in Co. Tipperary, who had emigrated to Australia. After working as a sheep

3. Dr Robert Collis to the *Irish Press*, 3 October 1936; quoted ibid., p. ix.

4. Kearns, *Dublin tenement life*, p. 34.5. Ibid., pp. 30-31, 169-70.

6. Judith Kiernan and Brian Harvey, 'The Mount Street Club: past, present and future,' November 1994 (DCLA, Ar/add/81/130).

7. Ibid.

8. Jeremy Williams, 'An Irish genius: J H de W Waller 1884-1968,' *Irish Arts Review* xii (1996), pp. 143-6.

James Waller

farmer and a miner, young Waller left Australia and came to Ireland to study engineering in Galway and Cork.

During the First World War he served with the Corps of Royal Engineers and was awarded a DSO and an OBE. While serving in Salonika, he developed what became his Nofrango system, the coating of tents with cement slurry, which developed into lightweight concrete. At the same time he built a jetty out of baskets filled with rocks, a system that he never patented although it has been used widely since. Just before the Armistice in 1918 he launched a thousand-tonne concrete barge named the *Cretarch*, which ended up on a French inland waterway.

After the war Waller was working in Iraq, where he came upon the great self-supporting sixth-century banqueting hall at Ctesiphon near Baghdad, which still seems to hang in mid air. It is the first inverted catenary vault ever devised. He adapted the idea as a building technique which he christened Ctesiphon, where huge curved areas are framed with hessian covered with liquid concrete or plaster and no supporting pillars are needed. The Irish Architectural Archive has a photographic album illustrating around five hundred Ctesiphon structures built under Waller's direction.

He devised further architectural inventions which were deployed worldwide. In Ireland, his most significant piece of surviving architecture is the Locke's Whiskey Bonded Warehouse in Kilbeggan, Co. Westmeath, which still amazes visitors to Ireland's oldest distillery; Jeremy Williams describes it as 'a colossal congested black jellyfish on a small island.'[9]

Through Waller's interest in cheap housing—a scheme designed by him survives at Loreto Avenue in Rialto—he became increasingly aware of the spectre of unemployment. In Dublin he was a partner of a contemporary named Alfred Delap, whose son, Hugh Delap, was a brother-in-law of Paddy Somerville-Large. Hugh Delap would play a major part in the development of the club, of which he would become one of its governors.

9. Ibid., p. 146.

Fifteen years younger than Waller, Paddy Somerville-Large was born in 1900 in Dublin, although he had a West Cork background. His cousin was the writer Edith Somerville. In 1922 he qualified as a civil engineer at Trinity College Dublin, after which he joined the Great Southern Railways Company, rising to be chief railway engineer.

His first assignments were the rebuilding of bridges destroyed during the Civil War, an experience that left him with a lifelong disapproval of de Valera, whom he blamed for the violence. In 1930 he advised the Great Northern Railway on the rebuilding of the Boyne Viaduct, where wrought-iron work was replaced with steel girders without interruption to the service. Castigating the memory of the great engineer Isambard Kingdom Brunel who located the railway around Bray Head, Paddy organised, with the help of an improvised rope chair, the buttressing of the line, which was in continual danger from erosion. In the 1960s he was involved in the building of the first drive-on ferry at Rosslare. Late in his career he strongly opposed the closing of the Harcourt Street railway line, correctly foreseeing its need when suburban development came to areas along the vanished line at Dundrum, Stillorgan, Foxrock, Carrickmines, and Shankill.[10]

Coming from an affluent background, throughout his life Paddy displayed a practical generosity. He consistently followed the advice of his father, a clergyman, who wrote: 'give all you can afford to relieve distress, but never lend, since the borrower always avoids and dislikes the man who has lent him money.' He supplied vital funding to the Irish Country Women's Association and its flagship, the Country Shop, and before the start of the Second World War lent his house to refugees from Germany and Austria. He gave initial money to the club, and five years later, in 1938, he and his brother, Becher Somerville-Large, would supply the finance that enabled the purchase of Larkfield, the Mount Street Club farm.

Many good ideas begin in the simplest way, and without doubt the initiative

10. Henry Boylan, ed., *A dictionary of Irish biography* (Dublin, 1998), pp. 406-7.

The first Board of Governors. November 1934.

Paddy Somerville-Large. 1964.

for the founding of the Mount Street Club came from discussions between these two men and a further group of concerned friends appalled by the poverty they saw around them. It is now impossible to verify whether it was Waller or Somerville-Large who put forward the club's structure. One would guess that the basic scheme came from the restless and energetic mind of Waller, a man who is remembered as having 'thousands of ideas.'

Robert Owen's co-operative philosophy

The planning of the club was heavily influenced by the early nineteenth century co-operative and socialist ideas of the Welshman Robert Owen.[11] In 1810 Owen took over the running of New Lanark in Scotland, a group of vast cotton mills near Glasgow which employed two thousand people, including hundreds of children brought there from poorhouses in Glasgow and Edinburgh. When Owen first arrived at New Lanark, children from as young as five were working for thirteen hours a day in the textile mills. He stopped employing children under ten and reduced their labour to ten hours a day, decisions which were regarded at the time as extraordinarily liberal. Before he took over the mills, conditions among workers enduring long hours and drudgery were deplorable. Education and sanitation were neglected, families lived in one room, and drunkenness was common.

This wretched situation would change under Owen's direction. His principles, which he would lay out in a series of books and pamphlets, had a basic simplicity—if you treated your workers well, not only would they benefit, but commercial success would also be assured. His ideas of reform were not original, since they had been tried out elsewhere in Europe. But their success, and his insistence on the importance of the formation of men's characters from their earliest years, had a far-reaching influence. His workers became healthy and content and their relationship with their boss remained excellent; drunkenness and illegitimacy became almost unknown. New Lanark

11. R. A. Davis and F. J. O'Hagan, *Robert Owen* (London, 2010).

made money. Under Owen's direction its operations developed with such satisfaction that over the years it attracted visitors who included statesmen, social reformers, and even Nicholas, later the czar of Russia.

Among Owen's innovations that attracted Waller's attention was his use of 'tallies' or tokens for the exchange of goods. He opened a shop where his workers could buy items of good quality at little more than wholesale prices. Many employers of the time operated what was known as the 'truck' system, whereby workers had to buy shoddy goods at top prices. Outside New Lanark the 'truck' system was to continue up until the 1830s when it was stopped by legislation.

Owen's practice of selling quality goods at basic prices and passing on savings to his workers formed the basic ideas for the co-operative stores that continue to this day. Many of his ideas were imitated elsewhere in Britain and America with varying degrees of success. In the twentieth century the Kibbutz movement in Israel was based to some extent on Owenite community plans.

In Ireland in the early nineteenth century one such experiment at Ralahine in Co. Clare worked as well as anything devised by Owen, but lasted for a pitifully short time. Owen first visited Ireland in 1822, invited by a group of progressive landlords. In the following year he returned to give a series of lectures on his ideas about communal peace and prosperity. Listening to him in the audience was an unsteady landowner with a gambling problem named John Scott Vandeleur. He owned an estate in Co. Clare named Ralahine which consisted of 618 acres of which a third were cultivated, the rest being rough pasture and bog.[12]

Vandeleur must have listened carefully to Owen and absorbed his ideas. However, he did nothing about them for a number of years until agrarian unrest reached a dangerous degree in Co. Clare. In 1831 a house on the Ralahine estate was raided by a group of terrorists dressed as women who called themselves Lady Clare's Boys and shot dead Vandeleur's steward.[13] This incident convinced Ralahine's landlord that the solution to agrarian unrest was a commune similar to those he had heard about from Owen's lectures nine years before.

He invited over from England an eccentric socialist named Thomas Craig who agreed to become secretary of the Ralahine Agricultural and Manufacturing Co-operative Association. Craig and his wife Mary, who hadn't a word of Irish between them, were coming to 'the most disturbed and lawless place in Ireland.' Within six weeks of their arrival four murders had taken place locally, and Craig himself was told a grave was waiting for him.[14] Nevertheless, for a very short time he made a startling success of the Ralahine enterprise.

The commune he developed consisted of fifty-two members in its first year, far fewer than the Owenite recommendation of five hundred individuals. It included a number of children and orphans. In its second year the numbers would increase to eighty-one. Craig stressed the importance of education and introduced innovations such as a potato washer, a horse-drawn reaping machine, and a huge ash-lavatory whose contents could be wheeled away into the bog. The latter was said to have saved the commune from the cholera epidemic of 1831.[15]

Craig wrote, 'The perfect health and freedom from disease of our members were the results of combined causes—sanitary precautions, nourishing diet, cleanliness, and the happy cheerfulness and contentment arising from our social surroundings, dances, and weekly amusements.'[16] He wrote proudly how Ralahine 'became as "a city set on a hill" and attracted the attention of men

---

12. James Connolly, 'An Irish Utopia' in Edward Thomas Craig, *An Irish commune: the experiment at Ralahine, County Clare, 1831–1833*, with essays by James Connolly (1910) and Cormac Ó Gráda (1974) (Blackrock, 1983), pp. 183-4.

13. Craig, *An Irish commune*, p. 11. The principal text is *The Irish land and labour question, illustrated in the history of Ralahine* (London, 1893), an account written by Craig in his old age, republished in an abridged form in Dublin in 1920.

14. Ibid., p. 21.

15. Ibid., p. 83.

16. Ibid., p. 84.

of all classes.' Like those who went to New Lanark to observe Robert Owen's reforms, at Ralahine 'noblemen, landlords, thinkers, and writers visited us to discover how far our system would promise a solution of the difficulties with which Ireland was afflicted.'[17]

At Ralahine alcohol, tobacco, and snuff were banned, together with the use of nicknames. Gambling in any form was forbidden.[18] The prohibition of gambling at Ralahine was deeply ironic, since Vandeleur's own habit led to the collapse of the commune in its third year when its members were evicted after Vandeleur had lost all his possessions. They were left to struggle in their own miseries, while Craig and his wife returned to England where Craig had a long career over most of the nineteenth century, engaging in leftist political movements. James Waller was aware of the Ralahine enterprise; there is an account of the short-lived experiment in the Mount Street Club's *Journal* of March 1941.

Setting up the club

Initially those who supported Waller in the founding of the Mount Street Club, who would become its governors, consisted of members of the professional class, mostly in business, described as 'busy men employed in various capacities giving all their available time to this experiment of several years.' Paddy Somerville-Large became the chairman and J. J. Newcome the secretary. For the first year there were twelve governors, the majority of whom were Protestant; among the exceptions were Newcome; Father William Burke of St Andrews, Westland Row; and Terence de Vere White, who acted as the club's solicitor prior to taking up a literary career. The growing diversity of the governors is evident in a list published in 1938 which includes a harbour master, an ex-tea planter, various parish priests, and even a train driver. By that year a third of governors were Catholic.

From the beginning it was stressed that the club should be strictly nonsectarian as well as nonpolitical. The founders stressed that their aim was to tackle unemployment. They considered that 'the evils caused by prolonged unemployment—mental and spiritual depression and distress, loss of hope and health, demoralisation and plain hunger and cold suffered by the unemployed themselves and their families; the enormous loss to the community in terms of manpower, skill and production—are evils of the first magnitude.'[19]

The governors would oversee the members of the club, although the members themselves would be responsible for its running, and would themselves decide who was worthy of admission. According to the initial pamphlet published at the time of the formal opening at the end of 1935, they would enjoy the amenities of 'a social, recreational, occupational Club which caters specially for the needs of the unemployed and casually employed men.' By their own initiative members would 'find occupation for their wasted hours and so keep themselves fit.'[20]

A premises would have to be found for them. It was Waller who discovered a dilapidated old hotel at 81 and 82 Lower Mount Street, which, the governors decided, would initially be rented on a twenty-five year lease. The location in Mount Street was considered excellent—a short distance away from the slums, yet central. An early photograph shows a handsome-looking building with large bay windows. The hotel consisted of two adjoining houses, each with three floors and a basement as well as stables and outbuildings which were perfect for conversion to workshops, and premises for physical exercise and games. The actual hotel rooms were large and would provide 'the comforts of warm, cheerful club rooms' where members would be able to read and write. Importantly, members would be served one square meal a day. Hot baths would also be provided.

Such plans were all very well, but the houses were in terrible condition.

---

17. Ibid., p. 79.

18. Ibid., pp. 33-42.

19. *The Mount Street Club—with introduction by The Right Hon. Lord Mayor of Dublin Ald. Alfred Byrne, TD* (November 1935).

20. Ibid.

Renting was a matter of courage, since, according to J. J. Newcome, 'we had no money, only ideas.'[21] He remembered how 'it was a very wet day when we went to take over possession and the condition of the outer offices was deplorable—a large hall at the rear of what was formerly livery stables was roofless and the whole scene depressing enough to give us the "willies." However, we were now committed and there was nothing else to do but try to get going.'

The wretched appearance of number 81 gave Waller the idea for a popular joke, which was immediately adopted to much hilarity. 'Jim was determined that it should not convey a gloomy picture, or contain any suggestion of charity or re-habilitation...The most exclusive and self-regarding society in the city was probably the Kildare Street Club. So Jim suggested to the Board of Governors that the new venture should be called "The Mount Street Club." The name was adopted by unanimous acclaim and Dublin had gained another famous club.'[22] A number of the governors were themselves associated with the Kildare Street Club.

The dilapidated condition of the premises is evident from the various tenders and specifications offered to the governors. Many of the roof timbers were rotten. Slating, flashing, replacing of gutters were necessary, in addition to repairs to boundary walls.

Waller not only supervised the work of restoring the building, but was also able to persuade a group of contractors to work for the club without much recompense. His biographer described his method.

> In order to get the help needed to do these things the technique was to ask, for instance, the Master Builders to send representatives to a meeting, explain to them the idea, and offer them the privilege of assisting—by doing the necessary reconstruction work free of

21. J. J. Pollard, 'The origins of Mount Street—work to do,' *The Mount Street Club Journal* (1945).
22. Ibid.

The Mount Street Club, 81 Lower Mount Street.

81 Lower Mount Street. 1938.

charge! And it was in this way that the building was re-wired, heating installed, the whole building painted, and even a radio provided! The organisations concerned were rewarded by seats on the Board of Governors and a good deal of incidental publicity. Jim was a tremendous salesman for this idea; he wrote copiously on the subject, addressed meetings and bullied his friends into helping. His trump card was to offer them the privilege of doing something constructive.[23]

Electrical and radio traders were rounded up, together with drapers and heating and plumbing engineers. At the same time work was found for a considerable number of unemployed men. Waller's tactics resulted in the acquisition of 'such commodities as building materials, carpenter's materials, drapery, leather, tools, coal, bread, newspapers and provisions of different kinds.' With little money the governors were able to achieve their initial objective in just over a year. The speed and enthusiasm of Waller and his cofounders in obtaining outside help bordered on the miraculous.

Contributors included the Master Builders' and House Builders' Associations who carried out extensive repair work. The Electrical Contractors' Association supplied electricians for rewiring and lighting. Central heating came from the Heating and Ventilating Engineers' Association. A number of firms, including A. H. Masser Ltd, T. G. Bedwell, Messrs Stewart and Lloyds and Messrs Potter Cowan, as well as the Merchant Drapers' Association, contributed large quantities of materials, while timber was obtained from the Timber Importers' Association. Waller also stated that 'a host' of private individuals 'have given us quantities of most valuable second-hand materials, as well as financial assistance.' They included the Royal Institute of Architects, Woolworths, and Messrs Crean, soap manufacturers.[24]

By the official opening at the end of 1935 the premises consisting of 81 and 82 Lower Mount Street was rewired, repainted, and equipped with central heating. Near the kitchen was a large dining room or main hall which could, in due course, seat several hundred men. Workshops were equipped; there was a barber's shop, a small laundry, and a gymnasium with attendant showers. The buildings were put on display to the public, who could inspect them between ten-thirty in the morning and six-thirty in the evening. 'We most heartily invite all who are interested or even casually curious to take an early opportunity of visiting the club.'[25] With any luck some of these visitors might contribute to its upkeep.

The principles of the club

Initially the club's aims were modest. It did not pretend to cure unemployment, but 'by providing the means whereby unwanted hours may be profitably and pleasantly spent' it could 'appreciably supplement the measures at present taken by the State.' It would attract a membership of two hundred men by stages, fifty at the outset.

The club would be run on five principles. The first principle stated that the club was to be managed by the members and for the members, acting through a house committee elected every six months. However, 'general control will be exercised by the Governors' Committee.' This required explanation. 'To a certain degree…the Governors are trustees for the public, hence the provision that general control shall be exercised by them. The real function of the Governors is to arrange for the provision of the means by which the normal activities of the Club can be pursued.' The control and management of the club would be vested in the governors. They could be pleased that a start had been made and the club would open with a small number of members enrolled by the end of 1934.

The second principle emphasised that the club would not be run on the lines of a charitable institution. 'Each member will pay a weekly subscription

23. Ibid.

24. Ibid.

25. *The Mount Street Club* (1935).

and also for his meals, games and any materials he may use in the occupational activities of the Club such as carpentry, etc.'

The third principle declared that 'payment by members were to be made by service. Standard coin: one hour's service.' This principle, the basis of the tally system, was considered to be of the greatest importance. Members of the club would pay for their needs and material benefits, not in cash, but in time. Hours worked per week rather than any rate of payment per hour would be the earnings of what was first described as 'special currency.'

It was Waller, with Robert Owen and Thomas Craig in mind, who came up with the idea of using, instead of cash, a 'tally' which was earned for an hour's work. At Ralahine, Craig, following Owen's idea, had been responsible for a system of tokens or 'Labour Notes' with which the members of the commune were paid. As Owen had recommended, they could be used to buy goods on the premises, or exchanged for money if members wished. The Ralahine 'Labour Notes,' which could be converted into money on demand, were printed on pieces of cardboard, representing one day's, a half-day's, a quarter-day's, an eight-of-a-day's or a sixteenth-of-a-day's labour.[26] This form of barter would be noted by Waller and adapted for the Mount Street Club. Tallies earned by members would have no value outside the club.

A member of the club would initially pay one tally for his subscription, and one tally a week thereafter. Accumulated tallies in excess of the subscription, each representing an hour's work, would be exchanged for food, clothing, tobacco, and a range of commodities and services which in the following years would greatly increase.

Because of tallies, it was claimed that money from outside went much further than if it was paid directly to an unemployed man. Waller's biographer explained how 'one pound might buy a pair of shoes, but could also buy the materials for three pairs made by the members and paid for by them in time and labour.'

It was important that work done by members should not affect outside industry and employment and antagonise unions, who were later hostile to the club's ideals. The inward nature of the tally system, a currency confined to members, would ensure that commodities made within the club would not compete with goods produced in normal industry.

As the basis of the club's economics, bringing in a large measure of freedom from outside support, the unusual idea of the tally was also important in attracting the attention of the press. The novelty of this paper currency had a news value that would repeatedly appeal to the public reading of it in press reports. The tally system would continue until well after the Second World War, ceasing sometime in the mid-sixties.

The fourth principle of the club stated that the club would be financed 'as far as possible without appealing to private firms or persons.' It was emphatically distancing itself from charity. 'It is felt…that many who would support it individually are already doing all that their means will allow to help old established and more deserving charities. There was no intention of benefiting the unemployed at the expense of the old and the sick.'

Groups, rather than individuals, would unite to provide the club's needs, and guarantee the club's running expenses 'both in cash and kind.' A fine line was drawn between charitable donations and such voluntary contributions and from the beginning the distinction seems fairly blurred. But already it was seen to be working, since Waller had nudged the Master Builders' and Housebuilders' Associations into rebuilding a large part of the club's premises, in the year before the club was launched.

The members were faced with a formidable set of rules, over thirty of them, of which the most important embodied the fifth of the five principles: 'The Club shall be non-sectarian and non-political, and any member taking part in any religious or political discussion on the premises shall be expelled.'

Alcoholic liquor and gambling would not be allowed on the premises. The governors had observed how Dublin was in the midst of a gambling craze where queues of poverty-stricken men and women waited outside betting

26. Craig, *An Irish commune*, pp. 74-5.

THE MOUNT STREET CLUB
81 LOWER MOUNT STREET - DUBLIN

Do You Know
THAT THERE ARE STILL 100,000 MEN WITHOUT WORK IN THIS COUNTRY?

Why
SHOULD THESE MEN NOT CONTRIBUTE TO THEIR OWN SUPPORT AND THAT OF THEIR DEPENDENTS?

You Are Asked
TO CONSIDER THE POINTS SET FORTH IN THIS SHORT FOLDER—

To Support
A MOVEMENT THAT HAS BEEN PROVED CAPABLE OF ENABLING MEN WHO ARE UNEMPLOYED TO CREATE WEALTH BY CO-OPERATIVE METHODS.

The Mount Street Club
AIMS AT PUTTING UNEMPLOYED MEN IN A POSITION TO PRODUCE THEIR OWN REQUIREMENTS AND THEREBY TO CONTRIBUTE MATERIALLY TO THE WELFARE OF THE WHOLE COMMUNITY.

★ *"Unemployment is fundamentally the most serious of all the problems that this country must face in consequence of the War."*—MR. LEMASS.

★ *"Social services should always aim at preserving self-respect and independence.... There is a danger that certain forms of charity may demoralise and encourage people to persist in the ways of shiftlessness. Care is needed to prevent undiscriminating forms of charity."*
—THE MOST REV. DR. BROWNE, Bishop of Galway.

Mount Street Club Appeal leaflet. 1942.

saloons, and groups of unemployed played cards for high stakes along the docks, scenes which were taken for granted.

John Cullinan, appointed resident superintendent at the outset, whose salary was paid by the governors, was made responsible for the day-to-day running of the club, for the behaviour of its members, and for assisting and directing them in their duties and activities. He worked with the house committee, and between them they were responsible for discipline and supervisory duties, in addition to advising the governors. He lived on the premises with his wife and daughter; the latter, like her father, was employed by the club and received a salary. No members of the club actually lived in Mount Street, but would attend there on the days of the week that suited them.

A memorandum was prepared addressed 'to all whom it may concern, that is, to every citizen of Dublin.' It revealed that prior to the club's opening the governors had obtained sufficient funding to pay the rent, and meet running expenses for some months after the official launch. In due course there would be arrangements for 'indoor games, such as cards, chess, dominoes etc.' In the stables and out-buildings where, it was envisaged, there would be space for 'games, physical exercises, music, and such occupations as carpentry, boot repairs etc.' was accommodation for a laundry, a barber's shop and bathing facilities. A gymnasium would be fitted with a shower bath. In addition, 'benches will be equipped at which the members may repair their furniture and make new furniture for their homes, and facilities will be given for them to repair their boots and those of their families.'[27] These plans were formulated well before the Mount Street Club's official opening in November 1935.

The opening of the club

The Mount Street Club for the Unemployed opened formally at its premises at 81 Lower Mount Street, Dublin, on 5 November 1935 at 5p.m. By that date the buildings had been renovated and the club itself had been functioning

27. Ibid.

for over a year. From a start of twelve members it had recruited sixty men who, through the tally system, had been able to produce a large share of necessities for themselves and their families. Compared to official unemployment statistics, the number might seem piteously inadequate, but at this stage the actions of the club were considered justified in keeping even a small number of Dublin's unemployed off the streets and giving them the means to do something to help themselves. The idea was appealing, and already there was a waiting list for those who wished to apply and to follow the strict rules that governed their qualification for membership.

The ceremony was conducted by the lord mayor of Dublin, Alfred Byrne, TD, known for his charitable works among Dublin's poor. He is remembered as a small dapper man with a three-piece suit and a fob watch and chain straddling his waistcoat. A pointed grey moustache and shining patent leather shoes contributed to his elegant appearance, enhanced on such an occasion by his sparkling chain of office, a dazzling piece of what would now be described as 'bling.'[28]

Byrne's support for the club was emphasised by the introduction he wrote to the booklet specially published to coincide with the opening. In the following years, he would allow the use of the Mansion House for the club's annual meetings.[29]

The large attendance at the opening included members of the Dáil and Senate and members of the public, among them Kathleen Clarke, the widow of the revolutionary leader Tom Clarke, the artist Jack B. Yeats, and the young Erskine Childers, whose father had been shot during the civil war. After a speech by Byrne, Paddy Somerville-Large, the chairman of the board of governors, outlined the club's initial history, affirming that 'they were trying to fill a man's day instead of his night, and to keep unemployed men off the streets and let them see they could do something for themselves.' He emphasised that

28. *Irish Times*, 5 November 1935.

29. *Irish Times*, 18 January 1939.

<u>SERVICE REQUIRED OF MEMBERS.</u>

From the foregoing it will be appreciated that each
member will be required to work at least eight hours per week
in order to pay his subscription and for one meal per day.
The work available will be domestic duty inside the club:
such as preparing and cooking food, cleaning and decorating,
clerical work, hall porter, etc.

Outside, the service will be principally the distribution of
pamphlets and the collection of goods, stores, etc. for the
Club.

Service required of members. 1938.

THE TALLY

For every hour a member works, that is, renders service to the Club as a
whole, he receives one Mount Street Tally. This document is a piece of paper,
not unlike a tram ticket in appearance :

THE MOUNT STREET TALLY.

The question at once arises—What is a tally worth ? It must at least
be exchangeable for something the member considers it worth while to
work for one hour to obtain. If it does not command *at least* this par value,
work will cease and the Club go out of business.

Journal. 1938.

THE MOUNT STREET CLUB IDEA
CO-OPERATIVE SELF-HELP

THE STORY of the Mount Street Club begins with a small group of people who came together in November 1934 to seek a practical method of relieving unemployment. They had considered various aspects of the situation—the inadequacy of a bare " Dole," the psychological effects of prolonged unemployment, and the fact that voluntary charitable effort could not be expected to cope with the situation. They believed, rightly, that the average unemployed man is ready and willing to work. And from that belief emerged a new idea—the idea that jobless people should be enabled to produce their own major necessities by co-operative effort.

A start was made without delay. In December 1934 the idea was explained to a group of unemployed men, and a number of these became the first members of the Mount Street Club. The next task was to equip these men with the means of production—premises, land, tools, raw materials, administrative and technical direction. Through voluntary effort, and with the help of funds contributed by the public, this was accomplished, and the subsequent history of the Club has been one of development and expansion.

A landmark in the growth of the Club was the purchase of a farm in the Spring of 1939 ; this made it possible to produce a greatly increased volume and variety of foodstuffs. As time went on the range of products and services available to members gradually widened. Already the method of self-help by co-operation has been proved practicable beyond question ; and the Mount Street Club can no longer be regarded merely as a " Club for Unemployed Men." It is the demonstration of a System by which jobless men can raise the standard of living for themselves and their dependents by the work of their own hands. These men earn no money; instead they share among themselves everything they produce, each in proportion to his industry.

Membership of the Club has been limited to 250, because funds have not so far been available to provide the necessary workshop accommodation, land, raw materials and implements to enable a larger number to participate in the benefits of the movement. But even this limited membership, together with dependents, means that about 1,000 people are being provided with food, fuel, footwear, clothing and recreational facilities. The achievements may be gauged from the fact that with £4,500 and gifts in kind contributed by the public in 1940, goods and services to the approximate value of £13,000 were produced and distributed.

Already similar Clubs have been formed in Waterford, Cork and Limerick. The Mount Street Club Idea has been recognised as a workable plan for the relief of unemployment. Given the necessary funds, its scope is limited only by the number of unemployed who are willing to help themselves.

Mount Street Club Appeal leaflet. 1942.

the club's role was complementary to what was already being done elsewhere. It was not a place where any work would be done which would be in the smallest degree competitive with the work that was being done by ordinary employed men outside. Neither was the club an employment exchange, its only object being to assist the unemployed in any way they possibly could. Its guiding principle was service in return for help.[30]

The question of expense was brought up carefully. Somerville-Large thanked private individuals and individual firms 'who had rallied to the support of the club, and particularly the various business enterprises through whose generosity the club had been made ready for occupation.'

Moving a vote of thanks to the Lord Mayor, Councillor Martin O'Sullivan specifically mentioned 'the group of private gentleman by whose efforts the club had been brought to its present state…for many of them had put their hands deep into their pockets to support the project.' At least £3000 had already been spent in renovating the premises in Mount Street, and it was calculated that £2000 would be needed for expenditure during 1936. According to Waller, 'the club could get on splendidly' with this annual amount.

30. *Irish Times*, 6 November 1935.

UNEMPLOYMENT, CHARITIES, TRADE UNIONS, AND THE WORKING MAN IN DUBLIN IN THE 1930S
II
Sarah Campbell

There are...a very large number unemployed [in Dublin], but I think that there can be no poverty so absolute as poverty in a large city like Dublin. In a rural district a person, no matter how destitute he may be, will not starve, as a rule, but in Dublin a person could be starving in one room in a tenement dwelling while people in other rooms would not even know, and if they did know, probably would not care. You have that impersonal atmosphere existing in the city, which makes poverty here a particularly severe condition to be in.[1]

Introduction

The impact of the world economic depression, which began towards the end of 1929, was experienced somewhat later and less severely in Ireland than in the industrialised countries.[2] That said, the impact and effects of the depression in Ireland were profound and compounded by local factors, such as the economic war with Britain,[3] as well as the lay-off of labourers on completion of housing and road-making schemes, and army demobilisation. Prices for agricultural products fell steadily, the cost of living rose, and there was a large increase in the numbers unemployed. The average weekly number of persons on the live register[4] in 1933 was 72,000, of whom only about one-third were claiming unemployment insurance benefit.[5] An indication of the extent of the hardship being experienced was the fact that in March 1933 there were approximately 126,000 people in receipt of home assistance[6] as against 48,000 in March 1926.[7] By the end of the decade, unemployment stood at 105,000 and 80,000 people were on outdoor relief.[8]

It was generally acknowledged that Dublin was the 'storm centre of the unemployment problem' in the country.[9] This chapter examines the extent of the unemployment problem in Dublin in the 1930s and the official government response to it. When Fianna Fáil came to power, their social and economic achievement between 1932 and 1938 was, in the circumstances, impressive on the face of it.[10] There was a significant increase in the amount of social legislation passed, much of it aimed at improving or alleviating the conditions of the working class. This legislation will be discussed, but a more significant effect of unemployment was not the legislation aimed at countering it but rather the social impact it had on working-class people. While much of the legislation did improve the lot of many of the poorest in Dublin society, it did not provide a proper standard of living by any means. This chapter will, therefore, also examine the economic and social challenges faced by the unemployed in Dublin during the thirties.

1. Seán Lemass in *Dáil Éireann deb.*, xxxvi, col. 729 (28 November 1930).

2. Department of Social Welfare, *Report of the Commission on Social Welfare* (Dublin: Stationery Office, 1986), pp. 32-3.

3. The economic war was a retaliatory trade war between the Irish Free State and Britain (1932-1938) which was initiated when de Valera's government refused to pay so-called 'land annuities' — a disputed item in the Anglo-Irish settlement of 1921—and which led the British Treasury to seek payment instead through penal 'emergency' tariffs on Irish imports. The Irish government responded by imposing similar taxes on British imports.

4. The live register is used to provide a monthly series of the numbers of people registering for unemployment assistance/benefit. While it is specifically not designed to measure unemployment, one of its main purposes is as a short-term trend indicator of unemployment.

5. Department of Social Welfare, *First report of the Department of Social Welfare 1947–49* (Dublin, 1950), p. 17.

6. Under the Local Government (Temporary Provisions) Act, 1923, the conditions governing receipt of outdoor relief were revised and the scheme was renamed home assistance.

7. Dept of Social Welfare, *Report of the Commission on Social Welfare* (1986), pp. 32-3.

8. *Dáil Éireann deb.*, lxxiv, col. 1835-36 (9 March 1939). See also *Irish Times*, 18 March 1939.

9. *Dáil Éireann deb.*, xxxvii, col. 615 (26 February 1931).

10. J. J. Lee, *Ireland 1912-1985: politics and society* (Cambridge, 1989), p. 195.

The extent of the problem

There was a perception in the late 1920s that unemployment in Dublin was worsening. A St Vincent de Paul report for 1928 stated that there was a 'continuance of the severe distress which our members have noticed during the past three or four years. A feature of this new condition is the continuance of the need for assistance in almost undiminished volume over the summer season.'[11] In 1929 the charity reported that 'the work of visiting the poor in their homes tended to become unduly heavy owing to the great dearth of employment in the city.'[12]

Mel Cousins argues that while the problem of lack of or insufficient work had existed for centuries, 'unemployment' and 'the unemployed' were terms that were invented in the late nineteenth century.[13] National governments have tried to counter rising unemployment rates by intervening actively both in the regulation of the labour market and in the provision of social benefits. These efforts have two main objectives: fostering employment and reducing the number of unemployed in the country; and limiting and possibly avoiding the negative consequences of unemployment in terms of poverty, precariousness, social exclusion, and lack of social cohesion.[14] The first of these objectives was addressed with relief programmes; the second, through legislation aimed at reducing hardship. The 1930s began with the Poor Relief (Dublin) Bill, 1929, and closed with the Public Assistance Act (1939). Perhaps the most significant piece of social legislation came almost midway through the decade with the Unemployment Assistance Act (1933).

The Poor Relief (Dublin) Bill, 1929

The Poor Law was an attempt to come to terms with some of the problems arising out of widespread poverty in Ireland in the early nineteenth century. The original poor law in 1838 had been confined to indoor relief but outdoor relief had been introduced during the Famine. This payment, however, was effectively abolished a decade later. Yet the level of outdoor relief payments gradually increased from 1859 onwards, and by 1913 the majority of paupers in Dublin were still relieved in the workhouse, although the numbers on outdoor relief had grown steadily.[15] The early 1920s saw the abolition of poor law unions in the Irish Free State (with the exception of Dublin) under the Local Government (Temporary Provisions) Act, 1923. The reforms included the separation of the treatment of the sick entirely from poor relief, the establishment of county homes for the aged and infirm, and the separation of treatment for 'the mental defectives in workhouses, unmarried mothers and children.'[16] All restrictions on outdoor relief were abolished and assistance was granted to the able-bodied and children under the new name of home assistance.

The annual numbers in receipt of relief varied, falling from 23,700 in 1924 to a low of 18,056 in 1926 before rising significantly to 26,500 in 1928.[17] The Poor Law Commission, which was established in 1925 to recommend a permanent system of poor relief, examined in particular the position in Dublin. A special committee of the Senate was also set up in May 1929 to address the case of Dublin, as 'the existing provision for the relief of unemployment is inadequate, and the method of administering home assistance to the wives and families of the unemployed and those in distress calls for investigation without delay.'[18] The committee recommended that legislation should be passed immediately

11. Society of St Vincent de Paul (hereafter SVP), *Report of the Council of Ireland*, 1928, p. 9.

12. SVP, *Report of the Council of Ireland*, 1929, p. 36.

13. Mel Cousins, *The birth of social welfare in Ireland, 1922-52* (Dublin, 2003), p. 22.

14. Marco Giugni, ed., *The politics of unemployment in Europe: policy responses and collective action* (Surrey, 2009), p. 2.

15. National Archives of Ireland (hereafter NAI), Guide to the records of the Poor Law, http://www. nationalarchives.ie/research/research-guides-and-articles/guide-to-the-records-of-the-poor-law/ (accessed 28 December 2012).

16. Charles Eason, *Report of the Irish Poor Law Commission* (Statistical and Social Inquiry of Ireland, 1928), p. 17.

17. Mel Cousins, 'The politics of poor law reform in early twentieth century Ireland,' *MPRA Paper* 5535 (University Library of Munich, 2007), p. 9. http://mpra.ub.uni-muenchen.de/5535/, (last accessed 28 December 2012).

18. NAI Taois/S 2887, Report of the Special Committee re Poor Law Relief (Seanad Éireann), 27 June 1929.

providing that, pending the adoption of a county scheme, the Poor Law Guardians in Dublin should be empowered to grant outdoor relief without the restrictions which were removed for the remainder of the country by the Local Government (Temporary Provisions) Act, 1923.[19] Seán T. O'Kelly, a leading member of Fianna Fáil, argued in the Dáil that 'something of this kind has been very badly needed in the City and County of Dublin, especially in recent years…There is not any part of the area under the Free State that has had as high a proportion of people in absolute want as the City of Dublin.'[20]

The bill was not wholly welcomed, particularly by Dublin Corporation, as well as by many deputies in the Dáil, who felt that an undue burden was being placed on ratepayers in Dublin.[21] J. J. Byrne (North Dublin) stated that the main argument for the bill was that the city of Dublin was only being asked to do what the rest of the country had been doing for years.[22] However, the bill, according to the estimate of the Dublin Union Commissioners, would cost the citizens of Dublin and the adjoining townships the 'gigantic sum' of £250,000 in addition to the amount already being expended on Poor Law Relief, which amounted to £264,000. Together the total would come to an annual charge of £514,000 on the ratepayers—'a dead weight charge upon the trade and industry of the city of Dublin which no other part of the country had to bear.'[23]

As might be expected, the implementation of the Act led to a significant increase in the numbers on outdoor relief in Dublin, which jumped from 11,900 in 1929 to 21,700 by 1934 before the introduction of unemployment assistance transferred significant numbers away from the home assistance scheme.[24] St Vincent de Paul noted the far-reaching importance the legislation had on its work in the city. There was a decrease of 48,301 visits paid by the organisation to the poor in the city of Dublin[25] and it noted that 1930 could be regarded as 'a turning point in the history of the Society in Dublin.'[26] The passing of the Poor Relief Act transferred the onus of providing against actual starvation for workless families to the public authorities, instead of charities like St Vincent de Paul.

The 1932 election

Neary and Ó Gráda note that the 1930s were years of political turmoil and economic crisis and change in Ireland.[27] However, unemployment had increased rapidly in the early 1920s. Mel Cousins argues that the Cumann na nGaedheal government had, in effect, no employment policy. Employment creation was seen as part of a broader fiscal or tariff policy.[28] The government was heavily criticised for its performance on unemployment. Seán Lemass, later Fianna Fáil Minister for Industry and Commerce, in particular, made lengthy speeches in the Dáil on the deteriorating levels of employment at the beginning of the new decade. In November 1930, he noted the alarming increase of unemployment in the previous year, which had risen from 17,126 in July 1929 to 23,990 in November 1930. What was more concerning, he stated, was that while the number of registered unemployed had increased, the number of persons in receipt of unemployment insurance benefit did not increase at the same rate, with only 50 per cent of the registered unemployed in receipt of benefit in November 1930.[29] When Richard Mulcahy, as Minister for Local Government and Public Health, introduced the Poor Relief (Dublin) Bill, 1931, which was to continue for a period of five years the Poor Relief

19. Poor Relief (Dublin) Act, 1929.

20. *Dáil Éireann deb.*, xxxii, col. 447 (30 October 1929).

21. See *Dáil Éireann deb.*, xxxii, col. 455-512 (30 October 1929).

22. *Irish Times*, 5 December 1929.

23. Ibid.

24. Cousins, 'The politics of poor law reform,' p. 18.

25. SVP, *Report of the Council of Ireland*, 1930, p. 50.

26. Ibid.

27. J. Peter Neary and Cormac Ó Gráda, 'Protection, economic war and structural change: the 1930s in Ireland,' *Irish Historical Studies*, xxvii, no. 107 (1991), p. 250.

28. Cousins, *The birth of social welfare in Ireland*, p. 35.

29. *Dáil Éireann deb.*, xxxvi, col. 726-7 (28 November 1930).

(Dublin) Act of 1929, Lemass noted that it was a 'fitting condemnation of the whole policy of the Executive Council.'[30] J. J. Byrne criticised Lemass's reading of the situation, however. He stated that there were more unemployed in Northern Ireland, Liverpool, and Manchester that there were in the Irish Free State.[31]

Although during its last two years in government, Cumann na nGaedheal was forced to mimic Fianna Fáil's economic policies, the 1932 general election offered a clear choice to the electorate. Cumann na nGaedheal devoted one grudging paragraph in its election manifesto out of fourteen to social and economic policy.[32] Fianna Fáil, on the other hand, concentrated heavily on social policy and economic issues, promising economic self-sufficiency and intervention in economic affairs, including the creation of 85,000 extra jobs in industry.[33] Sydney Minch (CnG, Kildare) observed that the one point that defeated those who stood for the Cumann na nGaedheal party in the 1932 election was unemployment. It was, he said, the best asset that the Fianna Fáil party had.[34] The verdict was electorally decisive. The electorate chose the party proposing sweeping constitutional, economic, and social changes. Fianna Fáil won 44.5 per cent of the vote and formed a new government with the backing of the Labour Party.[35]

While Fianna Fáil strode ahead with its programme of a 'more intense nationalism,'[36] unemployment became the pressing concern of the country. St Vincent de Paul noted that notwithstanding the removal from the books of their conferences in Dublin of many poor families whose needs were being attended to by the Poor Law Authorities, the number of families assisted in Ireland during 1930 increased by a couple of hundred. The increase, though small, was evidence that there was still widespread unemployment, and that their help was sought more readily than used to be the case previously.[37] The Society also noted that another class of case had emerged in which there was acute want for a short period, namely, where the man lost his employment and had to wait three or four weeks before receiving unemployment benefit.[38] Eamonn O'Neill (CnG, West Cork) stated in April 1932 that 'the question of unemployment transcends every other question that comes before this House at the present time. There are 80,000 people unemployed; there is an increasing number in the register of the unemployment exchanges every day… and we must realise that there are 90,000 people living on outdoor relief in this country.'[39]

Relief works and housing

Mary Daly notes that there is a long tradition of resorting to public works as a means of relieving distress and unemployment.[40] Mel Cousins argues that despite the range of reports available to the government and despite the greatly increased tempo of parliamentary opposition on social issues, the Cumann na nGaedheal government did little in most areas during the lifetime of the Fifth Dáil from 1927 to 1932.[41] The main area of activity was in relation to unemployment with the establishment in November 1927—arising from a

30. *Dáil Éireann deb.*, xxxvii, col. 610-11 (26 February 1931).

31. Ibid, col. 616. The figure stated for unemployment for the Free State was 25,000, while for Northern Ireland it was 29,000. With a much smaller population figure, this constituted a much higher level of unemployment in Northern Ireland.

32. Lee, *Ireland 1912-1985*, p. 169.

33. Mary E. Daly, *The buffer state: the historical roots of the Department of the Environment* (Dublin, 1997), p. 154.

34. *Dáil Éireann deb.*, xli, col. 68 (27 April 1932).

35. After a snap general election in early 1933, Fianna Fáil won 51 per cent of the vote and formed a majority government.

36. Daly, *The buffer state*, p. 154.

37. SVP, *Bulletin*, lxxxvi, no. 8 (August 1931), p. 236.

38. SVP, *Report of the Council of Ireland*, 1930, p. 26.

39. *Dáil Éireann deb.*, xli, col. 899 (29 April 1932).

40. For example, the Local Government Board was involved in organising relief works throughout the west of Ireland during the depressed years of the 1880s. Daly, *The buffer state*, p. 179.

41. Cousins, *The birth of social welfare in Ireland*, p. 46.

Dáil motion on unemployment—of a Committee on Unemployment chaired by Vincent Rice (CnG, Dublin South). The committee, in its final report, recommended a more coherent approach to relief works, advising long-term investment programmes, such as improving coastal roads, slum clearance, and improvements in water supplies or minor drainage schemes.[42] The committee reported that there were 78,934 persons living in one-room tenements (more than one-quarter of the total population of the city of Dublin) according to the 1926 census as compared with 73,973 persons in 1913. The report concluded that approximately fifteen thousand new houses would be required to meet the needs of the city and that no form of national activity afforded so great a field for the absorption of the unemployed, or would contribute to the betterment of the lot of the people, than a housing works and slum clearance programme.[43]

The housing problem in Dublin was acute, particularly for the working classes. In the early decades of the twentieth century, the city of Dublin faced a crisis in housing provision. Long years of neglect and economic stagnation, combined with a decaying fabric, had resulted in a severe working-class housing problem.[44] This situation had not improved by the 1930s. One deputy noted in 1932:

> Deputies in this House might remember that at this very hour thousands of women and children in this city are making ready to settle down for the night in rooms that are crawling with vermin, in rooms that are filthy beyond description, in houses that have been repeatedly condemned by the public authority as unfit for human habitation...There are families in Dublin tonight settling down in coal cellars under the street for their night's rest...There is scope there for the employment of seventy per cent of the unemployed in Dublin.[45]

While in opposition, Lemass outlined an ambitious public housing programme:

There are certain services for which we would like to see money provided on a much more lavish scale than has been provided heretofore, in respect of which we would place no limit upon the amount the minister of finance might seek to secure. The service of housing is a case in point. Apart from the wisdom of embarking upon large development schemes during a time of depression and unemployment, and for that purpose borrowing money, the social need for improved housing is so great that the problem should be faced as one of the first magnitude.[46]

During 1931-32, there was a substantial increase in grants sanctioned by the government for houses to be built under the Housing of the Working Classes Acts. The figure nearly doubled from £353,818 in 1930-31 to £603,786 in 1931-32.[47] Public works assumed greater significance when Fianna Fáil came to power in 1932. One of the first debates in the new Dáil in 1932 arose from a motion from Labour Deputy Dan Morrissey proposing that work or maintenance be provided to meet the immediate needs of the unemployed.[48] Expenditure on roads, housing, and sanitary services came to be assessed for their potential to provide jobs rather than as desirable for their own sake.[49] At the same time compulsory notification was required of jobs subsidised by public funds to the employment exchanges and branch employment offices, resulting

42. Ibid, p. 49.

43. Committee on the Relief of Unemployment, *1927 Final Report* (Dublin, 1928), paragraph 34.

44. Ruth McManus, 'Public utility societies, Dublin Corporation and the development of Dublin, 1920-1940,' *Irish Geography*, xxix, no. 1 (1996), p. 27.

45. *Dáil Éireann deb.*, xli, col. 675-6 (27 April 1932).

46. *Dáil Éireann deb.*, xxxv, col. 36-37 (28 May 1930).

47. NAI, Taois/S/2969 [B], Department of Local Government and Public Health Reports, 1931-32.

48. Cousins, *The birth of social welfare in Ireland*, p. 60.

49. Daly, *The buffer state*, p. 154.

Morgans Cottages, located close to Lower Mount Street. 1913.

Dublin tenements. 1913.

in the registration of jobseekers. The measure led to a massive increase in the numbers on the live register, from 32,000 in April 1932 to over 100,000 by the end of the year. As Mel Cousins notes, the measure disclosed the extent of unemployment and underemployment in Ireland and highlighted the need for immediate measures to respond to this issue.[50]

Seán MacEntee, as Minister for Finance between 1932 and 1939, was very conservative in fiscal and social policy throughout his ministerial career, opposing increased taxation and demands for state provision of social services. In 1934 MacEntee appointed a commission to examine banking, currency, and credit in the Irish Free State. Given the conservative composition of the commission, the conclusions of its report in 1938 were unsurprising: it criticised the government's social programmes, particularly housing, and also the sharp increase in the national debt.[51] However, although the report of the Commission on Banking Currency and Credit claimed that the government's housing schemes constituted a veritable public works programme, housing was regarded as desirable in its own right and was not viewed as part of a job-creation programme.[52] This contrasts, Mary Daly argues, with expenditure on roads, water, and sewerage where improvements in services appear to have been given low priority relative to efforts to provide employment.[53]

One of the first steps taken by the Fianna Fáil government in its first budget in May 1932 was to announce funding of over £2 million for unemployment relief works.[54] The 1932 budget provided £1.55 million in grants and loans for relief works and a further £550,000 for the Local Loans Fund.[55] Exchequer expenditure on employment schemes totalled £4,698,000 during the years 1932-39, most of it on programmes associated with the Department of Local Government: £901,000 on public health, £1,494,000 on roads, £147,000 on housing site development, and £982,000 on miscellaneous works, including parks.[56] In Dublin, 7,051 houses were built between 1933 and 1938.[57] Of all the houses built during the 1930s by Dublin Corporation, more than half were built in Crumlin,[58] which was situated in the Dublin suburbs. One of the main issues that arose with the building of suburban housing was the cost of the rent. At the time, Ruth McManus argues, it was recognised that only the more well-off members of the working classes could afford to live in the tenant-purchase suburban schemes initiated in the 1920s, and even then they often had to struggle to make ends meet.[59] The Society of St Vincent de Paul observed that the rents in general charged to the poor were 'outrageously high'—nearly all of the cases in Fairview were due to the high rents in the new areas, some as high as 15s per week.[60] Alfie Byrne, the Lord Mayor of Dublin, was critical of such high rents: 'There is no use talking about putting up houses at rents of twelve or fifteen shillings a week when the majority of those waiting for accommodation are a class that can pay about two shillings for a room.'[61] Not only that, but the cost of transport to the areas of employment was also a concern for those housed in the new housing developments. Thomas Kelly noted that 'The extremely small means of the persons we are called upon to provide accommodation for will be further burdened with the heavy cost of transport and the poorest sections would rather be closer to the centre of the employment where work is of a casual

50. Cousins, *The birth of social welfare in Ireland*, p. 60.

51. Deirdre McMahon, 'Seán MacEntee,' in James McGuire and James Quinn, ed., *Dictionary of Irish biography: from the earliest times to the year 2002* (Cambridge, 2009).

52. Daly, *The buffer state*, pp. 178-9.

53. Ibid.

54. Cousins, *The birth of social welfare in Ireland*, p. 60.

55. Daly, *The buffer state*, p. 181.

56. Ibid, p. 196.

57. *Report of inquiry into the housing of the working classes of the city of Dublin, 1939-43* (1944), Appendix 6.

58. Ruth McManus, *Dublin, 1910-1940: shaping the city and suburbs* (Dublin: Four Courts Press, 2002), p. 196.

59. McManus, 'Blue collars, "red forts" and green fields: working-class housing in ireland in the twentieth century,' *International Labor and Working Class History*, lxiv (2003), p. 46.

60. SVP, *Bulletin, Supplement for Irish Conferences*, April 1931, p. 4.

61. *Irish Times*, 7 May 1931.

nature.'[62] By focusing so heavily on this 'better class of dwelling,' Dublin Corporation was, in effect, turning its back on the most needy members of society. Even extensive suburban building would not enable any single slum area to be actively cleared, as the majority of the inhabitants were unable to afford the cost of living in the outer areas.[63]

The working man

At the turn of the twentieth century, the Dublin worker usually drew wages that effectively denied him and his family the standards of food, clothing, education, and housing enjoyed by his social superiors. But wide differences also existed within the working-class world. There was a vast difference between the artisan and unskilled labourer. Likewise, the casually employed, aged poor, and beggars were necessarily reduced to the degraded life of the slums, though considered fortunate if they escaped the workhouse.[64] The misery and degradation of a large section of the population of Dublin was all too apparent. It was impossible to deny the visible evidence of miserable housing conditions or to refute the painful record of death and disease. Over one-quarter of the citizens of Dublin in 1914 were in pressing need of the essentials of decent living.[65] Unfortunately, this statistic did not change much with independence. Cormac Ó Gráda argues that few Irish historians would deny that the Southern Irish economy performed poorly between the 1920s and the late 1950s. Indeed output and incomes grew so little during those decades that for most people in Ireland the economic benefits of political independence must have remained far from obvious.[66]

Life in the Dublin tenements was a constant struggle for financial survival. Most of the poor had minimal literacy and no job skills, and had to seek labour on a casual, sporadic basis. Steady employment was unknown to many people.[67] For that reason, the relief works were an important source of temporary income for most. Yet, most councils traditionally paid lower wages to workers employed on relief schemes than to regular road labourers.[68] The Labour Party, in particular, was vocal in its opposition to this tradition.

Speaking in the Dáil on 8 March 1933, Labour Party leader William Norton decried the practice and said he hoped the Fianna Fáil party would 'strangle the mentality that is enshrined in the idea of low rates of wages.' He went on to say:

> ...this rate of wages [24/- a week] is a scandalous one. It is a starvation rate and could not be justified by anybody except those who believe that poverty, misery and squalor must be the destiny of the working classes in this country. While on this matter I have looked up some statistics and I find that it costs 2/- a day to feed a pauper in the Dublin Union. Remember this is for food alone, to say nothing about housing and clothing. It costs 14/- a week to feed a pauper in the Dublin Union. But a man with his wife and six children is expected to be able to live on an extra 10/- a week and then they are not supposed to be paupers.[69]

In 1937 a national convention of delegates from various branches of the Unemployed Workers' Rights Association drew attention to the fact that the relief system needed serious attention, and called for all work of the unemployed to be paid at trade union rates. Delegates present said that the unemployed refused to submit to the new 'slave status.' They stated:

---

62. *Dublin Municipal Council Reports*, 'Report of the Housing Committee,' 28 May 1934, pp. 172-3.

63. McManus, 'Blue collars,' p. 46.

64. Joseph V. O'Brien, *Dear, dirty Dublin: a city in distress, 1899-1916* (London, 1982), p. 161.

65. Ibid.

66. Cormac Ó Gráda, *A rocky road: the Irish economy since the 1920s* (Manchester, 1997), p. 1.

67. Kevin C. Kearns, *Dublin tenement life: an oral history* (Dublin, 1994), pp. 29-30.

68. Daly, *The buffer state*, p. 183.

69. *Dáil Éireann deb.*, xlvi, col. 485 (8 March 1933).

Relief schemes are being carried out under conditions and wages that put the barbarians of Africa in the shade. Men were engaged in road making, land drainage, sewerage systems and the cultivation of agricultural produce at the princely wage of 27s per week. Who is there in the working class movement who would doubt the intention of the Government to extend this system of slave labour into every possible occupation at the earliest opportunity, thereby gravely menacing the established trade union standards and conditions?[70]

Income shortage was often compounded by bad management and debt was a major problem. Credit unions did not emerge until the late 1960s. When money was short, women habitually trekked down the street to the local pawnbroker. Pawnshops—known then as the 'people's bank'—became an institution in Dublin's tenement district.[71] Kevin Kearns notes that without the pawnbroker, the 'already precarious life of the poor would have been even more unstable.'[72] When a few pounds, rather than mere shillings, were needed, a person could always turn to the notorious moneylenders who abounded in tenement areas. Moneylenders charged up to 100 per cent interest and took children's allowance books as security.[73] One mother described her whirligig of debt—to the landlord, ESB [Electricity Supply Board], shop on the corner, moneylenders—as being 'as if my head and my feet are in a halter.'[74] Alcoholism or gambling were other thorns. Parents were occasionally in such dire straits that they refused to take their child from maternity hospital.[75] Dr T. W. T. Dillon summed up the vicious circle that existed for the unemployed and poor in Dublin:

The poor cannot keep clean, because they are unable to buy soap or fuel to heat water. With every month at unemployment their position becomes more desperate, more hopeless, until they finally join the ranks of the unemployable. The mother starves herself to feed the children and, in a very high percentage of cases, is found on examination to be suffering from nutritional anaemia. The children fall behind in school and gradually slip down to a social status even lower than their parents...At the age of 18 they are replaced by some other unfortunate and join the ranks of the unemployable proletariat. There are families in Dublin in which the second generation is now well advanced on that dreary road.[76]

Social and health policy in the early days of the Free State can only be described as austere. Small voluntary and community organisations concerned with social distress and poor housing emerged from the nineteenth century onward, often with a religious motivation. An interesting feature of Dublin city in the 1920s and 1930s was the close bond that existed between the Catholic Church and the working class.[77] By far the largest and most enduring of the charities was the Society of St Vincent de Paul. Such was the level of activity by the Society in the course of these years that Judge D. J. O'Brien was able to state that 'the most striking thing' about the work of the Society was that 'there is not a single street, lane, alley or court in Dublin city that is not directly under the jurisdiction of some Conference of the Society.'[78] Indeed,

70. *Irish Times*, 25 March 1937.

71. Kearns, *Dublin tenement life*, p. 31.

72. Ibid.

73. David Gwynn Morgan, 'Society and the schools,' *Commission to Inquire into Child Abuse*, 4 (2009), paragraph 3.12, p. 204.

74. Ibid.

75. Ibid.

76. T. W. T. Dillon, 'The social services in Éire,' *Studies: An Irish Quarterly Review*, xxxiv, no. 135 (September 1945), p. 331.

77. Éamonn Dunne, 'Action and reaction: Catholic lay organisations in Dublin in the 1920s and 1930s,' *Archivium Hibernicum*, xlviii (1994), p. 109.

78. Ibid, pp. 114-15.

the Society in Dublin during these years often 'stood between hundreds of families and complete destitution.'[79]

As the effects of the economic war began to take hold, Myles McIver and Charles Buckley of the Irish Unemployed Workers' Movement appealed in 1936 for the government to improve conditions for the unemployed:

> It is admitted that this winter is the most severe we have experienced for the past twenty-five years. Grave hardship exists in the homes of the poor. Thousands of unemployed are on the borderline of starvation, and, unless something is immediately done to assist them in relieving their unhappy lot, the Dublin Union will claim many of them…Every item of food has reached the dear stage; rents in thousands of cases are exorbitant. Boots and clothes are out of the question. There is not sufficient relief being received by the unemployed man to buy food.[80]

The Unemployment Assistance Act, 1933

Perhaps one of the most important pieces of legislation that was passed in the 1930s, as far as the working class was concerned, was the Unemployment Assistance Act. J. J. Lee argues that though Fianna Fáil's economic policy helped increase employment outside agriculture, unemployment continued to remain a chronic problem.[81] In November 1932 Lemass submitted a memo to Éamon de Valera (President of the Executive Council) outlining his views on the economic situation and the need for drastic remedies to address the position. Lemass argued that the fullest possible industrial development could not employ 100,000 unemployed without an export market. Accordingly, he proposed a major expansion of the public works programme, which would be carried out under direct government control, rather than using local authorities. His proposals were designed to ensure the employment of all unemployed in public works pending their absorption into industry.[82] Both Cousins and Daly question how genuine Lemass's proposals were, suggesting that the document may have been an attempt to shock de Valera into abandoning the Economic War.[83] A week later Lemass submitted a further memo to de Valera. He recalled that they had frequently discussed the steps which must be taken to provide for the unemployed and had, more or less, accepted responsibility for giving effect to the principle of 'work or maintenance' insofar as it may be practicable to do so.[84]

This was the basis of the Unemployment Assistance Act, which came into effect in April 1934. The provisions of the unemployment insurance code were found to be inadequate as they were subject to two important limitations. A person had to be employed for six weeks before becoming entitled to one week's unemployment benefit, and benefit could not be paid for more than twenty-six weeks in any one year. In addition, those employed in agriculture were not covered by the unemployment insurance acts.[85] According to the 1926 census, that included almost two-thirds of the employed population in the Free State.[86] By 1933 only about one-third of the unemployed qualified for the insurance-based unemployment benefit.[87] Very substantial numbers were therefore reliant on public works schemes or on the locally administered 'home assistance,' which Lemass commented, because of the 'taint of pauperism' associated with it,

79. SVP, *Supplement for Irish Conference*, February 1930, p. 5.

80. *Irish Times*, 18 January 1936.

81. Lee, *Ireland 1912-1985*, p. 195.

82. Cousins, *The birth of social welfare in Ireland*, pp. 60-61. See also Daly, *The buffer state*, pp. 184-5.

83. Ibid.

84. Cousins, *The birth of social welfare in Ireland*, p. 61.

85. Department of Social Welfare, *Report of the Commission on Social Welfare* (1986), p. 32-3.

86. Central Statistics Office, *Census 1926 Reports*, Vol. 10, Chapter III, p. 26 (http://www.cso.ie/en/media/csoie/census/census1926results/volume10/C,1926,V10,ChapterIII.pdf, last accessed 28 December 2012)—almost two-thirds were registered as 'producers.'

87. Brian Nolan, *Ireland and the 'minimum income guarantee': a review of Irish social assistance provision in the light of the EU recommendations on minimum income* (Dublin, 1995), p. 27.

deterred many people from applying for it.[88] Not only that, but the wide variations in assistance given from one area to another were undesirable, and it was felt that the responsibility for financing such assistance should be a national rather than a local one. The Unemployment Assistance Act transferred the obligation of providing relief to the able-bodied unemployed to central government, and harmonised the amounts payable and the means test applied.[89] Unemployment assistance would be payable to all unemployed people but excluding persons under 18 and over 70, persons on unemployment insurance, people maintained by their families or who would ordinarily be maintained by them, and, for a period of six months, persons who refused suitable employment, voluntarily left employment, or lost employment through misconduct.[90]

Lemass argued that the Act was the biggest attempt at social legislation attempted in the country for a long time.[91] The Society of St Vincent de Paul noted that the effect of the Act had considerably reduced the need of families for material assistance by the Conferences, particularly in Dublin.[92] Nevertheless, the problems that existed with the Act did not go unnoticed. In more than one instance in the debates on the Bill, it was judged as being too carelessly and too loosely thrown together.[93] Most notable were the restrictions placed on who could access relief. While the scheme included for the first time the unemployed agricultural worker, and on the face of it applied to all, Mel Cousins points out that subsequent clauses effectively excluded the vast bulk of women, the assumption being that the normal state of affairs was that they were dependent on their husbands. Single women (spinsters) and widows could only qualify if they had dependants or if they had been insured for at least one year in the four years prior to the claim.[94] Single men were not much better off—the Irish Unemployed Workers' Movement pointed out in 1936 that 'The pittance being doled out to single men at the Labour Exchange is, in many cases, nothing more than insulting. Many single men, because of having no permanent home, receive nothing.'[95] Cumann na nGaedheal TD Paddy Belton described the bill as pauper legislation. The Labour Party regarded it as inadequate. The trade unions received the bill with a measure of favour, but said it was regarded only as a halfway measure.[96]

But another concern was that the relief provided by the Act was insufficient to alleviate distress. At the Fianna Fáil Ard Fheis in 1934, one speaker expressed the opinion that the allowance of 12s 6d for a man with a family in an urban area was insufficient and suggested that an allowance be made per head for each child.[97] A report by the Sick and Indigent Roomkeepers' Society stated that during 1934 the expenditure in relief of deserving cases amounted to £3,155 19s 5d; the number of families assisted was 4,871, consisting of 20,735 persons. Compared with 1932, these figures showed an increase of £307 in the amount distributed and of 244 in the families assisted.[98] St Vincent de Paul observed that poverty was still prevalent in areas like Coolock and Artane owing to unemployment, and that it was necessary to supplement relief or to assist temporarily in the intervals between the making of a claim for state assistance and the actual receipt of it.[99] Fine Gael TD Peadar Doyle brought up the waiting period issue in November 1934, remarking that there was general dissatisfaction with it.[100] The Society of St Vincent de Paul also noted that there was a number of families living almost continuously on the

88. *Dáil Éireann deb.*, xlix, col. 1652 (27 September 1933).

89. Nolan, *Ireland and the 'minimum income guarantee,'* p. 27.

90. Cousins, *The birth of social welfare in Ireland*, p. 63.

91. *Irish Press*, 15 November 1934.

92. SVP, *Report on the Council of Ireland*, 1934, p. 26.

93. *Irish Times*, 23 September 1933.

94. Cousins, *The birth of social welfare in Ireland*, p. 64.

95. *Irish Times*, 18 January 1936.

96. *Irish Times*, 23 September 1933.

97. *Irish Press*, 15 November 1934.

98. *Irish Times*, 22 June 1934.

99. SVP, *Report on the Council of Ireland*, 1934, pp. 72-4.

100. *Dáil Éireann deb.*, liv, col. 211 (15 November 1934).

borderline of starvation in 1936, and 'unemployment, high rents, low rates of assistance and an altogether unsatisfactory system in the administration of the Poor Laws…[were] the main causes of distress.'[101]

Another key issue was that while the cost of living continued to rise, the unemployment assistance rate remained the same. In 1937, at a Dublin Board of Assistance meeting, Dr Joseph Hannigan requested that the government, in light of the alarming rise of prices (since 1933 the cost of living of the average family of six people had gone up by 8s 9d per week), grant a general increase of 20 per cent in unemployment benefit.[102] However, the government could go no further. Lemass acknowledged that while the estimated cost of the Act—£1,250,000 a year—had proved fairly accurate, there could be no modifications of the Act which would increase the cost, without having clearly in mind where the money was to come from.[103]

The organisation of the unemployed

J. J. Lee has argued that Fianna Fáil's social and economic achievement between 1932 and 1936 was, in the circumstances, impressive. It halted, despite the partly self-inflicted wounds of the economic war, the slide into the economic abyss that appeared to threaten in 1931, and thus blunted the potential appeal of political extremism.[104] Indeed, this was a trend that was prevalent in Britain during the same decade. As unemployment there climbed to almost 3.5 million by 1932, the response was a series of hunger marches by which the unemployed sought to draw attention to their plight. The impotence of the British government also encouraged the growth of extremist political parties— the British Union of Fascists led by Sir Oswald Mosley and the Communist Party of Great Britain which started to attract young intellectuals to its core membership of industrial workers.[105]

Everywhere the unemployed were organising. Belfast became a focus in 1932 with the Outdoor Relief strikes, where over 30,000 people, in a show of mass unity of the working class, took to the streets and went on strike. When it eventually ended, the strikers had won big cash increases on their pay. The preconditions normally conducive to successful political extremists did exist in the Free State in the 1930s. Jobless workers formed the Irish Unemployed Workers' Movement, an offshoot of the National Unemployed Workers' Movement, which was established in 1921 in Britain to draw attention to the increasing numbers of jobless following the First World War. Feargal McGarry argues that the Irish Unemployed Workers' Movement was a communist 'front' organisation and controlled by the Communist Party of Ireland.[106] The movement was quite active during the 1930s in mobilising the unemployed for mass action. They organised a number of protests[107] but, overall, failed to make any significant impact on policy.[108] Diarmaid Ferriter argues that despite a strike in the building industry in 1937 (the biggest in the history of the state) it was not until the late 1940s that labour militancy emerged.[109]

Plus ça change

One piece of important legislation in the 1930s, which was designed to improve working conditions, at least of juvenile and female labour, was the

101. SVP, *Report of the Council of Ireland*, 1936, p. 74.

102. *Irish Times*, 15 April 1937.

103. *Irish Press*, 15 November 1934.

104. Lee, *Ireland 1912-1985*, p. 195.

105. K. K. D. Ewing and C. A. Gearty, *The struggle for civil liberties: political freedoms and the rule of law in Britain, 1914-1945* (Oxford, 2000), p. 214.

106. Feargal McGarry, *Irish politics and the Spanish Civil War* (Cork, 1999), p. 88.

107. Following a refusal by Seán Lemass to receive a deputation from the movement, members of the movement organised a march to Leinster House. The march was banned and the protesters were baton charged by the Gardaí. *Irish Times*, 15 November 1934.

108. The movement supported the Belfast Outdoor Relief strikers in 1932 and a march was organised in solidarity to mark the one-year anniversary in 1933. *Irish Times*, 23 September 1933.

109. This can also be attributed to trade union weakness and infighting. Diarmaid Ferriter, *The transformation of Ireland, 1900-2000* (London, 2004), p. 373.

Conditions of Employment Act (1936). The main reforms for the working class were the introduction of a nine-hour day and a forty-eight hour week. It became unlawful to permit a female worker to start earlier than 7 a.m. or finish after 8 p.m. (except in certain jobs, such as bread-making or domestic service). Industrial work for women and juveniles on a Sunday or a public holiday was outlawed.[110] These restrictions, particularly on women workers, were very much in keeping with the belief that a woman's proper place was in the home. This belief would be further enshrined in the 1937 Constitution.

The conditions of extreme want and destitution continued throughout the 1930s, despite social welfare legislation to alleviate hardship caused by unemployment passed during the decade. The Public Assistance Act of 1939 was an attempt to consolidate the existing law relating to the relief of the poor by local authorities. The Poor Relief Commission had proposed such an amending and consolidating statute.[111] With the passing of the Act, which widened the scope of earlier legislation and provided both general and medical assistance to eligible people, a member of the Society of St Vincent de Paul expressed hope that the new legislation would noticeably 'improve the lives of poor families':

> The Act is an act of the widest scope. It extends and modernises what was known in the bad old times as poor relief and it appears to me to be right to say that in the carrying out of our weekly visitation, if we know the details of what the Public Assistance officer can do, we will be able to do more for the poor.[112]

Such hopes were not realised. According to O'Cinnéide, the Act of 1939 tidied up the law but it reiterated the old Poor Law principles and procedures, as updated by the Local Government (Temporary Provisions) Act of 1923, and did not alter the existing home assistance service in any significant way.[113]

Conclusion

By 1939, after seven years of Fianna Fáil governance and at the beginning of the Second World War, the unemployment situation did not appear to be easing at all. Ferriter notes that by the 1940s agriculture still directly employed almost half of the active work population and by the late 1930s it seemed clear that Fianna Fáil's economic policies had reached the end of their shelf life.[114] Lemass despaired, stating, 'It is undoubtedly correct that we have grave unemployment here.' But, he noted, 'the gravity is not due to the fact that unemployment has increased in recent years—it has not increased—but to the fact that it has persisted despite many efforts made to reduce it. We have had large-scale public works, widespread housing programmes, and also it persisted despite the success of the industrial policy in providing new sources of employment.'[115]

Yet, Neary and Ó Gráda argue that while unemployment persisted at the end of the decade, employment actually expanded between 1932 and 1938. While the increase was unspectacular, it probably represented the first sustained increase in numbers employed since the Famine and was comparable with any subsequent six-year increase.[116] Cousins makes a similar point, adding that the numbers of those employed, insurable under national health insurance, increased from 355,000 in 1933 to 415,000 in 1937. The expansion of public works and Fianna Fáil's policy of industrial development led to a sharp fall in the numbers on the live register, from an average of 119,500 in 1935 to 81,800 in 1937.[117] This improvement, according to Neary and Ó Gráda, goes a long

110. Conditions of Employment Act (1936).

111. Department of Social Welfare, *Report of the Commission on Social Welfare* (1986), p. 34.

112. SVP, *Bulletin*, 89:12 (December, 1944), pp. 13-15.

113. O'Cinnéide, 'Poverty and policy: North and South,' *Administration*, xxxiii, no. 3 (Institute of Public Administration, Dublin, 1985), quoted in *Report of the Commission on Social Welfare* (July 1986), p. 34.

114. Ferriter, *The transformation of Ireland*, p. 372.

115. *Irish Times*, 8 April 1939.

116. Neary and Ó Gráda, 'The 1930s in Ireland,' p. 255.

117. Cousins, *The birth of social welfare in Ireland*, p. 72.

Dublin Tenements. 1911.

Courtesy of Dublin City Libraries

way towards explaining the substantial working-class support won by Fianna Fáil during the 1930s.[118]

Yet, a white paper on national income and expenditure for the years 1938-44 revealed that roughly the top 3,000 took 5 per cent of all income in 1943, suggesting that not enough was being done to decrease the gap between rich and poor.[119] It would appear that during this decade, most official efforts pointed to the reduction of unemployment, perhaps based on the assumption that the most dramatic consequences of unemployment are located at the economic rather than the social level. While industry may have expanded and the numbers on the live register had decreased as Ireland faced into the 1940s, T. W. T. Dillon, writing in 1945, observed that:

> The present system of relief in Ireland, and particularly in Dublin, still has most of the disadvantages attached to the old poor law and is in addition both inadequate and wasteful. The main defect in the old poor law was that people were made to feel that poverty was a sinful thing and that the poor had lost their rights as human beings. They could be imprisoned under inhuman conditions in the workhouse, or they might receive from a reluctant authority just enough to prevent them from starving. The change of name in our cities has not changed the conditions to any important extent. The poor are still granted by a reluctant authority just enough money to prevent starvation; and if they are unfortunate enough to be without a home, they are still shut in under subhuman conditions in the old poorhouse with a new name.[120]

118. Neary and Ó Gráda, 'The 1930s in Ireland,' p. 255.

119. Ferriter, *The transformation of Ireland*, p. 372.

120. Dillon, 'The social services in Éire,' p. 330.

THE FIRST DECADE OF
THE MOUNT STREET CLUB
III
Peter Somerville-Large

Even before the Mount Street Club opened, the founders had made careful plans for how the club would function. At the outset it was envisaged that membership would be limited to 'about thirty or forty' although, according to an appeal made to possible donors, there were plans to accommodate 'several hundred' members in due course.

The first founder members were chosen with great care 'for upon them will fall the responsibility of getting the club organised and establishing within its walls that spirit which is essential for harmonious working.'[1] Upon these men would be the responsibility of getting the workings of the club going smoothly, after which new members would be invited to join.

The club would expand as the governors would indicate there could be an increase in numbers. Meanwhile, entry to the club was made particularly difficult. Major James Waller had been in the army, and he was introducing something in the form of military discipline. As if he were joining a prestigious regiment, a man would have to prove himself before he was accepted. He would be part of a voluntary co-operative system in which he would be given some say, while, at the same time, adhering to its strict rules in which there was a measure of compulsion.

The governors would instruct the superintendent to post the number of vacancies on the club notice board and the date when a ballot would be held to fill them. Candidates had to be unemployed or casual workers, without restriction as to age. A member of the club who wished to propose a candidate for membership had to obtain a form from the superintendent and find a seconder; the candidate would then have to be elected by ballot. The completed form would be put up on the notice board at least six days before the ballot, which would be carried out in the superintendent's presence.

A successful candidate would be put on trial for three weeks before approval. The secretary of the house committee, formed to advise club members, observed in later years how 'the new member on probation should be helped as much as possible...Most of us remember our first few days in the Club; we were glad of a few hints, a little encouragement and a friendly word of welcome. Such an attitude with new members would bring out the best that is in them, and do much to make them valuable additions to the working life of the Club.'

Members were judged in the performance of their work by Superintendant James Cullinan or his deputy. However, discipline was principally maintained by unpaid officials chosen by members themselves. Gross misbehaviour might result in expulsion, but simple disobedience or incompetence would not condemn any member in this way.

A majority of those who applied to join the club were unemployed married men, often with large families, whose social welfare benefits were inadequate to provide their dependants with an acceptable standard of living. A member would still be able to draw the dole, and as he was officially unemployed, he had to spend part of his week reporting to the Labour Exchange and follow up job possibilities in conventional employment. He would have to work at least eight hours a week for the tallies that would pay his subscription and a daily meal. 'There's nothing for nothing in the Mount Street Club' was a repeated slogan of Waller's. As he observed in an early club newsletter:

> There are two classes of unemployed; the unemployed worker and the unemployed. Of these two classes, the former greatly outnumber the latter; but unfortunately the existence of the slacker greatly prejudices the position of the would-be worker.
> There is also a third class who does even more harm. He is the

1. *Tally-Ho—The Journal of the Mount Street Club Society*, i, no. 3 (Autumn 1938; DCLAAr/add/81/243).

gentleman picturesquely called 'a bum' in America, who goes from door to door asking for work, and hoping that none will be offered.[2]

Maintaining the club would offer many hours' work, largely domestic duties such as preparing and cooking food, scrubbing, cleaning, decorating, and clerical work. A man would be employed as hall porter. Outside of the club, others would be required to distribute pamphlets and collect goods for necessities. In later years outside work would include work on allotments provided by Dublin Corporation.

Over the years numbers increased until the Mount Street premises had full capacity. Members came and went; by 1938 about 550 men had become members of the club, while 350 had left, for the most part because they had found employment.

The tally system

The high morale of the men in the club, noted by observers from the beginning, derived from the independence offered by the tally system. The tallies a man earned paid not only for his subscription, but for his meals, and all the other amenities that would be built up over the next few years and offered by the club. Each member, according to a booklet published in 1938 on the club's aims and achievements, 'pays for his meals and for all the products of the Club's industries, such as, clothing, blankets, boots, tinware, woodwork, vegetables and potatoes; he pays for his shave and haircut, his oculist, dentist and his music lessons; he pays to have his clothes mended, cleaned and pressed, and for his laundry; he even pays for the use of his towel and his bath.'[3] The laundry service included darning of socks 'to meet the needs of single members.' A married member, presumably, could rely on his wife for mended socks. All

2. J. H. de W. Waller, stencil newsletter (April 1937).

3. *The Mount Street Club in 1938—its aims, organisation, achievements and plans for the future* (Dublin, 1938).

THE MOUNT STREET CLUB SOCIETY.

THE RULES.

1. The provisional Rules of the Mount Street Society are hereby repealed as from this date.

2. The name of the Society shall be the Mount Street Club Society and its headquarters 81/82, Lower Mount Street, Dublin.

3. The members of the Mount Street Club Society shall be:-

   Those persons who apply on the form prescribed for the purpose and are elected to membership by the Council.
   Members on the 29th October, 1937 need not re-apply for membership.
   The election of members shall be confirmed annually by the Council.

4. The objects of the Society shall be:-

   (a) To assist in the carrying on of the Mount Street Club, by extending the knowledge of the work and methods of that Club; by collecting funds for the purpose of that Club; and by giving such aid and assistance to the Governors of that Club as may be decided from time to time.

   (b) As opportunity offers, to prepare for and assist in the foundation and maintenance of other Clubs to be organised on same basis and principles as the Mount Street Club.

   (c) To collect and distribute information in regard to the methods and work of other institutions and organisations dealing with unemployed men, with a view to the adoption of such improvements as may seem desirable.

5. The management of the Society shall be vested in the officers and council.

6. The officers shall consist of the Chairman of the Council, and the Honorary Secretary, both of whom shall be elected by the Council, and the Honorary Treasurer of the Mount Street Club.

7. The members of the Council shall consist of:-

   (a) Members not exceeding twenty in number who shall be proposed, seconded, and elected by the members at the Annual General Meeting.

   (b) Such other members as may be co-opted from time to time.

   (c) The Governors of the Mount Street Club (ex officio).

   The members of the Council shall hold office until the next general meeting of the Society and shall be eligible for re-election.

   Five members of the Council shall constitute a quorum.

Club Rules. 1937.

Boys' Pants	From	7	Tally
Boys' Overcoats and Jackets....	,,	20	,,
Men's Overalls		15	,,
Girls' and Children's Garments	From	5	,,
Suit or Overcoat cleaned and pressed		4	,,
Blankets (Woven on Club Loom)		15	,,
Pair of Socks		3	,,
Children's Stockings		3	,,
Socks, washed and darned		$1\frac{1}{2}$	,,
Boots and Shoes to order (Kip)		30	,,
Do. do. (Light)		38	,,
Boots, soled and heeled		4	,,
Kitchen Dresser to order	From	25	,,
Do. Table do.	,,	10	,,
Do. Stool do.	,,	5	,,
Domestic Tinware (according to article)	,,	3	,,
Potatoes, per stone		1	,,
Other Vegetables		$\frac{1}{2}$	,,
Pickles, Preserves (grown in Club Gardens)			
per jar		1	,,
Hire of Bicycles, per day		$\frac{1}{2}$	,,
Baths (subscription per week)		$\frac{1}{2}$	,,
Haircut		1	,,
Shave		$\frac{1}{2}$	,,
Tooth extracted....		1	,,
Pair of Spectacles to order	From	25	,,
Handcart of blocks, delivered		5	,,
Billiards (per half hour)		$\frac{1}{2}$	,,
Games (Club subscription per week)		$\frac{1}{2}$	,,
Ticket for Weekly Concert		$\frac{1}{2}$	,,

Club Shop Price List. 1941.

members paid for their needs by working; for every hour they worked they received a tally. Among Dubliners, the Mount Street Club had come to be known as the Tally Club.

With the increase in membership, the yearly issue of tallies during the first four years of the club's existence rose from 15,000 in 1935 to 92,500 in 1938. A list of the purchasing power of tallies included the price of a shave (half a tally), a tooth extraction (one tally), baths (half a tally a week), and an overcoat to order (sixty tallies). A pair of spectacles cost twenty-five tallies; spectacles could also be provided for the wives of members.

Dinner cost a tally. Two main meals were served in the dining room. The club was always proud to contrast the usual tea and white bread diet of the unemployed with the well-balanced meals available to members. Lunch, at 12.30 p.m., consisted of plain or home-made white or brown bread and butter, accompanied by tea; in 1935 the bakery was making yeast bread in addition to soda bread. Dinner was served at 5.30 p.m. A sample dinner menu offered bacon, cabbage, mashed potatoes, and tea. On Fridays members were offered fried fillet of fish with parsley sauce.[4] By 1938 the average annual number of meals served was 6,800.

The tally system was based on exchange . Occupations which members could undertake for tallies ranged from baking to rabbit breeding, cycle assembly and repairs, house repairs, and care of the house drainage. A barber provided thirty haircuts a week. There was an annual spring cleaning where the club would continue to be maintained in good conditions, and parts of the premises would be painted. Daily cleaning, scrubbing and polishing, bookkeeping, carrying messages, and serving meals earned tallies. An average 180 hours a week was spent on cooking; members had taken lessons from instructors. Three hundred and eighty hours at an average were spent on routine housework, and 195 hours on fuel chopping. Large quantities of firewood were collected, cut up, and sold to members. Men carrying club cards and wheeling handcarts went

4. Ibid.

around collecting goods donated by householders.

Generally speaking, a man had no control over the work he was offered, although he could make suggestions to the superintendent. Efforts were made to find men suitable work from the moment they became members; they were required to put on their application forms the jobs that they preferred to engage in. Since so many had joined who had never had a previous chance of employment, they had little idea of the sort of work that would suit them, and the club undertook to steer them in the right direction. It was hard for all skilled work to be undertaken by appropriate workers, although efforts were made in this direction. But governors and members alike boasted that results were good; a man who left the club to obtain a job seldom returned since he was too good a worker to lose his employment easily.

A typical day at the club was described in the 1938 booklet:

> From 11 a.m. until 5 p.m. 150 men may be all through the premises doing every kind of job, perhaps 20 or 30 in the gardens, and perhaps a few just chatting and reading the papers.
> They knock off for lunch at 12.30 and for dinner at 5 p.m.
> Unless the weather is very bad, no games are played until after 5 p.m.[5]

The carpenter's shop produced a large quantity of rough woodwork for use in the club and in members' homes. Another workshop concentrated on cycle repairs. By the end of 1937 club members could take advantage of a Legal Aid Bureau, sight testing and provision of glasses, and a 'Dental Clinic established through the kindness of a lady member of the Mount Street Society.'[6] Weekly first aid classes provided a small stream of members with first aid certificates. A blood transfusion panel had been set up, and already members had given twenty-five donations of blood.

Subsequently, according to the club's minutes, 'the best sewing machines' were purchased and it became possible for every member to use his tallies to get his boots repaired or buy a new pair. In autumn 1938 Waller noted that 'if the Club had done nothing else but make available for its members and their families, at the beginning of another winter, 300 pairs of boots and shoes, new or repaired, it would have justified its existence.'[7]

The club acquired a loom on which good quality tweed was woven by three club members, two of whom were 'very good weavers.' More important would be the development of the tailor's shop where a tailor came in to teach members to sew; soon they could earn tallies by repairing and altering suits and making pants and overalls. A suit made to order would cost a member seventy-five tallies. At a meeting of the council of the club society in 1938 made-to-measure overcoats sewn by the tailor's shop from tweeds woven in the Club were examined 'and created a profound impression of the progress made.'[8]

Knitting machines, including one devoted to making socks, provided further opportunities for work for tallies. There were classes in bookkeeping. A workshop was adapted for willow and cane work, where an average of three workmen would make willow armchairs, tables, baskets, and trays: items which were exclusively offered to club members and were in high demand. After Larkfield Farm was acquired in 1939, this cane furniture was necessary for equipping the premises.

Music was encouraged, and an entertainment committee arranged that during the winter months fortnightly—later weekly—concerts would be held where performers, including singers and musicians, gave their services free. The attendance was seldom less than two hundred, and the majority of the audience were the wives and children of members. An early 'enjoyable concert' in 1936 included performances from Delany's band, an accordion player, a conjuror, and a boy soprano named P. Coleman. The members and their friends and families who made up the audience paid half a tally to attend. The members could receive music lessons on a donated piano, as well as regular

5. Ibid.

6. *Tally-Ho—The Journal of the Mount Street Club Society*, i, no. 3 (Autumn 1938).

7. Typed and signed minutes of joint meeting of Mount Street Club and Mount Street Club Society, 26 May 1938 (DCLA, Ar/add/81/015).

8. Ibid.

singing lessons and dancing. In addition to these entertainments, the members held regular debates.

Every summer an excursion took place, usually to Killiney, for members and their families. In July 1936 a more ambitious outing was arranged for members and their families who travelled by train to Gormanston where a hall was available to accommodate 400 people for tea. Sweets, donated by Messrs Williams & Woods, were distributed while the Great Northern Railway offered a train taking four hundred people for a nominal sum. Gormanston became a regular destination for the annual excursion, but it was not always so successful. Three years later 'the day chosen…turned out to be the wettest of 1939—probably the wettest in the memory of many of the younger participants.' People were crowded into a large hall and served meals, and 'good temper and cheerfulness of all concerned succeeded…in turning what might have been complete disaster into at least an adventure.'[9]

In January 1939 it was announced that the two millionth hour was worked in the club since its formation. At the same time the 200,000th tally was earned by a member named Jim Gallagher, who received a special presentation to mark this landmark in the club's history.

Sports

Sport, games, and recreation were preoccupations of Waller, who considered that 'nothing, it is felt, will fit men for employment more quickly than work in the workshops during the day, followed by a regular course of physical training in the evening.'

From the beginning there was an emphasis in providing members with a variety of sports. It was felt that two of the worst features of unemployment, described as 'the big bad wolf,' were 'boredom, accompanied by a low standard of physical fitness which would not only render a man unfit for employment, but they make him morose, lethargic, dispirited and almost impossible to live with.'

9. 'Club Notes,' *The Mount Street Club Journal* (August 1939).

Serial No.)
of Appln.)_____/

Member-)
ship No.)_____

Membership Application Form   (when Elected)
(and Record Sheet)

Full Name of)
Applicant   )- -Age- - - - - - - - - -
                                                          Whether Married,
Address- -Single, or
- -Widowed- - - - - - - - - - -

Are you Unemployed, or Casually Employed?-- - - - - - - - - - - -
If Registered at Employment Exchange, Please State:-

   Classification No.- - - - - - - Qualification Cert. No.- - - - - - - -Book No.- - - - - - - - -

Are you in receipt of:-   (1) Unemployment Assistance?- - - - - - - - - - - - - - -
                         (2) Unemployment Insurance Benefit?- - - - - - - - -
                         (3) "Able-bodied" Relief Subsidy?- - - - - - - - - - -
                         (4) Home Assistance?- -
                         (5) Health Insurance or Disablement Benefit?- - - - -
                         (6) Old Age, or any other Pension?- - - - - - - - - - - - - -
                         (7) Any other Income?- -

Particulars of Dependents:-

	Name	Age	Relationship	Whether living with Applicant
1.	- -	- - - -	- - - - - - - - - - - - -	- - - - - - - - - - - - - - - -
2.	- -	- - - -	- - - - - - - - - - - - -	- - - - - - - - - - - - - - - -
3.	- -	- - - -	- - - - - - - - - - - - -	- - - - - - - - - - - - - - - -
4.	- -	- - - -	- - - - - - - - - - - - -	- - - - - - - - - - - - - - - -
5.	- -	- - - -	- - - - - - - - - - - - -	- - - - - - - - - - - - - - - -
6.	- -	- - - -	- - - - - - - - - - - - -	- - - - - - - - - - - - - - - -
7.	- -	- - - -	- - - - - - - - - - - - -	- - - - - - - - - - - - - - - -
8.	- -	- - - -	- - - - - - - - - - - - -	- - - - - - - - - - - - - - - -

Date of leaving Last Employment- - - - - - - - - - - -Duration of Same- - - - - - - - - - - - - - -

Name and Address of Last Employer- -
- -

Special Interests or Qualifications (if any):-
- -
- -

Sporting or Recreational Interests:-
- -
- -

If Proposed by a Club Member,
State Name- -

Give Names and Addresses (if you can) of) Name- -
Two Responsible Persons who would be   ) Address- - - - - - - - - - - - - - - - - - - -
willing to recommend you for Membership:)   - - - - - - - - - - - - - - - - - - -
                                           Name- -
                                           Address- - - - - - - - - - - - - - - - - -

I have been informed of the general Objects of the Club, and the
more important Rules applying to members have been explained to me. I
undertake, during my Probation, to acquaint myself fully with the Rules, as
posted up in the Club Premises, and to co-operate actively in the work of
the Club.
   Particulars taken by- - - - - - - - - - - - - -   (Signed)- - - - - - - - - - - - - - - - - - - -
                                                       Date- -

Membership Application. 1941.

Farm Menu for Week ending 4th January, 1941

DAY	BREAKFAST	DINNER	5.30 TEA
SUNDAY ...	Porridge Brawn Tea, B. and M.†	Stewed Mutton Carrots and Potatoes Tea, Potato Cake	Tea, B. and M. Boiled Rice
MONDAY ...	Porridge §Bacon Tea, B. and M.	Corned Beef Turnips and Potatoes Tea, Potato Cake	Tea, B. and M. Jam
TUESDAY ...	Boiled Egg Porridge Tea, B. and M.	Boiled Mutton Carrots and Potatoes Tea, Potato Cake	Tea, B. and M. Boiled Rice
*WEDNESDAY ...	Porridge Liver and Kidney Tea, B. and M.	Corned Beef Parsnips and Potatoes Plum Pudding Tea, Currant Cake	Tea, B. and M. Plum Pudding Currant Cake
THURSDAY ...	Porridge Liver Tea, B. and M.	Corned Beef Turnips and Potatoes Tea, Potato Cake	Tea, B. and M. Jam
FRIDAY	Porridge Fried Egg Tea, B. and M.	Colcannon Tea, Potato Cake	Tea, B. and M. Bread Pudding
SATURDAY ...	Porridge Brawn Tea, B. and M.	Roast Beef Parsnips and Potatoes Tea, Potato Cake	Tea, B. and M. Jam

* Wednesday being New Year's Day the menu was exceptional.

§ When supplies permit, bacon is served at dinner three times a week and fresh or pickled meat on three alternate days.

† B. and M.—Bread and margarine.

All the articles in the menus set out are, with the obvious exceptions, homegrown. All the meat used is killed and cured at Larkfield and all foods are prepared, cooked and served by the members. The bread, a proportion of which is wholemeal, is baked in the farm kitchen. The charge at Larkfield for full board, lodging and laundry is 32½ tallies per week. There is accommodation at the farm for 45 resident members.

Farm Menu. 1941.

A sports committee supervised those who agreed to take up sport and had to undergo compulsory courses of training. Members had to pay for their games and sports in the same way they paid for meals and boots—by spending tallies. Efforts to keep members fit included the provision of bicycles which could be hired for half a tally a day. Members could indulge in cricket, tennis, clock golf, swimming, and life saving classes. Exercises using the Sokol system of physical training had caught the eye of Waller. Sokol—from the Czech word for 'falcon'—was a movement of physical training founded in Czechoslovakia and highly popular in Europe at the time, so much so that the Nazis and the Communists would ban it and substitute training systems of their own.[10]

Evenings at the club were wholly given over to recreation. At the social evenings held on Wednesdays badminton, and deck tennis where a ring was thrown over a net, could be played in addition to table tennis where a prize was offered of five cigarettes. Billiards for half a tally per half hour were on offer, or a member could work for tallies looking after tables, cues, and marking. Draughts and darts were another alternative, or members could be seen 'probing for suitable fare on the shelves of the Club's library.'[11]

The 'first class' gymnasium, built in 1935, with members doing the work, was provided with gym equipment—a quotation from Elverys, the sports outfitters in Nassau Street, offered hand rings, a spring board, gymnasium mattresses or fibre mats and parallel bars 'very strongly made of ash, base and uprights fitted with special half-round wrought-iron inner brackets strongly bolted together…fitted with steel bars.'[12] The gymnasium incorporated a boxing ring which could be erected or taken down in a few minutes. This could also be replaced by a net for deck tennis or quoits. Attached to the dressing room were hot and cold showers.

Football matches were arranged, players affiliated to the Mount Street

10. R. J. Crampton, *Eastern Europe in the twentieth century—and after* (2nd ed., London, 1997), pp. 13, 236.

11. 'The Mount Street Club in 1938' (DCLA, Ar/add/81/145).

12. Quotation from J. W. Elvery and Co, weatherproof specialists and sport outfitters, 14 January 1937.

Amateur Football Club being trained by a professional footballer named F. Watters. A handball court, built by members in 1938, was regarded in the minutes as 'a notable achievement…when roofed and floodlit this would be one of the finest in the country.'[13] One of the club's expenses was insuring those who worked on this construction at a cost of four pounds.

Probably the most popular sport among members was provided by the boxing club. By 1938 the amateur boxing team was considered to be one of the most promising clubs in the country. In the League they won three section shields, while a juvenile, P. Scott, 'the son of a very popular member,' won the Six Stone National Juvenile Championship of Eire. In 1939 membership of the boxing team amounted to thirty-six men, so that the club had an entry at every weight from four to eleven stone.

Local people would attend tournaments, paying a shilling to watch. In a radio broadcast in 1997 a club member who gained a cup for being runner-up in a tournament remembered:

> My mother never liked the boxing—I would hide the boxing boots and gear and hope to God I would not get a black eye…if we had a little boxing tournament all the local people would go and see it they used to pay a shilling that's all…there was a league started and it was held in St Andrews Club in York Street and we put a team into that…I got runner up in that league—I have the cup… One night a week—on a Tuesday…Cigarettes were hard to come by and we would play table tennis and five cigarettes would be the prize…Deck tennis was played something like badminton and you threw the ring over the net—you couldn't let it fall you had to catch it…it was a beautiful game.[14]

After 1940 sports at Mount Street were supervised by a new governor, Dr Paul Piel, who oversaw the games department run by a committee of members. Dr Piel reported in the club's *Journal* on the success of handball, played in an 'alley which is second to none in Ireland' while the Boxing Club was 'one of the foremost of its kind in the City, and some of its juvenile members are well known to the sporting public.' He concluded that 'a man who can take a knockdown in the boxing ring and come up smiling for more or who can "cover up" and get out of a corner is fitting himself for the more serious fight of life.'[15]

Dr Piel was a surgeon of French extraction who lived and practised at 29 Harcourt Street. Not much is known of his association with the club or how he came to be a governor. He left his mark on Dublin life when in 1944 he established a charity golf competition in aid of the Mount Street Club. He donated a large, handsome silver cup which was first offered for competition in 1944 when the winners were L. Cunningham and N. Martin of the Royal Dublin Golf Club.[16]

Dr Piel decreed that the competition was open to all golf clubs in Ireland, but in practice, those who have taken part over the years have been associated with the Dublin area and its surrounds, such as Howth, Elm Park, Dún Laoghaire, Greystones, Sutton, and Woodbrook. With few interruptions, the Dr Piel Cup Golf Competition continued into the twenty-first century at different locations, the proceeds of the game going towards the funds of the Mount Street Club.[17]

The club shop

The club shop sold to members and their families surplus club-made goods, vegetables grown on the club plots at Merrion and Sydney Parade, and items

13. Typed and signed minutes of joint meetings of Mount Street Club and Mount Street Club Society (DCLA, Ar/add/81/015).

14. *The Mount Street Club*, RTÉ Documentary, 1997.

15. *The Mount Street Club Journal* (May 1940).

16. Memorandum on the origins of the Dr Piel Cup Golf Competition, c. 1996 (DCLA, Ar/add/81/474).

17. Ibid.

offered from outside by 'thoughtful well-wishers.'[18] A shop committee priced every item in tallies. It was the women of the Mount Street Society who inaugurated the Women's Shop Day in 1937, where the wives of members could attend the shop once a week and spend their husbands' tallies on the necessities they required. In its first year, wives spent over six and a half thousand of their husbands' tallies, which pleased the governors, who worried that members had a tendency to hoard tallies; they feared that this would result in debts for the club which could be called on unexpectedly.

Items for sale on the shop day included luxuries. Writing in *The Mount Street Club Journal*, Frank Watters remembered how 'my wife…bought a beautiful pair of the latest fashion shoes, so charming that it made me feel like singing: "lets be sweethearts all over again." They cost only four tallies; that meant four hours of my work but being a chivalrous sort of chap, the pleasure is mine.'[19]

The ladies' shop committee begged from donors ('ordinary well-meaning people') women's and children's clothes, and household goods such as sheets and blankets. According to Beatrice Somerville-Large, 'we'd wash them and mend them and we had everything stacked and once a week…the wives would come and children's clothes, of course, were very popular.'[20]

Kathleen Delap, wife of Hugh Delap, one of the most active governors after he was recruited in 1935, and sister-in-law of Paddy Somerville-Large, later recalled the contribution of 'kind shops:'

> There was a shop called Kelletts' [run by the father of the horsewoman Iris Kellett], they would give us materials—say, for instance, we would get a whole roll of tweed, maybe it was a colour

18. Typed and signed minutes of joint meetings of Mount Street Club and Mount Street Club Society (DCLA, Ar/add/81/015).

19. *The Mount Street Club Journal* (August 1939).

20 *The Mount Street Club*, RTÉ Documentary, 1997.

The Piel Cup.

that wasn't selling very well. We would have a working party in the house of one of our friends and we'd all make little boys' shorts or something like that out of the tweed. But they would also give us ready-made clothes, maybe the end of the line which wasn't doing very well.[21]

The introduction of wives of members to the shop proved immensely popular and Kathleen Delap remembered how 'we always seemed to have lots of stuff in the shop for them.' The shop created further opportunities for earning tallies since a delivery service became available to take heavier items of furniture and vegetables to members' homes.

After the acquisition of Larkfield Farm in Clondalkin, the shop was able to supply produce from the farm. 'How many unemployed men outside the Club can supply their families with such things as fresh milk, butter, brussels sprouts, and ducks?' queried a progress report in May 1940.

Tallies continued to be earned at Mount Street from tailoring, machine knitting, the boot shop, printing, and weaving. At Christmas 1939 forty-two men's overcoats had been made, fifty-seven towels hemmed, and two patchwork quilts had been assembled. Members who did not go out to Clondalkin to work at Larkfield continued to be employed in agricultural work in the city allotments, producing a variety of vegetables at the expanding club gardens.

The agricultural allotments

In 1935 Dublin Corporation presented the club with two allotments along the railway line out to Dún Laoghaire. There was a one-acre plot at Sydney Parade, while the other, at Merrion, consisted of about three acres. The offer was accepted dubiously, even by those who had the club's best interests at heart, since there was a widely held belief that men who had been born and raised in the city would be unable or unwilling to work on the land. The majority of club members were totally unskilled at gardening and had no idea of the work that was involved.

Using the allotments proved to be considerably more difficult than first envisaged, since both were in a poor state, particularly the three-acre stretch at Merrion which was badly drained, sour, and choked with weeds and rushes. Agricultural experts who inspected it declared that it was unfit for cultivation. The governors ignored them and members were put to work.[22]

By the summer of 1938 an average of 550 hours of work were spent by members in the vegetable gardens during the growing season. Both allotments had been drained, cleaned, and manured; in 1937 the fertiliser firm Gouldings supplied the club with a ton of special potato manure, sufficient for three acres of potatoes. The woodworkers at the club built a shelter at Merrion where gardeners could escape the rain. They were encouraged to 'occupy themselves useful under cover during showery weather on such work as the cutting up of firewood and preparing seed-boxes.' Various nurseries supplied seeds, plants and agricultural implements at cheap prices.

Soon the governors considered that no branch of the club's activities showed more satisfactory results.[23] Car drivers on the Blackrock road and passengers looking out of train windows could admire rows of neat, well-tended plots. One enthusiast, Professor Joseph Johnston, speaking in the Senate in 1938, declared, 'they have made a wilderness out at Merrion…a wilderness which is also a marsh—blossom like the rose.'[24]

In one year, 1938, eighteen tons of potatoes were grown, along with vast amounts of cabbages, and lesser crops including 200 bunches of carrots, six hundredweight of turnips, celery, leeks, broccoli, cauliflower, and pickling cabbage, destined for the club's dining room. Vegetables from the allotments gained second prize at the 1938 North Dublin Horticultural Society Show against all comers.

21. Ibid.

22. *The Mount Street Club in 1938*.

23. Typed and signed minutes of joint meetings of Mount Street Club and Mount Street Club Society (DCLA, Ar/add/81/015).

24. *Seanad Éireann deb.*, xxiv, col. 294 (13 December 1939).

Governors D. Kellett, P.T. Somerville-Large, A. Plumer, J. McNamara and J.J. Newcombe at the Mount Street Club Allotment at Sydney Parade. 1941.

The Mount Street Club Farm. 1941.

Far more importantly, those who had dug among the weeds at Merrion and at Sydney Parade had demonstrated that, contrary to general opinion, men who had been born and bred in the city were quite capable of becoming agricultural labourers. The plots were popular among members, who learned rapidly, and repeatedly asked for further opportunities to be associated with the land.

At first the amount of vegetables produced on the two allotments met the whole demand for the club's meals, in addition to the surplus being sold at the shop. But it soon became clear with the club's increasing membership that they could not provide enough vegetables for both the meals cooked at the Mount Street premises and those sought for by members for their families. The Club had become a victim of its own success; it could not recruit further members. Observing how well members had taken to working on the land, the governors conceived the idea of acquiring a farm.

Even after the farm at Larkfield was well established, an average of ten to fifteen men continued to work at the plots. In 1940 a further garden of two and a half acres became available at Stillorgan Road. The Sydney Parade acre had good soil and was suitable for all sorts of vegetables. The plot at Merrion continued to be troublesome; however, it was stated in the *Mount Street Club Journal* that 'a friend who runs a riding-school gives us the manure, MacGuiness, with his pony Alice, carts it out, many of the members dig well and seem to enjoy the work.'

The Mount Street Club Farm

In December 1938 the club purchased Larkfield, a farm situated in what was then a leafy stretch of countryside just outside Clondalkin village. Its purchase had been signalled in the third issue of the club's first newsletter, *Tally-Ho*, with an article by Paddy Somerville-Large, chairman of the board of governors, entitled 'The Next Step' in which he explained that the premises in Mount Street had reached their full capacity. In order to expand, the governors were considering buying a farm, providing funds could be raised.[25] Larkfield comprised 120 acres together with a Georgian house. It adjoined the main bus and tram routes, while a railway station was half a mile away. There were extensive walled gardens and thirty additional acres were rented from Dublin Corporation.

The price of the farm was £3,600, and while this was held in trust for the club, payment was advanced from the pockets of Paddy Somerville-Large, and his brother Becher Somerville-Large, an ophthalmic surgeon who was one of the club's governors.[26] But money was needed to furnish and stock Larkfield. The total expenses were £6,500 in cash, of which £2,500 was capital expenditure, with running expenses of about £4,000.[27]

The first Mount Street Club Farm Week devoted to the raising of capital for the farm was opened on 11 January 1939, by the ever-sympathetic lord mayor, Alfred Byrne. An information bureau offered literature describing the club and the farm, and a series of auctions and raffles were conducted of goods largely donated by various businesses.

Altogether Farm Week had raised £1,570 towards equipping Larkfield with machinery, including a tractor, two ploughs, three harrows, a manure distributor, a mowing machine, a reaper and binder, and other equipment. For the cattle herd a milking machine was required, together with separator and churn. The animals—cows, sheep, pigs, and poultry—had to be bought. The farm needed stables, hen houses, and all manner of miscellaneous tools. Fruit trees were to be planted. Rates had to be paid, electricity installed, and a lorry 'or similar vehicle' was essential.[28]

Another Farm Appeal, a general appeal for capital, followed Farm Week with press announcements, leading articles, posters, and a broadcast appeal,

---

25. P. T. Somerville-Large, 'The next step,' *Tally-Ho*, i, no. 3 (Autumn 1938).

26. Private information.

27. 'Financing the farm—progress of the appeal,' *The Mount Street Club Journal*, i, no. 1 (May 1939).

28. Typed and signed minutes of joint meetings of Mount Street Club and Mount Street Club Society (DCLA, Ar/add/81/015).

A few Facts showing what unemployed men can do when they work together to produce their own needs

● Within the limits of its space and financial resources the Club is open to all unemployed men who are willing and able to help themselves.

● The present capacity of the Club enables it to cater for about 1,000 persons in all, including dependents of members.

● New members are elected by existing members.

● With the Club premises in Dublin, a farm with about 170 acres of land and a bog in Co. Kildare, practically every essential item of food, fuel, clothing and other necessities is produced by the members.

● For example, last year's wheat crop will provide 60,000 2-lb. Loaves.

● Everything produced by the members is shared among themselves in proportion to the work done by each.

● All work done is acknowledged by the issue of " Tallies." One Tally acknowledges one hour's work.

● Tallies, and tallies only, can purchase the commodities and services produced.

WHY THEN DO WE NEED YOUR MONEY ?

BECAUSE————

Unemployed men can make boots and shoes; *but not without leather*.

They can grow food; *but require land, seed, manure and implements*.

They can make suits and overcoats and can weave cloth; *but yarn and trimmings must be bought*.

They can win turf to keep their homes warm; *but they must have tools, transport and supervision*.

In addition to essential raw materials, skilled supervision and transport, many other items, such as rent, rates and taxes, must be paid for in hard cash.

When times improve and the activities of the Club can be more fully developed, its scope will be widened and an increasing number of the requirements of members will be produced.

Mount Street Club Appeal leaflet. 1942

while a booklet was sent by post to individuals, business organisations, and professional bodies. Clergy of various denominations were approached to hold a 'Mount Street Sunday' on which a special collection would be made and congregations would be informed of the project.

The Club's misfortune was that the purchase of Larkfield came at a difficult time just at the beginning of the Second World War, referred to in Ireland as the Emergency. Naturally public donations were not as generous as had been expected, and during the following years the club was repeatedly obliged to look for funding. As expenses in running Larkfield increased, and the public, impoverished by the demands of the Emergency, proved to be less generous, the club would always be behind in its money requirements.

The club's *Journal* included regular descriptions of the progress of Larkfield over the years of the Emergency. The first number, in May 1939, appeared just two months after a farm manager, Mr Keena, was appointed to run the newly acquired farm under the guidance of a farm committee. It described the ploughing of thirty acres without horses, which had not yet been acquired, the development of poultry and increasing number of eggs, and the outstanding success of the farm, the dairy. Efforts were made to build up a tuberculosis-free herd and ten cows were producing milk consumed by members and their children. As yet, hot water had to be boiled and proper cooking and hot water facilities were urgently required. At this stage the farm accommodated about twenty members in dormitories; others came out from Dublin by bus every day and returned to the city after 6 p.m. supper. The account concluded, 'Two months ago this farm was empty; for years it has produced no food of any value to the country; today it is bringing health and happiness to a few men; tomorrow it will enable hundreds of people to provide themselves with an abundant diet of first class food.'[29]

In spite of ongoing financial problems, the farm would persevere. In December 1939 Senator Joseph Johnston, a professor from the University of Dublin, moved in the Senate that the Land Commission should offer suitable estates in its possession to the Mount Street Club, a move that never took place. During a long speech, in which he detailed the aims and achievements of the club, he described a visit he had made to Larkfield several weeks earlier in the autumn. 'There were 37 workers in constant employment there, living and sleeping on the premises and having the time of their life, not only in industrious exertions during the day and in the games and recreation which they enjoyed in the evening.'[30]

One of the first people Professor Johnston met was:

> the dairy-man or dairy-boy who, six months ago, was a messenger in the city and became unemployed in that capacity. After joining the Mount Street Club, he became one of their specialists in looking after cows, having never had anything to do with cows before…He is now by way of becoming an expert in dealing with the milk in the dairy, keeping the vessels clean and sterilised, and doing other highly technical and responsible work. He is only one of several persons who have found specialised occupations which they are carrying out successfully there.[31]

Professor Johnston described the silo tower 'made to their own specification on a plan which Major Waller, one of the directors of the club has devised… This use of grass silage for winter feeding is one of the things which is going to make all the difference to the success of our agriculture.'[32]

The third issue of the *Journal*, appearing in December 1939, contained an account of the remarkable development of the farm during the previous six months. The weather had been good that summer and the crops of oats and potatoes that had been harvested were satisfactory, as were 'first class

29. *The Mount Street Club Journal*, i, no. 1 (May 1939).

30. *Seanad Éireann deb.*, xxiv, col. 295 (13 December 1939). Professor Johnston's speech occupies columns 286-306. The motion was withdrawn the following day (ibid., col. 420).

31. Ibid., col. 297.

The Mount Street Club Farm. 1941.

The Mount Street Club Farm. 1941.

cabbages' and other vegetables. The dairy continued to be successful. Pigs, sheep, and cattle raised for slaughter had been processed in a newly fitted-up abattoir. The forge, cow sheds, and fowl houses were nearing completion. A hundred and fifty hens were already hard at work, laying an average of 300 eggs a week.[33]

The actual premises of the attractive old house had already been improved considerably, an echo of the work that had been done to Mount Street five years before. A water supply was laid on, and hot and cold water was supplied with adequate washing and laundry facilities. By now dormitories were fitted out, beds bought, and general repairs had been conducted throughout the farm house. The library, sports room with billiard table, and a dining hall where wireless had been installed were provided with fires every evening for resident members. The place had a pleasant 'homely' atmosphere which was attributed to the efforts of Mrs Keena, the superintendent's wife, who had been appointed lady superintendent.

In May 1940, the *Journal* reported on the previous winter which suffered 'the hardest and longest frost in living memory,' adding that 'not for one single working hour did work cease or serious alteration in the pre-arranged programme take place.' All during the bad weather members had taken part in 'very useful and difficult work...carried out with field drainage, hedges, gates and tree felling.' Eighty acres of tillage and twenty acres for potatoes were ploughed, and a ploughing match open to Co. Dublin took place on the farm where the club won the premier award.

This issue described how past the trimmed front hedge and through the newly painted gates with their chiselled inscription 'Mount Street Club Farm' had trotted the County Dublin Harriers who had arranged their last meet of the year at Larkfield. 'We provided afternoon tea for our guests and the start of the Hunt—close on 100 riders—was a sight whose brilliance will not be easily forgotten by those who witnessed it. Our sincere and grateful thanks are due to the Members of the Hunt Club for their generous "Cap."'[34]

For five years from the outset of the war, a simple escape from unemployment was to be had by crossing the Irish Sea and taking up wartime work in factories in Great Britain. As a result, as the Emergency progressed, members of the club and those who worked at Larkfield tended to be older men. Their experience on the farm meant that they 'were passing from our fields into regular agricultural employment.' Already in the harsh winter of 1939 the oldest member at the farm was seventy-two years old and he '"stuck to his guns" through the hardest part.' The *Journal* for May 1940 reported that fourteen members of the club 'secured work of an agricultural nature during the past 6 weeks.'[35]

In March 1941 the chairman of the farm committee reported 'with pride' that all men working on the farm were over military age or had been rejected as medically unfit for the fighting forces. 'In addition our "Roll of Honour" of men who have joined up stands at 31. Records show that 145 men have spent some time on the farm during the year 1940 and I am confident that all left fitter and better men in every respect.'[36]

There was accommodation at Larkfield in dormitories for forty-five resident members who were charged thirty-two and a half tallies per week for full board, lodging, and laundry. A farm menu for the week ending 4 January 1941 included porridge, liver, and tea for breakfast, mutton and corned beef served with carrots, turnips, and potatoes for lunch, and tea, bread, and margarine served at 5:30. 'All the articles in the menus are, with the obvious exceptions, home grown. All the meat used is killed and cured at Larkfield and all goods are prepared, cooked and served by the members.' Every *Journal* described the progressive success of crops, ranging from wheat, oats, and barley, through an abundant range of vegetables and fruit which included apples, gooseberries, strawberries, and grapes.

32. Ibid., col. 303.

33. *The Mount Street Club Journal* (December 1939).

34. *The Mount Street Club Journal* (May 1940).

35. Ibid.

36. *The Mount Street Club Journal* (March 1941).

The farm management decided to acquire a herd of pure-bred Kerry cows and by January 1941 fourteen heifers had been purchased. The aim was to have sufficient cows to provide 'an adequate supply of milk for members—and especially their children. Milk is, perhaps, the Club's most precious product.'

During the Emergency, the club undertook a new venture: turf cutting. Imported coal carried across the Irish Sea was in short supply and its price had risen considerably by the end of January 1941, when Taoiseach Éamon de Valera announced: 'In the coming spring every sod of turf it is possible to cut and save should be saved, so that next winter there will be such reserves as will enable as many homes as possible to do without coal, substituting turf wherever that can be done.'

The club had taken these words to heart and had already examined the possibilities of producing enough turf for the club and farm in addition to the requirements of members. The Turf Development Board offered access to a turf bank at Lullymore, Co. Kildare, in the heart of the Bog of Allen. The aim of the club was to cut a thousand tons of turf.

Between thirty and forty members from Dublin were asked to volunteer to go and live at Lullymore Lodge, which was described as standing on an oasis in a desert of bog. 'It was no small thing to ask of city men to go for months to such a place; to do unfamiliar work in, to many of them, fantastic surroundings. But those who volunteered realise that they are pioneers, in the limelight, and that in a very real sense the whole Club will stand or fall by their success or failure.'[37]

James Sheridan, one of thirty greenhorns, describes setting out across the bog at Lullymore with *slean*, spade, lunch, and a barrow. 'All I could see about me was bog and still more bog.' In a morning he learned to strip a bank—cleaning away the sods and mulch from the top of the turf and leaving it ready for cutting. After tea, boiled on a turf fire, he had another lesson on using the *slean* and cutting away the sods. 'It was lovely and cool on the feet standing on the turf, for the sun was very strong and our bare arms were beginning to turn brown. When stopping time came, after 5 o'clock, I knew at last that I was making headway.'[38]

A canal barge was hired to take the turf from Lullymore up to Mount Street Bridge where it was unloaded. Not only did it supply heating and cooking for the club and farm, but it was also sold to members for a tally a bag.

Additional funding was necessary for Lullymore, and a Mount Street Club Turf Production Scheme was initiated and aimed at the generosity of the public. 'If sufficient funds were available, a greater number of unemployed men would be enabled to spend many weeks in healthy out-door work—desperately urgent PRODUCTIVE work. Will you make this possible?...4d will warm an unemployed man's home and cook his meals for a Day...£3 will do this for Six Months...DO IT NOW!'

The purchase of Larkfield had come at an singularly unfortunate time, at the beginning of the Second World War, which initiated a long period of financial difficulty. By 1941 it was already evident that the operations of the club were increasingly hampered by conditions caused by the war. Costs increased steadily and many raw materials became unobtainable. For example, cloth could no longer be woven at the tailor's shop in Mount Street, while the boot and shoe department was confined to mending.

Meanwhile prices steadily increased, running costs increased, and raw materials were difficult to obtain. There were minor difficulties in running the club in Mount Street—for instance, a shortage of petrol increased the difficulties of getting supplies of left-off clothing to the shop. Laundries, whose carts were pulled by horses, were co-opted into delivering parcels addressed to the Mount Street Club after summons by the donor with a phone call or a postcard.

In Dublin the slums were as terrible as ever. The country was no better. The editorial of the *Journal* of March 1941 reminded its readers that 'tens of thousands of our fellow-countrymen in this most fertile and favoured island

37. *The Mount Street Club Journal* (April-June 1941).

38. *The Mount Street Club Journal* (July-September 1941).

TURF (continued)

ducible cash expenditure on equipment, food, transport, technical supervision and many other things may well approach £1,000.

Such a figure may seem surprising, until it is remembered that the *minimum* production hoped for is a thousand tons—and that the price of normally won turf in Dublin next winter is going to be very far above £1 per ton.

Two things seem certain : first, that every ton of turf that can be won will help to make the difference for some family between misery and comfort ;

second, that the unemployed and the very poor will be quite unable to afford to buy *in the open market* sufficient fuel for their needs.

Production at Lullymore, if the work is blessed by fine weather, need only be limited by funds. That hoped-for thousand tons could be doubled or trebled with much less than a proportionate increase in cost, since much of the expenditure need not be duplicated.

But the money is not there. And this seems a pity.

MOUNT STREET CLUB TURF PRODUCTION SCHEME

- The scheme, which is already in operation on Lullymore Bog, is estimated to yield approximately **ONE THOUSAND TONS OF TURF.**
- This figure could be much greater if sufficient funds were available. It could be doubled for a comparatively small increase in total cost.

- **IF SUFFICIENT FUNDS WERE AVAILABLE,** a greater number of unemployed men would be enabled to spend many weeks in healthy out-door work—desperately urgent **PRODUCTIVE** work.

- Will you make this possible? In round figures, here is what your money can do, provided you put it to work on Mount Street Club lines :—

4d. will warm an unemployed man's home and cook his meals for .... **a Day**

2/6 will do this for .... **a Week**

10/- will do this for .... **a Month**

£1 will do this for .... **Two Months**

£3 will do this for .... **Six Months**

- Compare these figures with what your money could do if you were to buy turf yourself—even in bulk—and **GIVE** it to those who need it.
- Here, then, is a highly efficient way of increasing—*now*—the total turf production of our country. And remember that it is *total* production that will count next winter, for the whole country cannot hope to produce too much.

- But time is very short. Every day that you hesitate means one day's production lost. So

DO IT NOW!

Subscriptions to the Turf Scheme should be sent to:

THE HON. TREASURER, THE MOUNT STREET CLUB, 81 LOWER MOUNT STREET, DUBLIN.

Cutting turf at Lullymore. 1941.

Mount Street Club Turf Production Scheme. 1941.

have never consumed a really satisfying and well-balanced meal. All this is well known.'[39]

Beatrice Somerville-Large, who had trained as a social worker, remembered visiting a tenement during the Emergency where a family of eight children lived with hardly any furniture in the room except a table and an old mattress and dirty rags for blankets:

> I used to spend my time at the Coombe looking for orange boxes for the babies and I remember one woman who used to go and pick cinders by the boat club—the children in their little carts and they would pick through the cinders for their fires.[40]

But because of wartime opportunities across the Irish Sea, this woman 'was in clover when her man had gone to England.'

Postwar decline

After the Second World War, and later under the leadership of Seán Lemass, Ireland began to turn the corner towards economic recovery. Soon there would be more jobs and better welfare payments and as a result these postwar conditions which would transform society, affected the ethos and running of the club. State assistance for the unemployed improved, especially for married men, increased emigration offered opportunities particularly for single men, and membership of the club steadily declined. However, the Mount Street Club continued to operate Larkfield until the farm's eventual acquisition by Dublin Corporation in 1973.

Christy Mahon, who came to Larkfield in 1957 when he was ten years old, recalled:

> it was run on a system—there was a bell outside in the yard— the man that was in charge of the house, he rang the bell every morning outside in the yard at half eight—it also rang at half twelve that was to stop for dinner—it rang again at half one after dinner also, the bell rang at five o'clock—that was for five days a week. It rang at half twelve on Saturdays—no one worked

Saturday afternoon or Sunday apart from the people in charge of the animals. Everybody went to their jobs, everybody knew their jobs, they were all interested in their jobs, there was no problem, the majority came from farming backgrounds and that's why they were there...they enjoyed it. There was about twenty rooms in the house altogether—including the kitchen and dining room and recreation room, they were very well looked after, men looked after the kitchen, men would make the beds and the doing out of the rooms every day and looking after the dining area and the man in the charge would see the fires lit so that men could sit round the fires at night...and there was also recreation facilities...snooker tables and pool tables...darts, rings...card games and then the television came in.

Mahon remembered the harvest ball:

That would be held around October or November—it always was held after the crops were saved...they never had much machinery....The harvest ball would involve all the members of the club, the governors, all the neighbours...it would be a great night—there would be a meal and a dance and all, it would go on to at least four or five o'clock and the meal would be cooked on the premises and Guinness's would send out three or four barrels of beer every year...very very popular...there would be a band there...The women would come from around that particular area around Clondalkin to Lucan.[41]

For more than thirty years the Governors would endeavour, not only to keep the original values of the Mount Street Club intact, but to keep up the struggle

39. *The Mount Street Club Journal* (March 1941).

40. *The Mount Street Club*, RTÉ Documentary (1997).

41. Ibid.

for its survival in a changing world. The strategies that had worked well in
the desolate times of the 1930s suddenly lacked relevance. The use of tallies
instead of cash, and the old structural rules that had governed everything
from choosing new members to barring intoxicating liquor, began to seem as
anachronistic as edicts governing an ancient order of monks. The workshops
had served their purpose and when there was work available for salaries men
did not wish to work on the allotments or at the farm.

In the early 1970s the history of the club underwent a dramatic change
when Dublin Corporation decided to purchase Larkfield and turn its acreage
into a housing scheme that would transform Clondalkin. By then land values
had risen immeasurably since the purchase of the farm in 1938. Larkfield was
sold to the corporation in 1972 and finally closed in December 1973. After
the club paid off the original loan by the Somerville-Large brothers, it was
left with a little more than £190,000 in cash. This windfall, invested with
the Commissioners of Charitable Donations and Bequests for Ireland, would
create new and different problems for the club.

By the time of Larkfield's demise, numbers had dwindled on the farm and
those who remained were elderly men. 'When it was closed down there was
fifteen of us altogether. Some of them kind of knew before that it was going
to close and got jobs before that...and more of them would have gone into
institutions...most of them roughly would have been around sixty.'

Mahon, among them, was wistful:

> I always realised that it was a fantastic atmosphere and a fantastic
> place...six acres of orchards, plums trees, raspberries, gooseberries,
> black currants—all of them were picked and the jam was made
> every year...the smell of the fruit and the likes of the gardens...it
> was another seasonal thing that you would never forget and there
> was very few places you would see that size of orchards...a very
> big greenhouse with tomatoes...then the recreation, it was like
> a holiday camp...I was terribly disappointed and despondent to

think of such a place so well organised that it would have to go for housing—why would you have to build on a place like this?[42]

42. *The Mount Street Club*, RTÉ Documentary (1997).

A VISION TO TRANSFORM UNEMPLOYMENT
IV
Colin Murphy

A modest beginning

One day in the early 1930s a small group of Dublin men fell to discussing the city's social ills. The newly free Irish state was experiencing its first global economic crisis and its premier, Éamon de Valera, had chosen that moment to launch an 'economic war' with Britain. Unemployment was soaring. These men were not at risk of unemployment; they were educated, accomplished, well-to-do, and mostly Protestant. But they were 'improvers' in the Victorian mode; men who believed that their station in life gave them an obligation to work for the betterment of society.

'Why not get some place where men who are out of a job could go in out of the rain, sit down, and have a read of the daily paper?'[1] one of the men said. But when that man had finished reading the paper, what then? He would want something more substantial than a game of backgammon. And what of the place where he was reading the paper—how could most be made of the clubhouse? And so the idea took hold of a kind of co-operative, where the unemployed members would teach each other new skills and trade their produce with each other. In a city recently scarred by civil war, the founders knew they would have to keep politics out of it; and, as Protestants, they knew it could founder were it to be perceived as a proselytizing venture: so politics and religion would be barred. The men found a premises and then a name: it would be a good joke to style it like one of those stuck-up gentleman's clubs, they thought, and so it was called the Mount Street Club.

The Mount Street Club's origins were modest. But its ambitions would not remain so.

'The most perfect scheme of social service yet conceived'

'For the first years of its existence the Mount Street Club made no attempt to put before the public its aims or achievements,' reflected the founders, in an introduction to the first issue of the club's journal, in May 1939.[2] Perhaps that was false modesty; the record suggests they were astute in cultivating political and media support. The day before the official launch, in November 1935, they dined as guests of the Dublin Rotary Club in the Metropole Restaurant, where they were formally welcomed by the Fine Gael TD Walter Beckett, and canvassed support. The launch was hosted by the lord mayor, Alfie Byrne, who proselytized ardently for the club and wrote the preface for an elegant pamphlet published by the club to announce its aims.[3] The launch was attended by numerous members of the Dáil and Senate, and was covered in the newspapers.

Journalists were welcomed, and even invited, to the club. A 'special correspondent' from the *Irish Times* called it 'one of the most interesting experiments ever tried in Ireland.'

> The basis of the Mount Street Club…is labour, not charity… None of the men is shame-faced, like the men in charitable institutions; he is working, and taking pride in his work…If a slacker comes along in the hope of free meals and recreation, he leaves very rapidly, as soon as he realises that these things must be paid for by honest work.[4]

1. This account is based on J. J. Newcome, 'The origin of Mount Street,' in *Work to do: a survey of the unemployment problem* (Dublin, 1945), pp. 107-8.

2. *The Mount Street Journal*, i, no. 1 (May 1939), p. 3. National Library of Ireland. My thanks to Barry Houlihan for his research in the National Library.

3. *The Mount Street Club with introduction by the Right Hon. Lord Mayor of Dublin, Ald. Alfred Byrne, T.D.* (Dublin, 1936).

4. 'Mount Street Club: new hope for the unemployed,' *Irish Times*, 10 June 1937.

P R O S P E C T U S.

THE   MOUNT   STREET   CLUB.

The Club has now completed its fourth year.

Its OBJECTS are:

    TO SUPPLEMENT THE ACTION OF THE STATE. in rendering
    assistance to unemployed men by providing means whereby:-

1.   The GENUINELY unemployed worker may BY HIS OWN
    EFFORTS raise his standard of living and that of
    his dependants.

2.   Such men MAY RETAIN their SKILL & INCREASE
    their COMPETENCE as WORKERS.

3.   Such men may build up THEIR PHYSICAL, MENTAL
    and MORAL CONDITION.

4.   Such men enjoy simple AMENITIES OF LIFE
    previously denied to them and by their CO-OPERATIVE
    ACTION relieve the BOREDOM & TEDIUM that is
    inevitably associated with the condition of unemployment.

The SPONSORS for this Club recognise:-

1.   That State action unassisted by the voluntary
    co-operation of individuals and corporate bodies can
    never wholly achieve the amelioration of the hardships
    incident with the condition of unemployment.

2.   That all citizens of Goodwill sympathise with the
    <u>willing worker</u> who can find no place in industry, and
    with his dependants, and are sincere in their desire
    to help them both.

Prospectus. 1938.

The *Evening Mail* agreed. 'The marvel of the Mount Street Club is that men are unchained from idleness. We want more Clubs on the lines of this admirable institution.' In the *Irish Independent*, the playwright and journalist David Sears wrote that he 'came away full of admiration for the most perfect scheme of social service yet conceived.' That the club was conscious of the value of such coverage, and probably cultivated it, is clear from the fact that cuttings were compiled in a memo sent to the Taoiseach's office later, when the club was seeking public funding.[5]

In November 1938 the *Irish Times* ran an editorial endorsing the club, in response to correspondence from founding member J. H. de W. (Jim) Waller:

> We hope that Mr de Valera's Government has not overlooked the theory which underlies the Mount Street Club. If a few private individuals could evolve an organisation which employs more than 120 men daily…surely the idea is worthy to be adopted on a public scale.[6]

By then, the club's founders had become interested in precisely that: how to have their idea adopted on a larger, national scale. They founded the Mount Street Club Society to support the club and launched a journal to disseminate their ideas. They encouraged other groups to follow suit and announced a fund to support them. They made a promotional film and ran an advertising campaign on Radio Éireann.

These actions may have been ambitious, but they were nonetheless conventional: they were the kinds of things organisations do when they seek to 'scale up.' But the founders then contemplated a further step, one with which they were not intrinsically comfortable: they sought public funding and

5. Work of the Mount Street Club, typed sheet headed 'Mount Street Club. Press Extracts,' 30 Mar 1938-4 Nov 1939 (National Archives of Ireland, Department of the Taoiseach: Private Office Records, TSCH/4/98/8/47).

6. 'Work for work,' *Irish Times*, 10 November 1938.

lobbied for a radical change in the state's response to unemployment. The Mount Street Club, they suggested, could be the seedbed for that change. Ultimately, they would be unsuccessful; nonetheless, their intervention opens a window into a time when Ireland was riven by ideological tensions that were a microcosm of the vast rifts on continental Europe.

Catholic action

It was an extraordinary age. The Great Depression had seeped out from the United States. Nazism and fascism were ascendant in Europe. Communism was growing in force. Spain had collapsed into civil war. There was a global crisis in capitalism, and 'men all over the world were seeking a new social order,' as historian John Henry Whyte surmised.[7] On continental Europe, Catholics responded to these ideological and existential crises with a new social movement, rooted in two papal encyclicals.

In *Rerum Novarum* in 1891, Pope Leo XIII had advocated that Catholics seek to improve social conditions in a context of class harmony, as opposed to the class warfare advocated by socialists. Forty years later, in 1931, Pope Pius XI returned to this theme in *Quadragesimo Anno*, subtitled 'On Capital and Labour.' He proposed a socio-political system based on the principle of subsidiarity, in which social functions should be conducted by the smallest or most local organisations possible: industries should be organised in 'vocational groups' or 'corporations' in which employers and employees would collaborate.

Across Europe, Catholics responded with a surge in new social initiatives, in part responding to the same underlying conditions that were motivating socialists, in part as a defensive strategy against the encroachment of socialism. As Whyte has it: 'Caught between the anarchy of traditional capitalism on the one hand, and the totalitarianisms of left and right on the other, Catholics

---

7. John Henry Whyte, *Church and state in modern Ireland 1923-1979* (2nd ed., Dublin, 1980), p. 68. I have relied on Whyte for the discussion that follows.

THE MOUNT STREET CLUB

FOR MEN WHO ARE GENUINELY UNEMPLOYED

(Founded at 81 Lower Mount Street, Dublin. November, 1934)

You are invited to provide funds to finance the
MOUNT STREET CLUB FARM
and other developments set forth below.

The responsibility of making this appeal has been undertaken on account of the widespread support that has greeted the proposal, and letters of approval have been received from (amongst others)—SEAN F. LEMASS, T.D., Minister for Industry and Commerce ; W. T. COSGRAVE, T.D. ; THE RT. HON. ALFRED BYRNE, Lord Mayor of Dublin ; W. E. WYLIE, Esq.

The Club has now completed its fourth year. Its objects are to supplement the action of the State in rendering assistance to unemployed men by providing means whereby :—

1. The **Genuinely** unemployed worker may **by his own efforts** raise his standard of living and that of his dependants.
2. Such men **may retain** their skill and **increase** their **competence as workers.**
3. Such men may build up **their physical, mental** and **moral condition.**
4. Such men may enjoy simple amenities of life previously denied to them and by their **co-operative action** relieve the **boredom** and **tedium** that is inevitably associated with the condition of enemployment.

The **Sponsors** of this Club recognise :

1. That State action unassisted by the voluntary co-operation of individuals and corporate bodies can never wholly achieve the amelioration of the hardships incident with the condition of unemployment
2. That all citizens of Goodwill sympathise with the *willing worker* who can find no place in industry and with his dependants, and are sincere in their desire to help them both
3. That heretofore it has been impossible to distinguish the man who suffers the miseries of enforced idleness from the man who prefers to live in a state of self-imposed indolence ; there has thus been a well-nigh insuperable barrier placed across the Path of Goodwill and Good Citizenship—a barrier that has been the cause of untold suffering
4. That so long as we cling to our conception of freedom, buying and selling our services as we will, there must always be some proportion of our man-power not immediately engaged in production. To cast this aside to rot is madness ; to conserve it and to build it up is sanity and good business.

The **Mount Street Club** has now emerged from the experimental stage, and while **It does not claim to be a complete solution** to all the problems arising from unemployment, it does provide means whereby many of the *disabilities of the genuinely unemployed* may may be removed, the wastage of national man-power arrested and the foundations of Society materially strengthened.

Further, by its characteristic conditions of Membership which offer no attractions to the work-shy, those who support the Club do so in full confidence that their help goes to the **genuinely** unemployed.

The Following is Published for the Information of Intending Subscribers

The Club caters for unemployed men who want to work : it is non-political and non-sectarian.

Founded in 1934, the Club has now (December, 1938) reached a stage where the work provided amounts to 13,500 hours per month, or **162,000 Hours of Work per Annum.** This work is all undertaken voluntarily by the Members.

The men work at a variety of indoor occupations and, principally, in the Club's Gardens. Tweed, knitted goods, tailored garments, boots, shoes, rugs and blankets, together with potatoes and vegetables are produced in quantity and are all passed on to the men in exchange for work through the medium of the MOUNT STREET TALLY—a token currency, only obtainable by work in the Club and one which can only be expended in the Club. In addition the tally purchases : services of dentist and oculist ; meals ; shave and haircut ; music lessons ; sports, such as boxing, football and handball ; games, such as badminton, billiards, etc. ; hire of cycle.

The principle object of the Club is to enable men to make and keep themselves fit physically and mentally, to keep employment when they get it : the priceless boon of employment in these days of keen competition is out of the reach of the man who is unfit. The Club has succeeded in a remarkable degree in this : up to fifty members have obtained work in one week.

The present membership is about 300, and is necessarily limited by space available. For further information see booklet entitled *The Mount Street Club* in 1938, post free from :

The Hon Secretary, Mount Street Club Society, 81 Lower Mount Street, Dublin.

The Scheme is Specially Recommended to all Sections of the Business Community and to Private Individuals, Great and Small.

Subscriptions will be specially welcome from **Banks, Insurance Companies, Business Houses, Professional and Commercial Associations,** and all **Corporate Bodies** whose **Executives** realise the fundamental necessity of **Social Stability** and the dangers and wastefulness which no country with a large unemployed population can escape.

The Sum Required is too large and the **Privilege of Participation** too great to leave all to the individual subscriber.

Nevertheless, it must not be supposed that subscriptions by individual subscribers are not welcome ; the reverse is the truth. The individual subscriber in his thousands is necessary not alone for his financial help, but because it is essential that the main body of citizens stand behind this movement if the members are to continue to take a genuine pride in their Club.

THE FARM PROJECT.

The Club has now outgrown its premises and its supplies of raw materials. It must, in the common interests, be expanded and made more nearly self-supporting. The men have shown that they can work the land successfully and they ask for further opportunities for this class of work.

In the interests of Humanity, of National Industry, of Public Health, of Education, of Agriculture, of Defence, their request must be met.

A well-equipped Farm of **180 Acres,** formerly known as **Larkfield, Clondalkin,** has been secured. In future it will be known as **THE MOUNT STREET CLUB FARM,** and will be worked by the members of **THE MOUNT STREET CLUB** in the interests of those members and their dependants.

THE **PURPOSE** OF THIS APPEAL IS

1. Pay the purchase price of this farm.
2. Equip it with implements, stock and buildings.
3. Provide working capital.
4. Effect certain improvements in the Club.

The minimum estimated sum necessary is **£10,000**

and it is evident that a much larger sum may be usefully employed for the purpose if it is forthcoming.

The proceeds of this Appeal, less its cost, will be handed over to the Governors of The Mount Street Club, who have undertaken to accept the responsibility for spending the whole amount in the interests of the Members of the Club for the time being, and in the extension of the Club's activities along the lines of their declared policy of Agricultural Expansion. If sufficient support is forthcoming, it is intended to purchase and equip other farming property.

Subscriptions may be handed in to The Mount Street Club, 81 Lower Mount Street, Dublin, or may be sent by post to The Manager, Royal Bank of Ireland, Ltd., Foster Place, Dublin.

Cheques should be made payable to THE ROYAL BANK OF IRELAND, LTD.—A/c. The Mount St. Club.

ISSUED BY THE MOUNT STREET CLUB AND SOCIETY.

Governors : *Director* : E. M. McGUIRE, Dip. Soc. ; *Chairman*—P. T. SOMERVILLE-LARGE ; *Hon. Sec.*—J. J. NEWSOME, P.C. *Hon. Treas.*—J. McNAMARA. *Council* : *Chairman*—J. H. DE W. WALLER ; *Hon. Sec.*—H. A. DELAP.

WHO GIVES QUICKLY————GIVES TWICE

Church of Ireland Gazette. 1938.

WILL YOU HELP ?

EACH SHILLING contributed to the funds of the Mount Street Club enables its Members to produce (in return for their work in the Club Workshops, Vegetable Gardens and on the Farm or Bog) about 2s. 6d. worth of food, clothing, footwear and other articles and services for themselves and their families.

The unemployment problem is becoming more and more acute, and we appeal most earnestly to the public to support us in our efforts to make the benefits of this movement available to the vast numbers of unemployed men *who are willing to help themselves*.

If you are not already a subscriber, your support is needed now, as never before.

Contributions, both large and small, will be received most gratefully, and remember *EVERY SHILLING CONTRIBUTED MAY BE WORTH MANY TIMES ITS VALUE IN AN ENLARGED SCHEME OF SELF-HELP FOR THE UNEMPLOYED.*

★

YOUR HELP IS URGENTLY NEEDED

SEND YOUR CONTRIBUTION TO-DAY

TO THE HON. TREASURER,

MOUNT STREET CLUB, 81 LOWER MOUNT ST., DUBLIN

● If you live in Waterford, Cork or Limerick, you will probably prefer to subscribe directly to the Clubs in those cities. Your donation should be sent to: The Hon. Treasurer, Waterford Unemployed Men's Club, Airmount, Waterford; to W. T. O'Sullivan, Hon. Secretary, Cork Unemployed Men's Club, 35 Mary Street, Cork; or to the Hon. Treasurers, The Talbot Club, Lower Glentworth Street, Limerick.

YOUR DONATION WILL BE OFFICIALLY ACKNOWLEDGED.

Issued by the Mount Street Club Society, and printed at the Sign of the Three Candles, Ltd., Fleet St., Dublin

Mount Street Club Appeal leaflet. 1940.

believed that the Pope had shown them a way out.'[8]

Ireland, mired in its own political struggles and with, as yet, little tradition of civic action, had largely ignored this social movement; but in the 1930s, 'Catholic Action' belatedly arrived. And so, at the same time as the founders of the Mount Street Club were wrestling with their own response to the social evils of the time, Catholics—both clergy and laity—were embarking on new social interventions. One of the most prominent was Muintir na Tíre, founded by Fr John Hayes in Cashel; some of its guilds explicitly sought to tackle unemployment. The Tuam guild, for example, undertook a forestry planting project to give work to unemployed men.[9]

This created a contradictory environment for the Mount Street Club's work: on the one hand, it simply reflected a similar desire amongst Catholics as amongst the club's founders, a desire to intervene for the greater good; many Catholics responded enthusiastically to the club and there were Catholic board members from the beginning. On the other hand, the Catholic Action movement had a militant wing, which jealously guarded the preeminent status of the 'true Church' and was hostile to any attempt (whether by public institutions or by other faiths) to infringe upon its responsibilities. The Legion of Mary, founded by Frank Duff, had specialised in picketing charitable services run by evangelical Christian groups, accusing them of proselytizing; its picket against the Dublin Medical Mission on Chancery Place ran till 1989. The Mount Street Club was never targeted, and there is no suggestion that it was ever anything other than scrupulously ecumenical or secular. But on one occasion at least, it nonetheless found itself caught up in an ugly sectarian row, and it appears to have been monitored by the preeminent Catholic figure of the day, John Charles McQuaid, archbishop of Dublin from 1940 to 1972.

When the club sought to enlarge its reputation and seek public funding, in the early 1940s, its representatives found they had often to restate their basic

8. Ibid.

9. Ibid., pp. 67–9.

principles and reassure people that the club was neither Protestant nor British nor ex-military—nor, indeed, communist. During a Seanad debate on the club in 1939, the long-serving senator John Joseph Counihan had described the club, erroneously, as consisting 'mainly of ex-soldiers, men who are amenable to discipline, who will take orders and carry out their instructions.'[10] 'We have been accused of being communists several times!' wrote club founder and chairman P. T. (Paddy) Somerville-Large in 1944. 'However I don't mind what anyone thinks about us, as long as we can continue to exist and stir the social conscience...We don't mind how controversial it may be. We are much more interested in the idea and putting across the idea; than in the Club itself.'[11]

'People still have the most astonishing ideas about the Club,' honorary secretary J. J. Newcome would tell a public meeting in 1940, 'and I could start by telling you a list of the things which the Club is definitely not...Such criticisms as are made against us are usually the result of lack of knowledge or even, I am sorry to say, prejudice.'[12]

The natural leaven

It was into this context of a newly febrile Catholicism that the club's chairman, Paddy Somerville-Large, unwittingly stepped in May 1939, when addressing a meeting in Dublin. His audience, to judge from reports, consisted of fellow members of the Church of Ireland, and he spoke on the subject of their obligations to the wider community. 'We, the Protestants, are the educated people of this country, the natural leaven,' he said; his point appeared to be that, like the leavening agent in bread, the 'educated people' could help the masses around them rise. His intention was to galvanise his audience into philanthropic efforts similar to his own; his effect was to provoke a public relations crisis.

His remarks were apparently reported in the daily press[13] and, in June, the Catholic magazine *Hibernia* responded with a full-page article by W. G. Fallon under the headline 'The Bankruptcy of Protestantism?'[14] Fallon accused Somerville-Large of having a 'superiority complex' and of believing himself to be 'a member of the Church to which the educated people of Ireland belong.' He proceeded to dissect what he saw as Protestantism's track record in social intervention:

> If there are kindly and philanthropically-disposed non-Catholics—and there are numbers—who have a mind for the social and economic welfare of the masses, it is in spite of official Protestantism's admitted bankruptcy in such matters.

He did not intend to attack Protestant theology, he said, but he observed:

> The so-called Reformation contained the seeds of 'Individualism' and economic 'Liberalism,' other names for the chaos in which theological Protestantism has now unwittingly eventuated—divorce; birth control… Unemployment Exchanges; and wage slaves—the open wounds of our own times.

10. *Seanad Éireann deb.*, xxiv, col. 306 (13 December 1939).

11. Paddy Somerville-Large to Thomas Johnson, 16 December 1944 (National Library of Ireland, Thomas Johnson papers).

12. Statement on the progress of the Mount Street Club, September 1940 (DCLA, Ar/add/81/124).

13. Despite references to these reports by W. G. Fallon and in club correspondence, we have been unable to locate them.

14. *Hibernia* (June 1939), p. 4. W. G. Fallon was a barrister, previously a prominent member of the Irish Parliamentary Party, and a 'Supreme Advocate' in the Knights of Columbanus (according to John Cooney, *John Charles McQuaid, ruler of Catholic Ireland* (Dublin, 2003), p. 135). He was a contemporary of James Joyce at Belvedere College and earned himself a passing mention in A *Portrait of the artist as a young man*: 'A boy named Fallon from Belvedere had often asked him with a silly laugh why they moved so often.' (See the brief biography on the website of Bective rugby club: http://www.bectiverangers.com/the-club-mainmenu-5/197-james-joyce, accessed on 4 May 2013).

He concluded:

> If then in the face of modern perils, Protestantism's only
> contribution is benumbed silence, if its 'policy' is to yield ground
> without a protest whenever confronted by rank secularism—then
> let it be known, first as last, that we Catholics intend to man the
> whole line of trenches even though Protestant England's newest
> ally, Anti-Christ Russia, happens to be on the opposite side.

(One wonders what he might have said *had* he intended to attack Protestant
theology.) Fallon's article was followed by complaints to the club's board of
governors about Somerville-Large's reported remarks and his failure since
to clarify them by two prominent individuals in the club.[15] Gerald Elliott, a
governor, warned that Somerville-Large's comments about Protestants being
'the natural leaven' could lead readers reasonably to assume that the Mount
Street Club was the place where he intended to leaven. Rita E. Byrne, a dentist
who volunteered her services to members, wrote that Somerville-Large's
comments were 'offensive to me in my capacity as a Catholic and as a member
of the Council of the Mount Street Club Society,' though she acknowledged
they were 'out of character with Mr Large.' She continued:

> In so far as the Governing Board is composed of members of
> Mr Large's Church their support is tantamount to a repetition
> of the insult. In so far as the Board is composed of Catholics
> who supported it in face of its implications, I view their support
> with extreme distaste and profound contempt. I view further
> association with them in any venture, however laudable per se, as
> eminently undesirable.

---

15. Correspondence relating to speech by P. T. Somerville-Large (DCLA, Ar/add/81/077).

In onóir don Uachtarán
In honour of the President

Ba mhór ag an Taoiseach, thar ceann an Rialtais,

*The Taoiseach, on behalf of the Government, requests
the honour of the company of*

The Chairman of the Mount Street
Club Society, and Mrs. Somerville-Large

do bheith i láthair ag Fáiltiú i gCaisleán Bhaile Atha Cliath,
Dé Luain, an 25ú Meitheamh, 1945, ar 8 p.m.

*at a Reception at Dublin Castle on Monday, the 25th June, 1945,
at 8 p.m.*

R.S.V.P.

Beir leat an cuireadh seo
This invitation to be presented.

Invitation from the President to the Chairman. 1945.

Club workshop. 1941.

She resigned from the council of the Mount Street Club Society, but warned: 'I hold myself free to deal with the matter elsewhere.'[16]

Belatedly, the board and Somerville-Large moved to tackle the controversy. Somerville-Large offered to resign as chairman, but this was refused. He sought to explain himself in a letter to the newspapers, which was circulated in draft to the board for their comments. His speech had simply been a protest that 'the Protestant Church is not taking an adequate part in facing up to the difficulties and responsibilities of our times,' he said. His 'leaven people' comment had been intended to convey that:

> ...because the majority of the members of my Church have been given a decent education, they have no excuse for inaction; nor must the smallness of our numbers be put forward as an excuse, for just as a small quantity of leaven can assist a much larger body to produce something of great value, so a minority should take its place in the community of which it forms a part...I was quite unaware that the word 'leaven' could be regarded as having any significance of superiority or underhand influence, and intended nothing of the sort. No reference to or criticism of the members of any other Church was made or implied.[17]

The letter to the papers was not sent, apparently. Rita Byrne does not appear to have taken it into her head to do anything further, but Gerald Elliott persisted in challenging the official version of events. The club secretary, J. J. Newcome, attempted to placate him: 'There appear to be misunderstandings all round in connection with this most unfortunate affair,' he wrote. 'In the meantime, I would suggest that you forget all about it and have a jolly good holiday.'[18]

16. Letter from Rita E. Byrne to J. J. Newcome, 13 July 1939, Ibid.

17. Draft letter from P. T. Somerville-Large to newspapers, 29 July 1939, Ibid.

18. Letter from J. J. Newcome to Gerard Elliott, August, 1939, Ibid.

Elliott, holidaying on Achill Island, was unable or unwilling to forget about it, and duly resigned from the Board.

The Archbishop is watching

John Charles McQuaid, formerly president of Blackrock College, was appointed archbishop of Dublin the following year. McQuaid would become notorious for the extent of the surveillance he maintained over Irish civic and religious life; in 1955 he would form a Vigilance Committee, intended to report back to him on un-Catholic activity.[19] McQuaid was hostile to the idea of secular charitable work; in his first pastoral letter, in February 1941, he wrote:

> Hence any merely human approach to a solution…for our social problems, especially in what concerns the entire life of the poor, the sick and the children may indeed bring a certain momentary relief: it must, however, fail in regard to that which alone is permanent and divine, the supernatural aspect of our people's life.[20]

McQuaid must have been aware of the 'leaven people' controversy; in any case, he took an early interest in the Mount Street Club. His archive contains a number of documents published by the Mount Street Club, which would have been readily available; it also contains some internal government documents relating to the club's application for public funding, documents which are not in the club's own archive, and a typed list of the club's governors, accompanied by notes on their religious background and character traits.[21] Paddy Somerville-Large, for example, was 'very sincere' and 'rather idealistic' though 'very aloof from members, probably through shyness or because he cannot get close enough to understand them properly'; he had 'real ability, but is very dictatorial and tenacious of his own opinions.' Along with nine others of the governors for which there are notes (the document is incomplete), Somerville-Large was 'C of I'; two of his coreligionists were noted also to be possible Masons. Seven governors were noted to be Catholic, with further detail such as that for J. J. Newcome: 'brother a PP (parish priest) in a Wexford rural parish.'[22]

Later, as the government considered an application from the Mount Street Club for public funding, McQuaid corresponded with the president of the St Vincent de Paul Society, J. T. Lennon, about Mount Street. McQuaid's archive contains documents relating to the club's application which were not publicly available,[23] including a minority report by a member of the civil service committee that reviewed the application, recommending its rejection.[24] McQuaid's words to Lennon suggest that Lennon, or someone else, had called for him to oppose the club. McQuaid wrote:

> I cannot give approval to an Institute like the Mount Street Club, which, whatever its good work, of set purpose excludes the consideration of the Catholic Faith. At the same time, because this Institute is helping to relieve the distress of many Catholics in these times and because the Faith of these people is not being interfered with, I cannot regard it as advisable to oppose the Club by open declaration.[25]

19. Cooney, *John Charles McQuaid*, p. 308.

20. Ibid., p. 133.

21. 'List of Governers,' numbered 1-35, and accompanying sheet of notes (Dubin Diocesan Archive, DDA/AB8/B/XVIII/35/6/1-2). My thanks to Maggie Armstrong for her research in this archive.

22. See Cooney, *John Charles McQuaid*, pp. 308, 327 & 368 for further examples of McQuaid's 'vigilance,' which Cooney describes as 'a formidable espionage network' (p. 327).

23. 'Memorandum for the Government regarding the application of the Mount Street Club for state aid,' 28 May 1941 (Dublin Diocesan Archive, DDA/AB8/B/XVIII/35/5/1).

24. Minority Report by Mr John Dunne, 26 April 1941 (Dublin Diocesan Archive, DDA/AB8/B/XVIII/35/2/(1)).

25. McQuaid to J. T. Lennon, president of the St. Vincent de Paul Society, 2 May 1941 (Dublin Diocesan Archive, DDA/AB8/B/XVIII/35/4). It is possible, of course, that Lennon had called on McQuaid to give approval to the Mount Street Club, rather than to oppose it.

There is no evidence that McQuaid—or other Catholic interests—ever sought to oppose the club. That it was being watched so closely, however, indicates how high the stakes were in social and political debate at the time.

'A plethora of revolutions'

Nonetheless, the Mount Street Club's founders had considerable success in persuading Catholics both to join them and to lead similar ventures. In 1941 the club announced the establishment of a fund, totalling £1000, to help similar initiatives across the country. One of those to respond was a Redemptorist priest in Limerick, Fr J. J. Gorey, who was inspired to establish a similar club in Limerick, named after the Dublin Catholic ascetic Matt Talbot, who had died in 1925. 'We thought it better to make a start humbly and quietly,' Gorey wrote to the Mount Street Club. 'Limerick is a place where you could have a monster meeting, a plethora of revolutions and then apathy.'[26] The *Limerick Chronicle* editorialised that it was 'very reassuring to know that the undertaking has influential backing; the full support of the clergy—some of whom were the originators—[and] the industrial and mercantile classes.'[27]

A sociable aside in the correspondence between the Talbot Club and Mount Street captures something of the class and social affinity amongst the founders of these clubs. Writing on behalf of Mount Street, a Mr Maguire had made a reference in a letter to 'Rowing times'; from the Talbot Club J. J. Scallan wrote to ask 'if I have ever been in a boat race with you, as I was rowing with Shannon RC in 1898, 1899, in senior crews—fours and eights.'[28]

Other clubs were started in Cork and Waterford; an attempt was made to start one in Dundalk, but it failed. A particular supporter of the club within the trade union movement was Louie Bennett, the former president of the Irish Trades Union Conference; under her guidance, the Irish Women Workers' Union (IWWU) started a club for unemployed women and arranged that the goods produced in their club, primarily clothes, could be exchanged for those, primarily food, produced at the Mount Street Club.[29] In an article in the

IWWU's journal, *The Torch*, in March 1941, she wrote that the Mount Street Club 'has in it the germ of a method which may lift the whole problem of unemployment to a new plane…If the Trade Union movement would adopt the fundamental principles of this Club and put them into general practice, it could become a social service as valuable as National Health Insurance.'[30]

The spread of the club's idea appeared to have momentum, and for a time the Mount Street Club governors considered creating an umbrella organisation to facilitate the sharing of information amongst the various unemployment clubs, and to drive their shared ideal. But this idea disappeared from the agenda, as politics came increasingly to dominate their concerns.

A philosophy in action

Within a few years of its launch, the club had already outgrown the modest ambitions of its founders; it was now being conceived of, effectively, as a laboratory for developing solutions to unemployment, and a journal was launched to facilitate this. Initially, the club had been simply a private response to a locally-observed problem; increasingly, it was being conceived of in more political terms, as an exercise in civic leadership and policy development. As they put it in the first issue of the journal:

> We do not feel that we are amateurs, attaching ourselves unwanted to a scientific expedition, but rather scouts, offering our services in the opening up of a new route through uncrossed jungle.[31]

26. Fr J. J. Gorey to Mount Street Club, 14 November 1941 (DCLA, Ar/add/81/079).

27. Cited in draft article by Talbot Club, February 1942, Ibid.

28. J. J. Scallan to Mount Street Club, 30 November 1941, Ibid.

29. 'A new social service,' *Mount Street Club Journal*, iv, no. 4 (April 1941), p. 3.

30. Cited ibid.

31. *Mount Street Club Journal*, i, no. 1 (May 1939), p. 4.

THE
MOUNT STREET CLUB
JOURNAL

VOL.
1.
No.
1.

MAY

1939.

PRINCIPAL CONTENTS.

"A PHILOSOPHY IN ACTION."
THE PUBLIC AND THE CLUB.
FINANCING THE FARM.
DOGS.
THE CLUB TO-DAY.
   THE TRADES' UNIONS AND THE MOUNT STREET CLUB FARM.

CLUB NOTES.
WORKINGMAN'S VIEW OF
   THE MOUNT STREET CLUB.
1908—1938——A COMPARISON.
TWO MONTHS——

The first *Mount Street Club Journal*. 1939.

Or in the more grandiose words of the *Irish Times*:

> When the Mount Street Club began its career in 1934 people tended to regard it as a philanthropic freak. Now they see it as a philosophy – a philosophy in action. They realise, however dimly, that one of the great experiments of modern times had its inception here in Dublin four years ago, and since then has vindicated itself triumphantly.[32]

That philosophy was, of course, a political one; but, though they had been accused of being communists, this politics was not explicitly left-wing. Instead, like the Catholic Action movement, the Mount Street Club sought something of a middle way through the ideological debates of the time, where the state would facilitate social action by private groups. A draft article in the archive discussed this:

> It is easy to adopt the attitude that private individuals can do nothing and that the problem of unemployment is a matter only for the state…The increasing tendency to do this is one of the most unpromising features of our present democracy. The whole ideal underlying a democratic state is that it is composed of individuals, each of whom should contribute his share towards the progress of the whole…The formation of public opinion should come from below and not from above.[33]

The writer believed that such a group of individuals could 'give a progressive lead in the assistance of men who cannot find work'; after three years, the club's founders were coming to the conclusion that the 'self-help' principle

---

32. 'A philosophy in action,' *Irish Times*, 18 January 1939, cited in *Mount Street Club Journal*, i, no. 1 (May 1939), p. 3.

33. Draft report to A.G.M on third anniversary of the club, November 1937 (DCLA, Ar/add/81/136).

'must be the basis of any practical and constructive scheme.'

Elsewhere, an article advocating 'economic nationalism' argued that the only solution to large-scale unemployment was the provision of farms and factories 'in which the unemployed population would produce the greater part of their own needs.'[34]

In 1938, the Mount Street Club stepped explicitly into the realm of politics when two of its founding governors, J. J. Newcome and Paddy Somerville-Large, decided to run for election to the new Senate, as 'the only candidates on any panel seeking election to the Seanad solely on the supremely important issue of UNEMPLOYMENT...Its urgency and vastness raise it far above party politics and make it a national issue—if not THE national issue.'[35]

Their campaign literature elaborated on the reconceived purpose of the club and society: 'It is of the utmost importance that this unique movement should have every facility for expansion, for with its assistance the government of this country may be enabled to change the entire face of the Unemployment Problem by turning it from a dismal quagmire of waste and want into a national scheme of self-help with voluntary assistance whereby 'Unemployment' among able-bodied men will cease to exist.'[36]

Somerville-Large was defeated but Newcome was elected; it proved a pyrrhic victory, for that Second Seanad[37] served just a few months, till the general election of June 1938 brought the parliamentary session to a close. Both men ran again, but failed to get elected. 'The voting for this election was definitely on political lines,' noted a subsequent Club report.[38] (Seventy-five years later, many would argue that is still precisely the problem with the Seanad: that the second chamber has been 'captured' by the party political system.[39])

Newcome spoke in the Senate just twice. In a July 1938 debate on 'vocational organisation' he gave a clear statement of the club's vision, couched in language that now reads as rather paternalistic:

> The State, no doubt, has done, and is doing, a great deal for the unemployed, but we in the Mount Street Club feel that a great

deal can be done by public effort. We look on this great army as of great potential value to the country, in the same manner that the wise industrialist, when his machinery is not working, keeps it well oiled and ready to start at the word 'Go.' We feel that this great potential asset, the man-power of the nation, the men in reserve, should be kept in such a mental and physical condition that they will be fit to take their part when reabsorbed into industry.[40]

By September 1940, when the club organised a public meeting at the Mansion House, they would be confident in proclaiming, 'We have undertaken a colossal job of work, nothing less than the demonstration that unemployment as we know it with all its attendant miseries is quite unnecessary.' In part, that confidence emanated from humility: the club was asserting that its methodology should be the basis for a national scheme precisely because it had realised that it could do little to effect change in itself. 'We must face the fact that large-scale unemployment has become a problem beyond the scope of private effort and enterprise to alleviate, and all the Club can hope to do at present is to make a success of the demonstration which we have undertaken.' The moral impetus behind this was simple. In a democracy it was 'the duty

34. Mount Street Club, 'Considerations on the rational application of subsistence production for unemployed workers,' February 1938 (DCLA, Ar/add/81/143).

35. J. H. de W. Waller, *Every elector is entitled to know…, Seanad Elections 1938* (Leaflet), 1938 (National Archives, TAOIS 98 8 47).

36. Ibid.

37. By convention, this first post-1937 Senate is known as the Second Seanad, and that of 1922-1936 is known as the First Seanad.

38. Correspondence and memoranda relating to the Submission to Vocational Organisation, Draft memo, 1940 (DCLA, Ar/add/81/156).

39. Colin Murphy, 'Irish government moves to abolish senate,' *Pacific Standard*, 23 April 2011.

40. *Seanad Éireann deb.*, xxi, col. 327 (13 July 1938).

and privilege of the individual to think'; then, it was his responsibility 'to try out his theory in a small way if he can'; and if it worked, he should 'try to get other people to believe in and adopt it…The Governors of the Mount Street Club have now reached the last stage in this process; they have tried out their theory and find it works, even better that they had hoped.'[41]

A promising social experiment

The Club's founders had tried to get other interested citizens to adopt their model, and had sought to spread the word via the media and political debate. Now, they took the argument directly to the government. In April 1940, they wrote to request £36,500 in public funds. Their initial appeal was modestly phrased and emphasised the economics of their scheme: they calculated that a typical 30-hour week worked by a member generated a cost to the club of £20 in inputs and an output with a cash value of £52; therefore funding of £5000 'could achieve an output worth £13000.'

'The least that can be said for such a scheme is that it is preferable, on both social and economic grounds, to the distribution of a like sum in public relief,' wrote the Governors. If extended, they suggested, their system 'might be applied with success as an alternative to certain Public Employment Schemes for the relief of the Unemployed.'[42]

This request was not one with which they were entirely comfortable, however. They added:

> The Board are anxious that they should not be classed amongst those who apparently think the Government have unlimited funds at their disposal and it is not the duty of private individuals to take the initiative themselves and to do everything within their power to assist in the administration of the country.

The initial reply from the government, issuing on behalf of the parliamentary secretary to the Minister for Finance, Hugo Flynn, was negative, and reflected the (accurate) perception that the club was essentially a charitable activity driven by voluntarism:

> It appears to the Parliamentary Secretary that the limit of voluntary effort in the City of Dublin in respect of the Club has practically been reached, and that the extension of the project to any size commensurate with the problem of unemployment, even in Dublin, would involve very large subsidies from some other source. Having regard to the degree in which the measure of success which the Club has achieved has been due to the very special and enthusiastic nature of the voluntary service—financial and otherwise—that has been put behind it, the question of assistance from State funds for its extension presents very real difficulties.[43]

The governors refused to be knocked back, and Newcome corresponded regularly with the parliamentary secretary. He noted that the outbreak of war had both provoked a crisis for the club and presented an opportunity: the club was losing men to the Irish and British armies and to the British labour force, and faced rising costs, but the club's farm had the potential to contribute to national self-sufficiency. The farm, he noted also, had had particular and unanticipated success as 'a training school for farm labourers…During the past four weeks 14 men obtained agricultural employment in this manner.' The Club's 'vigorous efforts… should merit recognition as part of the Nation's essential work,' he suggested.[44]

41. 'Statement on the progress of the Mount Street Club,' September 1940, (DCLA, Ar/add/81/124).

42. 'Memorandum by the Mount Street Club to the Minister of Finance seeking allocation of public funds to assist the Mount Street Club,' 1939, (DCLA, Ar/add/81/125).

43. Letter on behalf of the parliamentary secretary to the Minister for Finance to J. J. Newcome, April 1940 (DCLA, Ar/add/81/155).

44. J. J. Newcome to the parliamentary secretary to the Minister for Finance, 20 June 1940 (DCLA, Ar/add/81/125).

The government finally discussed the club's petition in September that year; it agreed that an interdepartmental committee would review the Mount Street proposal and report back to cabinet.

In the meantime, however, the club appears to have had powerful advocates within government. The Taoiseach, Éamon de Valera, had responded directly to a radio appeal for the club the previous October, instructing his secretary to forward a cheque for £5 as a personal subscription.[45] After the cabinet's initial consideration of the issue in September 1940, his office wrote to the Department of Finance in October, November, December, January, and again in February, querying progress on the Mount Street issue. The Taoiseach 'desires that consideration of this matter should be expedited having regard to the pressing need for the relief of unemployment,' his private secretary wrote.[46]

In due course the Department of Finance opined that the Mount Street Club was 'fairly widely regarded as a promising social experiment'[47] and, despite a minority report by John Dunne from the Department of Industry and Commerce, the interdepartmental committee recommended that the club be given a grant in order to test the value of this experiment. The cabinet agreed, but the funding was just a fraction of the initial request: the grant would total £6000 and would be spread over years, being halved in the final year.

The governors were underwhelmed, although they ultimately accepted the grant: an unsigned draft document in the archive, clearly by one of the governors, noted that 'the proposed grant is quite inadequate for any enlargement of the experiment.' The evolution in their thinking was now explicit: no longer was Mount Street simply conceived of 'as an end in itself for helping a few people'; rather it was regarded 'as an experiment to demonstrate the desirability of adopting a system of cooperative self help for dealing with a very pressing unemployment problem.'

The Governors consider that their most important function is to convince the Government that most of the grave disabilities from which the unemployed and their families suffer at present, and many of the very undesirable social consequence of unemployment, can be overcome by the application of the system which they are demonstrating on a small scale.[48]

Elsewhere the club had further dealings with the state. In a submission to the Commission on Vocational Organisation, established in 1940 as a nod to the Catholic Action movement (though the Commission's final report would ultimately be rejected by the government),[49] the club's refocused ambition was boldly stated:

> The Governors of the Mount Street Club…are of opinion that if the Mount Street Club idea was put into operation throughout the country on a sufficiently big scale, that unemployment, as we know it, would rapidly disappear, and that the only representation required would be by the cooperative society which would take the place of unemployment.[50]

45. Mount Street Club to the personal secretary to the Taoiseach, 30 March 1938–4 November 1939 (National Archives of Ireland, Department of the Taoiseach: Private Office Records, Work of the Mount Street Club, TSCH/4/98/8/47).

46. P. Ó Cinnéide to the private secretary to the Minister for Finance, 17 February 1941 (National Archives of Ireland, Department of the Taoiseach: Mount Street Club: question of state assistance, TSCH/3/S11952).

47. 'Memorandum for the Government regarding the application of the Mount Street Club for state aid' (Department of Finance), 28 May 1941, National Archives of Ireland, Department of the Taoiseach: Mount Street Club: question of state assistance, TSCH/3/S11952).

48. Memorandum on Government Grant and related correspondence (DCLA, Ar/add/81/076).

49. Whyte, *Church and state*, pp. 106-9.

50. Draft memo for submission to the Commission on Vocational Organisation, undated (July-December 1940), (DCLA, Ar/add/81/156).

In early 1942 Mount Street received a further form of official endorsement when the Central Bank Act made legal provision for the club's tally system, making the use of tallies in clubs of the unemployed a legal exception to the general 'prohibition of unauthorised money.'[51] Seán T. O'Kelly, the Minister for Finance, confirmed that the subsection in question was inserted to meet the case of the Mount Street Club and similar clubs in Cork and Waterford.[52] Amendments were proposed in the Seanad to extend this exception to co-operatives and to parishes, but these were defeated, with Éamon de Valera explaining that tallies could only be allowed within institutions or tightly-delimited communities.[53]

Unlikely revolutionaries

In 1945 the club took a further step to affirm its position as an advocate and provocateur, with the publication of a report, *Work to do: a survey of the unemployment problem*,[54] which demonstrated its impressive facility for presenting relatively radical ideas in conservative design. The document sought official endorsement, via an introduction from the then Minister for Industry and Commerce, Seán Lemass ('Yours is great work, worthy of the praise and material support of all men of goodwill')[55], and invoked religious sentiment with an opening quote from the papal encyclical *Rerum Novarum*.

The published volume featured a light-hearted article by J. J. Newcome about the founding of the club,[56] but a draft version in the archives is more political. Casting his argument in conservative terms, he decried 'the general tendency to rush off to the Government for money for this, that, and the other untried scheme and to blame it for matters which could obviously be remedied by other people'; he complained that taxation was so high that it had 'become almost impossible for private individuals with the very best intentions in exceeding the world to raise sufficient money to do more than a very little.' Unemployment, however, was not one of those matters that could be remedied by private individuals. The solution, he suggested, was to apply the idea of the Mount Street Club 'on a much larger scale.'[57]

In this, the club closely echoed the style and substance of the great social reformer of the era, Sir William Beveridge. In 1942 the British social reformer had published the Beveridge Report, which would revolutionise the relationship between the state and citizens and serve as the foundation for the post-war welfare state in Britain. The main object of Beveridge's report was the reform of social insurance, but he declared that any comprehensive reform would have to rest on three principles: a free national health service; universal children's allowances; and the maintenance of full employment. The Churchill government was initially hostile to his plans, seeing him (correctly) as exceeding his terms of reference. But Beveridge spun the report brilliantly; by disseminating its core ideas in advance of its publication, he helped created a massive sense of popular expectation. His scheme, he said, was an attack on the 'Five Giants' that blocked the road to post-war reconstruction: 'want; disease; ignorance; squalor; and idleness' (in today's terms: poverty, health, education, housing, and employment). His report sold 100,000 copies in its first month and Beveridge was acclaimed a hero.[58]

Beveridge and the Mount Street Club's founders had much in common. They were middle- to upper-class. They drew their motivation from a fundamental belief that everybody should be treated with respect and enabled to live in dignity. They were liberal rather than socialist: their rhetoric focused on enabling men to provide for themselves, rather than on socialising and redistributing society's resources. And like Newcome, Beveridge often marshalled to his

51. Central Bank Act, 1942 (No. 15 of 1942).

52. *Dáil Éireann deb.*, lxxxvii, col. 546 (30 May 1942).

53. Ibid., col. 548.

54. *Work to do: a survey of the unemployment problem* (Dublin, 1945).

55. Ibid, p. 5.

56. J. J. Newcome, 'The origin of Mount Street,' Ibid., pp. 107-15.

57. J. J. Newcome, 'The origin of Mount Street', draft article, 1944 (DCLA, Ar/add/81/128).

58. Nicholas Timmins, *The five giants: a biography of the welfare state* (London, 2001), pp. 23-5, 40-44.

service what would today be considered the tropes of conservatism: he didn't believe in a 'Santa Claus state'; he stressed the responsibilities of the citizen as well as their rights; and he emphasised that the State should not 'stifle individual incentive.'[59]

Beveridge had a substantial, but mixed, impact in Ireland. He was invoked by Seán Lemass in the Dáil in 1943, in support of a new children's allowance bill[60] but, by the 1945 budget, the Minister for Finance, Seán T. O'Kelly, had gone to the trouble of costing equivalent measures for Ireland and found that, at £20 million, they were unaffordable. Ireland, he said, had less industry, higher unemployment, worse public health, and more dependants per head of household.[61]

'The Beveridge Proposals caused a thrill to all interested in The Mount Street Club,' wrote Jim Waller. 'Here was a doughty champion indeed giving battle on a scale never dreamed of: no David with single sling but a mighty Samson out to slay a whole squad of Great Giants in one operation.'[62]

If Beveridge and Mount Street were united in principle, though, they diverged in practice. While others had argued that Beveridge's proposals for expanded social welfare could not be afforded in Ireland, Waller argued that money was inadequate to what was essentially a moral task: 'Money alone will never keep The Giants away…it is essential at the same time to outflank the enemy by personal effort—Employment, or as it is sometimes called in Mount Street "congenial occupation" is the main armour of Mount Street.'[63]

Nonetheless, money would certainly have been needed to implement the Mount Street idea on a national scale; and money was sorely lacking. So too, by contrast with Beveridge, was popular mandate: the club managed to get one of its governors briefly elected to the Senate; in the United Kingdom, however, Labour had made the Beveridge proposals the basis for their 1945 election manifesto and were returned in a landslide.

Palliative or panacea?

By this time, as we have seen, the founders of Mount Street had radically

THE MOUNT STREET CLUB

reconceived the club's objectives and had sought to have its model adopted on a national scale. At the same time, they had apparently lost some confidence in the viability of the club at the scale on which it was originally conceived.

The labour market had changed radically, thanks to the war: emigration to the UK, as well as the option of joining the armed forces of either Ireland or the UK, had provided a natural escape valve for the pressures of unemployment. The result was a higher turnover of members and less availability of the kind of men that were needed to make the club work: 'unemployed men of an enterprising type' had sought work elsewhere, leaving the club to draw from an unemployed population that was generally 'older, less adaptable, and less inclined to give new ideas a trial.'[64]

The same problem was noted at the Waterford Unemployed Men's Club also, where applicants were 'of a less vigorous and more unskilled type and tend to be more and more of the class "unemployable" economically.' The Waterford club recorded the reasons for some of its members having left the club: of a sample of seventy-two, forty had left for work in the UK; twenty left for 'regular employment'; and twelve left to join 'the Forces' (it does not specify whether the Irish or British).[65]

At the same time, the inputs needed by these clubs had grown more expensive. The result was that their productivity fell—and with it, their sustainability, as they became more reliant on charitable donations.

The political context had changed too. The Beveridge Report and its consequent roll-out in Britain by the post-war Labour government had

---

59. Timmins, *The five giants*, p. 40.

60. *Dáil Éireann deb.*, xcii, col. 27 (23 November 1943).

61. *Dáil Éireann deb.*, xcvii, col. 40 (2 May 1945).

62. J. H. de W. Waller, 'Sir William and Mount Street,' in *Work to do*, p. 81.

63. Ibid, p. 82.

64. Draft memorandum for submission to Carnegie Trust, c. 1943 (DCLA, Ar/add/81/142).

65. Waterford Unemployed Men's Club Annual Report, 30 June 1942 (DCLA, Ar/add/81/082).

changed expectations for what the state would provide for its citizens. The Irish response to these social pressures was far more cautious, but nonetheless social supports were improving, albeit in piecemeal fashion. The result was that the club found it more difficult to recruit members: as they put it in a subsequent application for funding to the Carnegie Trust in Britain, which was refused: 'another cause of the fall in the number of members may be traced to the policy of giving unemployed persons the goods which they require without asking any effort from them in return.'[66]

During the course of their negotiations with the government over the three-year grant for Mount Street, the club had argued that the proposed grant was so small as to be ineffectual. What was the club going to do when the grant came to an end? the club's representatives were asked. They recorded their answer in a subsequent internal memo: 'It was stated that the Club would probably shut down if it was impossible in the next three years to convince the people that the present method of dealing with unemployment should be abolished.'[67]

Thus they had effectively raised the stakes: not merely were they now seeking to have Mount Street be the basis for a revolution in how unemployment was tackled; they also had apparently come to believe that, if this revolution did not happen, their continued work at the club was pointless.

That revolution did not happen. But what would it have looked like if it had? This was the premise of an intriguing article in *Work to do*, the book published by the club in 1945, by the former leader of the Labour Party Thomas Johnson. The article was titled 'Looking backward' and was a futuristic fantasy in which the author imagined he was writing a history of the club as seen from the year 1960. In this fantasy, Mount Street had started small but had rapidly expanded to become a national organisation:

> What began as one of many small scale private schemes of amelioration catering for at most two or three hundred members in its first few years, we now see a nationwide organisation, backed by the State, through which every man and woman as he or she

becomes unemployed almost automatically participates in the benefit of the scheme, which has become the beneficent protector of the working class as a whole![68]

How had this happened? He explained this by reference to the ideological and actual battles of the war:

One of the many unforeseeable consequences of the Second World War, this rapid evolution of the Mount Street Club idea was facilitated by the fact that influential sections of the public were timorous that reverberations from the revolutionary movements on the Continent of Europe might reach this country, and should, if possible, be warded off, even that the advent of the new social order in Britain and Northern Ireland, accomplished by comparatively peaceful means, should not be taken as an example for this country to follow![69]

From this distance, it is difficult to discern Johnson's precise intent. On first reading, his article appears to be a straightforward, Utopian vision of the Mount Street Club's potential; on closer reading, it appears satirical—not of Mount Street, per se, but of Irish politics. He implies that the success of Mount Street could only come at the expense of the failure of a broader left-wing project, such as that which would succeed in post-war Britain: Mount Street would be a palliative, not a panacea, for unemployment.

Despite the more expansive moments of rhetoric that marked the club's intervention in social policy in the early 1940s, the club had acknowledged that

66. Draft memorandum for submission to Carnegie Trust, c. 1943 (DCLA, Ar/add/81/142).

67. Draft memo to the governors of the Mount Street Club, 10 September 1941 (DCLA, Ar/add/81/076).

68. Thomas Johnson, 'Looking backward, 1960-1935,' in *Work to do*, p. 31.

69. Ibid., p. 32.

it was merely a palliative: it did not seek to reinvent the system that produced unemployment, but rather it sought to improve the facilities provided for the unemployed while unemployed. Representatives of the club appeared in 1944 before the government-established Commission on Youth Unemployment, chaired by the Archbishop of Dublin, John Charles McQuaid. McQuaid's transcript of proceedings contains the following exchange:

> McQuaid: 'Do I understand that your system is a palliative in time of unemployment, something like the system they have in America?'
> Mount Street: 'Yes, to a large extent it is.'
> McQuaid: 'If there was no unemployment your organisation would cease to exist?'
> Mount Street: 'It would cease to function.'[70]

Conclusion

The Mount Street Club won impressive support from the media, from what today is called 'civil society,' and from the political establishment: clearly Seán Lemass and Éamon de Valera were, at the very least, morally supportive of it. It addressed a problem that was urgent and extensive. Its aims and sensibility chimed, at times, with those of the influential Catholic Action movement. It was a moderate but ambitious initiative in a conservative country that was hostile to radicalism, of either right or left. Yet Mount Street received neither the funding nor the endorsement necessary to roll out its idea on a national basis. Rather than abolish the then-current method of dealing with unemployment via social assistance, the government gradually expanded it, providing enhanced welfare benefits for the unemployed and their dependants. At the same time, the post-war boom in the UK ensured that there was a ready outlet for the pressures of unemployment. Irish men and women continued to do as Peter Geraghty had done in the late 1930s, and as his daughter, Anna, would in turn do in the late 1950s. The Mount Street Club did not close down; as the stories of Peter Geraghty and Patrick Cummins show, it continued to provide valuable services to unemployed men through to the early 1970s.[71] But the 1940s would prove to have been its heyday, when, for a time, the club's founders dared to dream that another way was possible.

70. Minutes of evidence taken by the Commission from the Mount Street Club, Youth Unemployment Commission, 14 June 1944 (Dublin Diocesan Archives, DDA/AB8/B/XXVIII/451).

71. The stories of Peter Geraghty and Patrick Cummins are to be found in chapter 10 of the present work.

THE CLUB AND THE PUBLIC
V
Peter Somerville-Large

The Mount Street Club's carefully balanced system of pay and take could not work without outside assistance and contributions, never to be described by the word 'charity.' The time had come to bring in the general public. The aim of the governors might be that the club should be self-supporting, but for the time being, financial assistance from outside was imperative. There was a pressing need for contributions apart from those offered by private individuals, in addition to such bodies as the Master Builders' Association and the Merchant Drapers' Association and other business enterprises that had initially rallied in support of the club. The club needed willing helpers, which was the reason for establishing a Mount Street Society. It was hoped that a large membership would be attracted to join, 'persons of goodwill, regardless of age, religion or, political opinions.'

At much the same time as the formal opening in November 1935, the governors arranged the creation of the Mount Street Society, whose object was to publicise the club's ideals with the ultimate aim of starting other clubs in Dublin and extending them elsewhere throughout the country. Plans were ambitious: numbers would increase to a maximum capacity of 400 members who could be accommodated at the premises at Mount Street, and then other clubs would start in different parts of Dublin and throughout the country. A further meeting to launch the society took place on 20 November, once again presided over by the lord mayor.[1]

On this occasion Paddy Somerville-Large, chairman of the club's board of governors, gave a speech that emphasised the club was started 'with the object of establishing something rather different to apparently similar institutions in other places.' The theory they were putting into practice was based primarily on the belief that the average man out of work wanted a job and hated having to regard himself as the recipient of charity. There was no room in the club for the slacker or the beggar.

J. J. Newcome, the club's secretary, described in detail what had already been achieved. Even before the official launch, in the period from 1 January to 31 October 1935, 17,792 meals had been cooked in the club and one and three-quarter tons of bread had been baked. Members had bought 102 suits of clothes, 198 pairs of boots and shoes, and a large quantity of other clothing. Three hundred pairs of boots and shoes had been repaired by members for themselves and their families. They planned to embark on making their own boots—a 'splendidly finished pair' was passed around for inspection. Leather to make and repair boots and shoes was another item of the club's expenses.

Major James (Jim) Waller, another founder of the club, also spoke, emphasising that the system which had been devised during the past two years had already resulted in a profound improvement of the morale of members. 'When men reacquired the habit of doing something useful and tasted again the pleasure of healthy occupation they gradually regained hope and confidence.'

Waller became the chairman of the Mount Street Club Society; the secretary was Hugh Delap, whose quiet, insistent role did much to shape the club's future. A subscription to be enrolled in the society cost a minimum of five shillings a year for an ordinary member. While all the governors of the club were men, the society's committee included a number of enthusiastic women such as Muriel Gahan, the founder of the Country Shop. The society's early meetings discussed immediate plans to organise a publicity week, the first of many efforts to attract public support.

Application forms for membership of the Mount Street Club Society read: 'I acknowledge a personal interest in the mitigation of the disabilities suffered by those who cannot obtain work. I undertake to study the problem and to endeavour to interest my business and/or professional associates and my friends in it, and in the Mount Street Club.' Each form was accompanied

1. *Irish Press*, 21 November 1935.

Hugh Delap.

by a request for twenty similar application forms to be distributed among promising acquaintances.[2]

Practical good intentions were the only qualifications for membership of the society. There were those who could express them by a handsome donation as well. 'Such a one is very welcome,' declared yet another pamphlet issued by the club. Another's good will could be demonstrated by a mere penny a week, and he or she, too, would be very welcome. Those who did not or were unable to contribute money 'may turn to the chest of drawers or the press, the boot-rack or the cubby hole. There he (or she) may find some unemployed goods that will be highly prized in the home of some less fortunate citizen who does not even boast a chest of drawers...By such means may these folk demonstrate their goodwill and become esteemed members of this Society.'

The point was put across repeatedly. At the end of 1937 Waller was reiterating how 'to assist the Club a large number of people of goodwill must be ready to think and talk abut the Club, subscribe to it and give to the Society and to all those individuals and firms who had helped the Club by gifts of cash, goods or services of many kinds.' The club also received gifts of 'jam flour eggs rabbits etc...with the greatest gratitude.'

Regularly, society members, as well as the general public, were nagged. For instance, in October 1936, 250 copies of a general letter were distributed. 'Sir or Madam...Have you anything in your cupboards or lumber room such as clothing and boots for men women or children, furniture, blankets or any other articles surplus to your requirements...All goods received are placed in the common pool of the Club...suits are turned and repaired by the Club. Tailors-Boots are repaired in the Club, nothing is wasted...In anticipation of your kindness OUR COLLECTOR WITH CART WILL CALL TOMORROW.'

'Once again we are interested in your Banking Account,' members of the society were told at the end of 1938. 'Not in the pounds you possess, only in the pence! On New Year's Day your Bank will not open, but inside busy

2. Application for membership of the Mount Street Club Society.

REPERTOIRE No. 1.

The
Mount Street Club
Concert
Orchestra

President ———— Very Rev. Geo. W. Turley, P.P.

Hon. Musical Director ———— Mr. A. A. Kightly.

Hon. Secretary ———— Mr. J. J. Newcome, P.C.

Hon. Treasurer ———— Mr. John McNamara,

81/82, Lower Mount Street, Dublin.

The Mount Street Club Concert Orchestra.

THE ORCHESTRA.

Leader—MR. J. BYRNE.

1st VIOLINS.
Miss N. Rispin.
Miss L. Bodie.
Mrs. M. Byrne.
Mr. W. H. Irwin.

2nd VIOLINS.
Mr. E. K. O'Brien.
Miss M. Flynn.
Mr. C. Ward.
Mr. J. Cullinan.
Mr. D. Kelly.

'CELLO.
Mr. J. Pollard.

BASS.
Mr. E. Weatherill.

PIANO ACCORDION.
Mr. T. J. Daunt.

OBOE.
Mr. F. White.

FLUTE.
Mr. W. Corr.

CLARINET.
Mr. P. O'Reily.

TRUMPET.
Mr. A. Jones.

HORN.
Mr. J. Doyle.

DRUMS.
Mr. C. Tuite.

TYMPANI.
Mr. P. Hogarty.

LIBRARIAN.
Mr. J. Wilson.

PIANIST—Mrs. S. Etherington.

Ref. B72275. M2. J.T.D.,Ltd.,D.

officials will spend the day striking a balance…it is almost certain to contain pence. Will you give us these pence to help your unemployed fellow citizens?… Every five new pennies subscribed to the Mount Street Club can be turned by the Members' own work into 12 pennies worth of food, fuel or clothing for their children, their wives or themselves…The Club is not an organisation for dispensing charity. It provides a means for you to help your less fortunate fellow citizens to help themselves.'

The public response included a writer to the *Mount Street Club Journal* who described herself as 'just a girl earning thirty bob a week.' She contributed to the funds a penny a week. 'I do not miss this, but it enables me to have the satisfied feeling that I am helping to make life a bit brighter for somebody.'[3] About half of the members were working men and women among whom groups were formed, each member contributing a penny a week.

Firms such as Kelletts, Swastika Laundry, Wills Cigarettes, Bolands, Jacobs, and Guinness undertook to pay regular subscriptions. However, most guaranteed subscriptions would come from individuals, among whom was the eccentric and generous lawyer and raconteur Eoin O'Mahony, known to all as Pope O'Mahony. Others gave in kind parcels of clothes, flour, pots of jam, meat, and black pudding.

Publicity campaigns and events

From the official opening of the Mount Street Club in 1935, publicity was necessary to raise funds. It may have been Waller in his position as chairman of the Mount Street Club Society who came up with the idea to associate lilac with the club. After it was agreed that the club should have lilac as its symbol and be brought to the notice of the public, a street collection was held annually on what came to be known as Lilac Day. Not only members of the society, but even the governors volunteered as sellers, offering sprigs of lilac to donors.[4] Lilac Days increased over the years; by 1939 there were three on 3, 4, and 5 May. 'Buy a Sprig from one of our Collectors,' the public was urged. 'They are very Pretty Emblems and will Adorn You.'[5]

In the minutes of the society are suggestions for the use of extra collecting boxes during Lilac Week. Other ideas involved collections on boats coming from Holyhead and Liverpool, inside the gates of the Royal Dublin Society (RDS) Spring Show at Ballsbridge, and house-to-house collections where, the minutes noted, some of the ladies might prefer to select their own areas.[6]

In 1938 Lilac Day was supplemented by the renting of the Gaiety Theatre for a week for the production of a musical whose title and theme had particular relevance. *Lilac Time*, a pastiche operetta translated from a Viennese version of the story, concerns the fictionalised youth of the composer Franz Schubert as an impoverished student. Containing such musical gems as 'Oh the Maytime is a Gaytime,' 'Four Jolly Brothers,' and 'Maiden, Try to Smile,' it was first performed in London in 1922 where it ran for over 600 performances. There were numerous revivals, including the six performances run at the Gaiety in Lilac Week, 1938. Renting the theatre, paying for lighting and advertisements cost £400, and costumes a further £300. However, takings were around £900 and a profit of £260 was raised for the benefit of the club.[7] In addition, sprigs of lilac sold in the theatre provided further funding. The performances were considered 'of the very highest order of merit.'[8]

Every year in the same week at the Spring Show, the club took a stand, offered for a nominal price by the RDS where club members displayed their skills, such as sock making, boot making, and mat making. Club products,

3. *The Mount Street Club Journal* (August 1939).

4. Typed and signed minutes of joint meeting of Mount Street Club and Mount Street Club Society (DCLA, Ar/add/81/015).

5. *The Mount Street Club Journal*, i, no. 1 (May 1939).

6. Typed and signed minutes of joint meeting of Mount Street Club and Mount Street Club Society (DCLA, Ar/add/81/015).

7. Correspondence relating to Olympia and Gaiety performances (DCLA, Ar/add/81/253).

8. Typed and signed minutes of joint meeting of Mount Street Club and Mount Street Club Society (DCLA, Ar/add/81/015).

together with literature and photographs, were offered for sale with the inevitable sprigs of lilac. There was a similar stand at the RDS Horse Show.[9]

After the purchase of the farm at Larkfield, the club held its first Farm Week in January 1939. Members of the society formed a large part of the voluntary staff that handled the proceedings, which were run from 45 Grafton Street, an office donated by Messrs Booth Brothers who ran the Grafton Motor Company. An exhibition offered to the public was similar to those regularly held at the RDS, but aimed at those who did not usually attend the grassy lawns of Ballsbridge. Like the RDS stands, it demonstrated the club's produce and the acquired skills of members: the boots and shoes, furniture, knitwear, and other items made at Mount Street. The council of the society offered a special prize to members responsible for the best club exhibit. There were photographs, and designs submitted for the recent competition for the cover of the *Mount Street Club Journal*. A film was shown about the club, which would later be taken elsewhere to Cork and Waterford where the Mount Street Club idea would be taken up and other clubs formed in imitation. In the same premises on Grafton Street a series of auctions and raffles was conducted of goods largely donated by 'the Traders of Dublin' whose response was 'very gratifying.' Posters were distributed widely. The entertainments that ran during the week included a performance by Miss Mooney's School of Dancing at the Queen's Theatre.

All those connected with the club concluded that 'very many people have seen for themselves something of the work of the club, much misapprehension has been removed and many new friends made.' But they had to admit that financial rewards were disappointing:

From the small shopkeeper who brought us the most highly-priced article in his stock—a half-pound packet of tea—and tied around it a one pound note; from the hundreds of factory workers

9. *Tally-Ho* i, no. 3 (Autumn 1938).

04. 105.

TUESDAY 17th DEC 1946

MOUNT ST. CLUB XMAS SALE.

1. MEAL OF COTTON. WOOL.
2. DOVE PAN.
3. STUNG.
4. WONDER BOX.
5. 30 CARD TRICK.
6. BAFFLING BUNNIES.
7. 3 CARD TRICK.
8. EGG BAG.
9. COIN PRODUCTION.
10. EVAPORATED MILK. AND BANG GUN.

ASSISTANT: RONNIE.

REMARKS: THE ABOVE SHOW WAS PRESENTED TWICE.
THERE WERE ABOUT 15 PEOPLE AT EACH SHOW. THE SALE
ITSELF WAS TERRABLE, THEY HAD HARDLY ANYTHING TO SELL.
THERE FORE, VERY LITTLE PEOPLE AT THE SALE. I APPEARED IN
EVENING DRESS. NO MISHAPS.

Excerpt from the diary of magician Albert le Bas. 1946.

who are regularly subscribing their penny per week; from those who have handsomely weighed in with cheques for £100 we have experienced nothing but intense enthusiasm, patriotism and appreciation of the work. From the larger building concerns and from many of the well-to-do it must be admitted that, up to the present, the response has not been what we had hoped for.[10]

Beginning in the autumn of 1939, it became increasingly difficult to raise funds among supporters because of other demands arising from wartime requirements. As the Emergency continued, the inability of the club to publicise its activities to the same extent as formerly would increase. Many active members of the board were away on war work. They included Waller, who went to England and tried to enlist but was declared too old. Instead he did his bit designing huts, warehousing, and aircraft hangars for the War Office.

Back at Mount Street, programmes continued as usual. The *Journal* reported on social activities, the annual dinner and children's party, the whist drives, games, and tournaments. In particular, the winter series of concerts performed by 'numerous and talented artistes' held weekly on Fridays continued to be one of the club's most popular features. Musical societies, concert parties, dramatic societies, and dancing schools contributed their services for free. 'Our visiting artistes are always telling of their personal enjoyment and their feeling of privilege at appearing on the Club platform.' About half the audience were children. 'It has been pleasing to see the eagerness with which the members' children clamoured each week for admission to the Concerts and the enthusiasm with which, at times, they joined with the artistes in the singing of popular songs.'

In the winter of 1941 a more spectacular theatrical experience was offered when the manager of the Queen's Theatre arranged a matinee of the pantomime *Red Riding Hood* for the wives and children of Club members. Nearly five hundred mothers and children attended, singing the choruses along with the performers. At the interval performers mixed with the children in the auditorium and distributed sweets. 'At a subsequent meeting of the members' House Committee a unanimous vote of thanks was passed to Mr Gogan for his kindness in giving this splendid treat to so many children who might otherwise have been unable to see a real pantomime this season.'[11]

The original 1939 appeal, aimed towards financing the Mount Street Club Farm, brought in just under three thousand pounds. The renewed Wartime Campaign raised approximately a thousand pounds. The *Journal* of May 1940 told its readers that 'continued success is assured—provided—and it is well not to mince matters in these stern days—the Club receives the financial support it deserves; without that support it must cease to exist. That contingency does not bear thinking about.'[12]

In April 1941 a second exhibition, similar to that of the Mount Street Club Farm Week held two years earlier, took place on the same premises in Grafton Street, which was embellished with 'amusing mural decorations.' Over ten thousand people attended between 21 and 26 April. Once again there were diagrams, photographs, and demonstrations of the range of commodities produced at Mount Street ('furniture, baskets, wicker chairs, woven cloth, blankets, rugs, clothes woven and tailored in the Club, socks, shoes, ladies sandals and children's garments'). These garments 'of attractive design and excellent design' caught the eye of visitors who tried to buy them. In vain: 'No, I am afraid they are not for sale, unless' (with a smile) 'you are unemployed and have earned the tallies for them.'

From Larkfield came a handful of wheat from the previous year's harvest, and heaps of oatmeal, rhubarb, barley, and onions 'which caused more mouths than eyes to water, and were rather pointedly kept out of reach by a net of annoyingly small mesh!'

Throughout the week a series of distinguished speakers gave a series of

10. 'Financing the farm—progress of the appeal,' *The Mount Street Club Journal*, i, no.1 (May 1939).

11. *The Mount Street Club Journal* (February 1941).

12. *The Mount Street Club Journal* (May 1940).

LILAC
DAYS
1939

MAY 3rd, 4th and 5th

Buy a Sprig from one of our Collectors.
They are very Pretty Emblems and
will Adorn You.

When You buy them, You help the
Mount Street Club and Farm.

THE MOUNT STREET CLUB SOCIETY

81 LOWER MOUNT STREET, DUBLIN

Hon. Secretary: J. J. NEWCOME, P.C.   *Organising Secretary*: F. HOLTSBAUM

This Society was formed in order to unite all those who, while unwilling to remain inactive in the face of widespread unemployment, yet feel that an individual acting alone can do little that is constructive. Every person who is not eligible for membership of the Mount Street Club may join the Mount Street Club Society. The sole qualification necessary is the giving of practical assistance to the work of the Club.

To belong to the Society one need not be a subscriber to the Club, though naturally the majority of its members have joined in this way—and funds must always remain the greatest material need. In many other ways, however, the Club needs help, and in as many different ways the public can join the Society.

Some of the Society's most valued members have themselves suggested and introduced the methods whereby they work for the Club.

The Hon. Secretary will be pleased to hear from all who would like to help the Club, even though they may be unable to contribute to its funds.

The Mount Street Club Journal is published for the Society to enable its members to keep in touch with the progress of the Club, and all who read it can serve the Club by making its aims and methods widely known.

MOUNT STREET CLUB SOCIETY NOTES

THE Ladies' Shop Committee, at their monthly meeting on 4th April, had the pleasure of hearing Miss Louie Bennett tell them about the "Torch and Distaff Guild"—the Club on Mount Street Club lines recently established by the Irish Women Workers' Union.

An informal talk followed on the best methods of co-operation between the Guild and Club, particularly with regard to the making and repairing of clothes. Already the Guild are making clothes for the Mount Street Club, payment being in Tallies, which are subsequently exchanged by Guild members for potatoes, shoe-repairs and similar products of Mount Street.

Every Wednesday morning, when the wives of Mount Street Club members shop, it is possible to offer them a fresh selection of very attractive children's clothes, products of the Guild.

* * *

An appeal to those who sew or knit, and have a little time to spare, is made by the Shop Committee. "Please send us a postcard and tell us you will do something to help us now—knit a jumper, sew a child's petticoat, or—best of all—gather a work party together.

"We have the wool, and we also send out children's clothes, ready cut out; we can supply simple patterns for either. But we have neither the workers nor the money to stock the shop as we would wish.

"The members of the Club can make a great many things their families require, but raw materials are expensive and the demand for children's garments is inexhaustible. Collaboration with the Torch and Distaff Guild will be of great benefit in making available for Mount Street Club families many things that men cannot easily or economically make—and vice versa. But there is still room for all the outside help in time, raw materials and money that you can give.

"You are delighted when you have a successful shopping day and find just what you want; please make shopkeeping at Mount Street as great a pleasure for the members' wives by helping us in the way described—or by sending us any clothes you can spare, to be repaired or converted into something new.

"REMEMBER:

If you knit, we will send you wool and instructions.

If you sew, we will send you cut-out garments, ready to be sewn, and simple patterns.

If you cannot do either, perhaps you can collect—old clothes to send to the Club,—old friends to form a Work Party!

Mount Street Club Journal. 1941.

somewhat pompous talks ('Co-operative self-help is the valuable constructive principle which forms the basis of the work'). They included Thomas Derrig, the minister for education, the Rev. J. M. Hayes, founder of Muintir na Tíre, and J. J. Rowe, corporation allotments officer. When Luke Duffy, the general secretary of the Irish Labour Party, began his speech, he explained that he had another engagement in half an hour's time which compelled him to be very brief. 'He then spoke for forty-five minutes to an audience who had packed the hall, the majority without seats or even a wall to lean against, who listened with close and eager attention to every word.'[13]

There were many volunteers, more helpers than ever before, who spent long hours on the street with collection boxes. Sadly, once again the cash received was 'perhaps disappointing.' Times were harder than ever. Again the club had to be satisfied that the success of the week was gained in goodwill and knowledge spread abroad.

Appeals for further funding came in small ways detailed in the *Journal*. A duplicate contract bridge tournament took place in Engineers' Hall. ('Tickets, including refreshments 3/6d payable at door.') Whist drives were held regularly; so were bridge tournaments offering both duplicate and rubber bridge and 'most attractive prizes.' There was a dance at the Mansion House and a Midnight Matinee held in conjunction with the Jewish Youth Refugee Organisation. 'We have to thank Mrs Logan for a most enjoyable Whist Drive which she organised...on February 14th at the Parochial Hall, Cross Avenue, Blackrock. The attendance was good in spite of transport difficulties and the coldness of the evening.'

The Rathmines and Rathgar Musical Society put on the *Mikado* at the Gaiety to aid the club; the 'artistes' gave their services free, but there were expenses, including the hiring of the theatre, costumes, and scenery, so that the gains were modest. Further funds were raised in the same month at a whist drive held at the Country Shop with 'attractive prizes' and a bridge tournament which took place at Fullers of Grafton Street, tickets (including refreshments) five shillings. The Carrickmines Players presented *On Baile's*

Strand by W. B. Yeats. Whist and bridge drives raised cash, and so did an 'American tea' held at Larkfield. 'A DANCE in aid of the Mount Street Club will be held at Shelbourne Hall Merrion Row…8-12 p.m…Spot Prizes— Tickets 2/6 (PAYABLE AT DOOR).' Music was provided by the Mount Street Club Band.

Letters were acknowledged. 'Dear Sir, Enclosed please find four shillings towards the funds of your Club and may God bless your work for the men…' One donor described how she had 'searched the house yesterday for something suitable to send you for your shop, but failed rather depressingly. But I did find a treasured collection of bronzes, lost for twelve years. Enclosed, please, find cheque in gratitude.'

There were 'gifts in kind.' An extreme example was a hundredweight of flour bought, as directed by the government, by a well-wisher in the early days of the Emergency; it became evident that his family could not eat it and he was prepared to write it off as a total loss; then he thought of the club.[14]

Money continued to be an increasing preoccupation with the governors. Up until the purchase of Larkfield, the governors could consider the club as reasonably successful during the five years of its existence in providing goods and services paid for by the tally system. The system worked, and the club in Mount Street, and Larkfield in particular, might seem to be flourishing. But financial problems would continue to harass the club throughout the war and far beyond. At the time of the purchase of Larkfield some funding had come from the Department of Agriculture, but government funding proved to be insufficient.

Printed promotion

Written publicity for the club was initially directed by Waller. Among members of the society and club, the first report produced by 'stencil' appeared in April

13. *Mount Street Club Journal* (April-June 1941).

14. *Mount Street Club Journal* (February 1941).

1937, and after that appeared monthly. Waller observed with satisfaction that 'no greater tribute has ever or will ever be paid to the sincerity of the Irish worker's interest in the cause of his fellow-Irishman than the extraordinary eagerness with which the monthly bulletins issued by the Club were seized and read.'

In late 1937 the club acquired a small second-hand printing-press for members to do a variety of printing jobs, such as dockets, post cards for calling meetings, dance tickets, and programmes. The press also allowed the bulletin to be adapted into a newsletter which was named *Tally-Ho*. The first issue, in May 1938, coincided with Lilac Week. Hundreds of copies were distributed at the club stand at the Spring Show and at the performances of *Lilac Time* in the Gaiety Theatre, while further copies were sent to every member of the society and hundreds of other helpers who were not immediately connected with the club.[15]

The third issue of *Tally-Ho*, published in autumn 1938, contained a column on statistics which the club always liked to offer as direct information on its aims and achievements. The public was told that 183 hours were worked in the bakery in September and 877 loaves were baked. In the same month ninety-four pairs of shoes were repaired and eight pairs of boots and shoes were made. Over three thousand hours were worked in the allotments at Merrion and Sydney Parade and over four and a half thousand meals were provided at the club itself. The column concluded: 'similar figures could be shown for many other activities, such as messenger services, cloakroom and library attendants, cleaners, painters, boiler men and so on, but space does not permit.'[16]

Items in the Mount Street Club Member's Section in the autumn edition included the following: 'We are proud of the fact that the civic spirit is well to the fore in Mount Street. The members' Blood Transfusion Panel continues to function and frequent calls upon donors have been made in recent months. We are honoured, too, in having at least one hero amongst us and we refer here with pride, to the gallant action of James Donnelly. This member, at grave danger to his life, rescued a child from drowning in the Canal Lock at Mount Street Bridge…He is undoubtedly a credit to the Club.'[17]

A report on the history of the Mount Street Club written in 1994 considered the name *Tally-Ho* 'singularly incongruous.'[18] This might well be the case, but it should be remembered that Waller had a Wodehousian sense of humour which included a liking for puns. However, after the third issue he had second thoughts. Not only did he decide that the journal should be enlarged and improved 'very considerably,' but he invited suggestions for a new title. This would be the more sober *Mount Street Club Journal*, which would be delivered free of charge to all supporters of the club. Early issues would be printed in the usual way on the club printing press by club members, but later they would be produced by outside printing firms.

From the outset, the *Journal* presented its readers with personal insights into the club's development that were unavailable elsewhere. The first issue, which appeared in May 1939, described itself as 'devoted to the study of unemployment and all that it implies' and offered an account of work from a member's point of view. Frank Watters wrote:

> ...during my nearly four years of married life I have not, thank God, experienced the awful agony of seeing my wife and children hungry...My first job was in the plots of Sydney Parade where I was supplied with a spade and, the weather being lovely, I did one man's part in helping our good friend 'Mother Earth' to do her work. Since then I have performed various duties from the humble work of peeling potatoes (three hours work for three of us) to the more serious work of making concrete blocks. Sowing potatoes,

15. Typed and signed minutes of joint meeting of Mount Street Club and Mount Street Club Society (DCLA, Ar/add/81/015).

16. 'Club Statistics,' *Tally-Ho*, i, no. 3 (Autumn 1938).

17. 'Mount Street Club Members Section—House Committee Notes,' Ibid.

18. Judith Kiernan and Brian Harvey, 'The Mount Street Club: past, present and future,' November 1994 (DCLA, Ar/add/81/130).

weeding in the gardens, door porter are some of the many other duties where one can make oneself generally useful. In return for this I have helped myself to dinners, haircuts, a nice suit of clothes, many pints of good milk, etc.[19]

The third issue of the *Journal*, appearing in December 1939, contained, in addition to news of the club and the progress of the farm, a ditty sung to the tune of 'The Mountains of Mourne': 'At Eighty-one Mount Street there is a fine Hall, For all unemployed men to see when they call...'[20]

The *Mount Street Club Journal* initially appeared quarterly, but from 1941 it was published monthly. The prize-winning cover design by Miss Eileen Couglan showed a working man wearing a cap face forward, while a shadowy procession of similar figures marched behind him. The critical report of 1994 complained that 'the contents were strictly segregated as from Mount Street Club Society members, governors, members and general articles by public personalities...Many of the articles were idiosyncratic musings, often politicised, particularly after the start of the second world war.'[21] The *Journal* also reflected criticism of the club, particularly, and many articles defended areas of negative reaction to the club from outside, the authors feeling themselves to be genuinely misunderstood.

At some time towards the end of the war the *Mount Street Club Journal*, with its valuable insights into the development of Larkfield and the progress at Lullymore, and notes on the continuing situation in Mount Street itself ceased to be published. Other documentation appears to have become sparse. The surviving records, minutes, and correspondence that were held in the Mount Street Club premises were later transferred to the premises at Fenian Street. In 2006 they were admirably catalogued for the Dublin City Archives by Deirdre O'Connell and are now stored in the Dublin City Library in Pearse Street. In spite of gaps in the records, they offer a comprehensive record of the Mount Street Club's progress over the past eighty years, reflecting the immense changes in social conditions during that period. Together they form a unique insight into the needs of the working class in the 1930s and 1940s, and present material of significant value to social historians. A second uncatalogued collection of documents acquired by Paddy Somerville-Large is held by Paddy's son, W. B. O. Somerville-Large.

In 1997 RTÉ broadcast a programme on the Mount Street Club which included the participation of a few surviving people who were involved with the club either as members or as participants in the society from its early years. Among these, Kathleen Delap, widow of Hugh Delap, one of the most forceful of the early governors, and Beatrice Somerville-Large, Paddy's sister-in-law, recalled the activities of members of the Mount Street Club Society.

Reactions in the press

A week after its formal opening the Mount Street Club was mentioned in a sermon on Remembrance Sunday at St Patrick's Cathedral. 'The opening of the first Unemployed Men's Club is surely a sublimation of that quiet heroism which dwells in most people.' However, the opening had been performed with an amount of fanfare and publicity that initially left the press bemused. The club was regarded as eccentric, 'a philanthropic freak' in the words of the *Irish Times*.[22] But its unusual methodology—there was nothing else remotely like it in Ireland—would soon gain wide appeal.

In December 1935 a reporter from the *Irish Independent* whose article was signed with the initials 'D. S.,' called in to Mount Street and 'came away full of admiration for the most perfect scheme of social service yet conceived.'[23] D. S. wrote that if ever he was reduced to destitution he would gladly join the club without feeling in any way that he was sacrificing self-respect or independence.

19. Frank Watters, 'An appreciation,' *Mount Street Club Journal*, i, no. 2 (August 1939).

20. *Mount Street Club Journal*, i, no. 3 (December 1939).

21. Kiernan and Harvey, 'The Mount Street Club.'

22. *Irish Times*, 18 January 1939.

23. *Irish Independent*, 10 December 1935.

He had been in clubs of all kinds, rich and poor, and the Mount Street Club was as cheerful and pleasant company as any he had visited.

Members 'were obviously poor men by their dress, but except in the matter of dress they were no different in their attitude towards each other, and towards the club officials, from the members of my own club. They were quietly cheerful and happy—no forced gaiety.'

The reporter inspected the billiard room where a game was in progress, 'with the same sort of interested spectators, and the same kind of jokes being made as one would see and hear in any other club or billiard room. Other members were sitting chatting around a bright fire. The superintendent called two men to him and gave them some job to do. They were quite pleased, but in no way servile about it...because a job means a tally, the currency of the establishment.'

From his observations D. S. considered the experiment an unqualified success, and had become an enthusiast. 'It should be a pleasure and a privilege to the citizens to give...all the practical support they can...money, clothes, food, furniture, books; in fact anything useful that can be spared.'

Increasingly, observers, like the writer of an editorial in the *Irish Press*, found merit in the club's structure. 'The...Club...is giving new hope, new strength and a tougher moral fibre to those whom it enrols as members. The whole atmosphere...is one that is inimical to "lead-swinging" and to the work-shy mentality.'[24]

In 1938, when the club was well established to the admiration and participation of many members of the public, the *Irish Times* saw the club as 'a philosophy in action...One of the most important experiments of modern times had in inception here in Dublin...and since then has vindicated itself triumphantly.'[25]

The *Irish Press* looked back and agreed. 'The Mount Street Club is one of

---

24. 'To assist the unemployed,' editorial, *Irish Press*, 21 November 1935.

25. *Irish Times*, 11 January 1938.

The Committee, with Mr. George Braund, the Magician. Left to right, seated: Mrs. A. V. Barry, Mr. Louis V. Nolan, Mrs. R. P. Law, Miss Nora Fitzgerald (Dance Chairman) and Mr. R. P. Law. Standing are Mr. W. Martin Murphy and Mr. George Braund.

Mount Street Club Dance Committee. 1950.

——————— May 1940. ———————

The Mount Street Club Journal.

——————— Members' Section. ———————

House Committee

Chairman : P. J. Maguire.   Vice-Chairmen : J. Gallagher and H. Carney.*
Secretary : A. J. Keary.   Asst. Secretary : H. B. Evans.*

Committee

J. Byrne, C. Carthy,* P. Keogh, P. J. Lacy, J. Maguiness, P. Maguire,*
J. Merriman, E. McGrath, H. McIver, J. O'Connor, M. O'Rourke,* J. Smith.

Sports Committee

Chairman : J. Gallagher.   Secretary : P. J. Keane.

Committee

P. J. Lacy, P. Scott, P. J. Maguire, W. McGrath, J. Clarke, E. McGrath.
* Denotes Farm Committee.

EDITORIAL

By A. J. Keary (House Secretary).

Since our last issue we are pleased to say that we have been able to accommodate about 50 new members from a very big waiting list. Unfortunately our space is still limited and, much as we would like to accommodate more of the unemployed, we can only fill vacancies as they occur.

We of the House Committee are very pleased with the harmony that exists between new and old members. All are working to increase production, those in the Club to meet the requirements of the "farmers," who in turn are doing their share to keep us supplied with all our needs.

Difficulties due to last year's late start on the Farm have, we are pleased to say, been overcome and we are all looking forward to a plentiful supply to meet the heavy demands at this end.

Members are still talking about the "Question Time" hour at Radio Eireann on Christmas Eve, when the programme was taken over by a team of members from the Club and Farm. We are pleased to say that the team selected acquitted themselves admirably and were complimented by the commentator who remarked that they were "beyond his expectations." All the competing members received gifts, as well as the usual cash prize, through the generosity of a number of supporters of the Club.

We had a very successful season with our indoor sports, including Table Tennis and Badminton, the successful competitors duly receiving prizes. The concerts and plays, which were of an exceptionally high standard, were well supported by the members, wives and families, who showed their appreciation in no unstinted manner to the artistes who kindly gave their services.

The House Committee's term of office is nearly at an end and to the new Committee we extend our good wishes ; in particular the wish that they may receive the same helpful support from the members that has been our lot.

Mount Street Club Member's Committee. 1940.

those institutions which, born of the vision and initiative of one or two men, cast roots so deeply and so swiftly into the soil, that most from the moment of birth, their permanence seems assured…Statesmen and social reformers have given it their blessing; men of all classes and creeds are associated with it.'[26]

In early 1938 the governors felt confident enough to put forward the names of two candidates for election to the Senate. The candidates nominated were J. J. Newcome and P. T. Somerville-Large:

> Each has made a prolonged study of the unemployment problem in all its aspects and has been intimately concerned in the development and administration of the Club since its inception three and a half years ago. They therefore possess a special knowledge of this problem from a practical as well as the theoretical point if view…NEWCOME and SOMERVILLE-LARGE are the ONLY CANDIDATES representing the UNEMPLOYMENT PROBLEM.[27]

In the event Newcome was elected in April but defeated at the next election in August of the same year.

The Mount Street Club was not unique. In Wales the Brynmawr Experiment, a scheme to help unemployed Welsh miners, was conceived in 1934, the same bleak year as the club. Paddy Somerville-Large corresponded with the naturalist Peter Scott, who was involved with the Experiment, and considered that 'the account of the Club you started in Dublin…seems to be along very similar lines to our own.' By 1940 the ideas propounded by the Mount Street Club were attractive elsewhere in Ireland, and similar clubs were founded in Cork, Limerick, and Waterford.

During the 1940s Waller was in touch with Sir William Beveridge, author

26. *Irish Press*, 25 March 1938.

27. *The unemployment problem*, leaflet (Dublin, 1938).

of the Beveridge Report published in 1942, which set out a plan to overcome the five 'giant evils' of 'want, disease, ignorance, squalor, and idleness.' The report laid the foundations of the social revolution in Great Britain that came after the victory of the Labour party in the 1945 general election. Waller tried to interest Beveridge in a visit to Ireland. Although this never materialised, Beveridge's interest was valuable. The Plan was eagerly discussed at the club since many of its proposals had a common object with the club's principles.

Criticism of the club

Not everyone was happy about the progress of the club; perhaps there was a tinge of envy in the voices of dissent over the years. A belief persisted that production resulting from members' work took away the livelihood from unfortunates who were outside the club and faced unemployment. This was in spite of the fact that a firm principle of the club, one that was strictly observed, was that none of the items produced by members would be offered for sale to the public outside. Everything was for sale, but only to members and their families, and every item was paid for in tallies. No item would come into competition with anything commercially produced or threaten the employment of those already in jobs. No outside trader or worker would have anything to fear from the club's manufactures.

The formation of an organisation where members were separated from the governors who ultimately had full authority in the running of the club, as well as the religion of a large number of the governors, may not have helped the club's outside reputation. Nor did the evidence of Waller's military experience and its influence on the rules. From time to time the old slur was repeated with the implication that it was a development of an imperial army: 'We must remember that the club consists mainly of ex-soldiers, men who are amenable to discipline, who will take orders and carry out instructions.'[28]

The club had to deflect criticism that tended to arise from a belief that

---

28. Senator J. J. Counihan in *Seanad Éireann deb.*, xxiv, col. 306 (13 December 1939).

MOUNT STREET CLUB
SHOP COMMITTEE

A CONCERT

in aid of the funds of the Shop Committee

will be given at

LEINSTER HALL, HIBERNIAN HOTEL

On Tuesday, November 18th, 1941

at 8 p.m., by

THE GOOD COMPANIONS

assisted by

CLYDE TWELVETREES

Accompanist   MADGE BRADBURY

TICKETS (Reserved and Numbered)   3s. 6d.

Booking at Pigott & Co., 112 Grafton St.

members were merely employees of the govenors. This hostility was persistent and difficult to eradicate, and from the evidence of editorials in the *Mount Street Club Journal* continued to puzzle governors over the next decade. Time and again Waller and his fellow governors had to state that governors paid nothing to members, whose earnings were in proportion to the work they chose to do. The products of their work and the goods that were contributed through the society were only distributed among members and nothing was sold outside the cub. It was a hard lesson to get across to some sections of the public, suspecting a form of latter-day paternalism, that no governor or subscriber had benefited from association with the Mount Street Club.

Many critics were not prepared to investigate Owenite principles and the working of the tally system of co-operative exchange based on labour value. There were those who, reluctant to learn the club's functions when approached for support, believed that, contrary to Waller's repeated statements, the club was far too easy on the unemployed. It converted men, already disinclined to work, into slackers. The inference was that the unemployed should be tramping the streets looking for work, and the club's comforts interfered with such efforts.

More serious dissent came from the trade unions. Some were relentlessly critical, fearing that unskilled or semi-skilled men were doing the work of skilled mechanics who were not club members and were being underpaid. In the summer of 1939 an angry meeting of the Dublin Trades Union Council was attended by a trade unionist who acted as a spy and reported back to J. J. Newcome, the secretary to the club's governors. He gave full details of the 'divided opinion' arising from 'a very lengthy and lively discussion' that had taken place:

> The following are a sample of the questions asked:
> 'How did the Board of Governors come into existence?'
> 'Who are behind the Governors?'
> 'What would happen to Stock and Property—Buildings etc, if

Membership of the Club should cease?'...

One delegate at the meeting informed the Council that fascism had started the same way as the Mount Street Club...

A resolution was passed disapproving of the principle on which the Mount Street Club was conducted on the ground that the Club would not operate in the best interests of the Trade Union Movement.

An equally rowdy meeting at the club itself produced shouts from a deputation of trade unionists from the back of the hall that the club was composed of parasites and supported by parasites and that the country's problems would be settled at the barricades.

An exchange of letters followed between P. T. Daly, the secretary to the Trades Union Council, and Newcome. Daly wrote of the unions' distrust:

> Our deputation to your Club reported that the men were being paid by tallies which were apportioned on the value assigned to the work done, without any consultation or appreciation of the correct wages to be paid. They further reported that tradesmen's work was being done by persons who are not tradesmen.

Newcome wrote soothingly back on behalf of the governors, with the usual assurances that members were not taking the food out of the mouths of those less lucky than themselves:

> The Club consists of a group of unemployed men working co-operatively to provide some of the necessities of life for themselves and their families which are ordinarily denied to them. It cannot be too clearly emphasised that the members are in no sense employees of the Governors who are simply a body of voluntary workers engaged in an attempt to alleviate in a radical way the desperate condition of the unemployed.

A CHILDREN'S
DANCING MATINEE

WILL BE GIVEN BY

PUPILS OF

MISS MURIEL CATT

IN THE

GAIETY THEATRE

ON

Wednesday, 22nd May, 1940

at 2.15 p.m.

IN AID OF MOUNT STREET CLUB

Usual Theatre Prices 5/-, 3/-, 2/-, 1/-

Booking now at 120 Lower Baggot Street. 'Phone 63304. On and after 15th May, at Gaiety Theatre, Dublin.

Published by the Mount Street Club Society at 81 Lower Mount Street, Dublin, and printed by Dublin Printing Services, 126 Orwell Road, Rathgar, Dublin. Telephone: 95642.

Mount Street Club Journal. 1940.

THE CARRICKMINES PLAYERS

(IN AID OF THE MOUNT STREET CLUB)

Present

"ON BAILE'S STRAND"

A TRAGEDY IN VERSE BY W. B. YEATS.

CASTE

Pamela Waller, Rosemarie Holden, Lois Faulkner, June Waller,
Catherine Paul, Lorna Newton, Helen Deutch, Hilary Archer,
Heather Archer Rita Rutherfoord, Gina Watson, Cherry
Chaloner, Audrey Stevens, Susan Semple.

Followed by

"THE LEGACY"

A COMEDY IN ONE ACT BY MARIVAUX

CASTE

Lois Faulkner, Rosemarie Holden, Pamela Waller,
Torrence Large, Michael Maconchy, Jack Stevens.

TANEY PAROCHIAL HALL, DUNDRUM

Friday and Saturday, 24th and 25th May, 1940

AT 8.15 P.M.

TICKETS - - - - - - - 2/6 and 1/-

THESE PLAYS ARE PRODUCED BY PAMELA WALLER,
Blackberry Hill, Carrickmines, Tel. 84159,
with whom seats may be reserved.

Train from Harcourt Street, 7.30. Carrickmines, 7.36. Foxrock, 7.40.

Mount Street Club Journal. 1940.

Daly replied:

> ...our deputation says that as far as the relief of unemployment is
> concerned they fully sympathise...And if your work was confined
> to that, they would have nothing but praise for your endeavours...
> however...they feel it will be only necessary to point out that the
> danger of supplying in excess of the demand would mean the
> destruction of the trades, their arts and their crafts...if there is
> no attempt made to send men who are unskilled—or even semi-
> skilled—to do the work of skilled mechanics, and if there is no
> inducement held out to them to encroach on the rights of skilled
> workers, any objection this Council might ever have raised would
> be withdrawn.[29]

Hostility culminated in an incident which took place on 19 October 1939
when a carpenter who had been working for the club for some weeks was
called off from the job. The governors had to consider complaints from the
unions that the club was undertaking tradesmen's work and having it executed
by people who were not tradesmen. 'In addition the wages paid (tallies)
amounted to what was considered considerably below the general standard.'

The craft unions in Dublin were never happy with the workings of the
club or its principles. But they had to concede that the club's programme
was attracting support elsewhere; by 1940 similar clubs had been formed
in Waterford, Limerick, and Cork. In addition, the expansion of the club's
activities with the purchase of a farm further weakened the union's objections.

Support for the club came from one unusual source. Father Canavan, a
Jesuit from Milltown Park in Dublin, wrote to Somerville-Large:

> The fact that many people blame and misrepresent Newcome and

29. Correspondence with trade unions 1939-43 (DCLA, Ar/add/81/081).

APPLICATION FOR MEMBERSHIP OF THE MOUNT STREET SOCIETY.

To The Honorary Secretary,
The Mount Street Society,
81, Lr. Mount Street, Dublin.

Dear Sir,

My friend..
has asked me to join the Mount Street Club.

I acknowledge a personal interest in the mitigation of the disabilities suffered by those who cannot obtain work. I undertake to study the problem and to endeavour to interest my business and/or professional associates and my friends in it, and in the Mount Street Club.

I desire to be enrolled as a member of the Mount Street Society and enclose 5/- subscription for the year ending the 31st December 1937.

Please send me 20 application forms.

Signed...
(Please state whether Mr. Mrs. or Miss.)

(Full address)...

....

....

Date....................

Note:- The minimum subscription for an Ordinary Member is 5/-.

Application form for the Mount Street Club Society. 1937.

yourself is almost proof that you are doing good work. We Jesuits are used to this sort of thing, and I am delighted to welcome you to our company. Most people have the bourgeois mind; they want to be respectable without self-sacrifice. Some philosopher told Alexander that it was a kingly thing to be abused when one did well...Stick it out and answer as little and seldom as possible.[30]

On the whole the public were impressed, if not awed, by the club's achievements. In 1939 the editor of the *Evening Mail* pointed out how it provided a 'brilliant' example of what could be done by pooling resources and willing co-operation:

It enables the unemployed worker to provide, at least in a measure, for himself and his family by his own labours; it allows him to enjoy comforts and pastimes that were denied to him before the Club came into being; it gives him the feeling of satisfaction and happiness that follow conscientious and fruitful work; and it enables him to retain his skill at his occupation while he is unemployed.

In December 1939 the *Mount Street Club Journal* proclaimed: 'The chief bye-product of the Mount Street Club is called happiness.'

30. P.T.Somerville-Large, private correspondence.

FEBRUARY, 1941   **THE**   PRICE 3d.

MOUNT STREET CLUB
JOURNAL

Winter on the Club Farm

IN THIS ISSUE:—

LARGE-SCALE AGRICULTURE
THE REMEDY FOR URBAN UNEMPLOYMENT
BY THOMAS JOHNSTONE

Mount Street Club Journal. 1941.

HEALTH, WELFARE, HOUSING, AND WORK SINCE 1939
VI
Mary E. Daly

The Emergency[1] and the Dublin working class

Ireland remained neutral during World War II, but people's lives were seriously disrupted. Dubliners fared significantly worse than rural households when it came to coping with shortages of food and fuel, not to mention higher prices and a wages freeze. They had few opportunities to grow vegetables, keep chickens, or catch rabbits, and while some had access to turf banks in the Dublin mountains most families had to buy fuel. Coal, which was commonly used for heating and cooking, was not available for personal use, and the turf, which was substituted, was often damp and difficult to light. Gas was only legally available for limited hours in the day—to cook a midday dinner. The Glimmer Man—the gas company employee, who checked if people were using gas outside the permitted hours, became a notorious figure in Dublin folklore.[2] On a more serious note, Dublin also suffered several bombing raids; thirty-four people were killed, ninety wounded, and 300 homes destroyed or seriously damaged when German bombs landed on the North Strand in May 1941.

Wartime restrictions began to bite in 1941. The volume of goods moving through the port fell sharply as Britain cut Ireland's supplies of essential imports in the hope that this might persuade the government to abandon neutrality. Shortages of timber, iron, and copper brought most construction to a halt; many factories closed or operated only part-time. In November 1939 the Department of Industry and Commerce had estimated that the number of unemployed in Dublin could quadruple to 100,000 because of the war.[3] This proved unduly pessimistic. Many Dubliners joined the Irish or British forces, because this gave them a living; others found jobs in Britain. Men from rural Ireland were prevented from emigrating during the war years if they had worked in agriculture, but no such restrictions applied to Dubliners, and war work in Britain saved many families from destitution. During the war years, Dublin had the second-highest rate of emigration, after Mayo.[4] Applicants had to obtain a British work permit, which involved a tough medical examination and delousing before they left Ireland.[5] Irish Shipping, the state-owned line founded to secure Ireland's wartime supplies, recruited many Dubliners, especially from the Ringsend-Irishtown area; 135 crewmen were lost at sea during the war.[6]

Despite the large number who emigrated or enlisted in the armed forces, the government remained concerned about unemployment. Young unemployed Dubliners were sent to the country to work on wartime turf schemes, but young men recruited to work on Clonsast bog in Offaly absconded en masse, as did those constructing bog roads in Kildare and the Wicklow Gap. This is not surprising; the projects were in isolated locations, and the labourers were housed in primitive barrack-like conditions.[7] Government concern persisted: in 1943 they established a Commission on Youth Unemployment, chaired by Dr John Charles McQuaid, the archbishop of Dublin. Its report (which finally appeared in 1951) suggested that youth unemployment was not a

1. The Emergency was the term used to describe the years of the Second World War. It is taken from the 1939 Emergency Powers Act, introduced when the war began, which enabled the government to act swiftly by making an emergency order without the need for specific legislation.

2. Clair Wills, *That neutral Ireland: a cultural history of Ireland during the Second World War* (London, 2007), pp. 247-8.

3. Gerry Fee, 'The effects of World War II on Dublin's low-income families 1939-1945,' Ph.D. diss., University College Dublin, 1996, p. 18.

4. Fee, 'The effects of World War II,' p. 38.

5. For a graphic description see James Deeny, *To cure and to care: memoirs of a chief medical officer* (Dublin, 1989), pp. 77-9.

6. Robert Fisk, *In time of war: Ireland, Ulster and the price of neutrality, 1939–45* (London, 1983), p. 278.

7. Mary E. Daly, *The buffer state: the historical roots of the Department of the Environment* (Dublin: Institute of Public Administration, 1997), pp. 279-83.

serious problem in rural areas. But 'the young person in a city "with nothing to do and all day to do it" is in very much greater moral danger than his country counterpart. The bigger the city the larger is the number of such young persons and the greater their moral danger.'[8]

Long-term unemployment brought family poverty, illness, and low morale. In 1943 *The Bell* described a man who had been unemployed for several years as 'far from contented. He hankers for a real pay envelope on Fridays.' He had hoped to work in England but was rejected because of his poor sight; rejection left him with 'a kind of apathy.'[9] Most of the responsibility for this family of six children, aged thirteen years to ten months, fell on his wife. They lived in a two-room tenement, which was scheduled for demolition, with no gas; water was carried up two stories from the yard, which also contained the only toilet, shared with five other families. They survived on home assistance, supplemented by meals from charitable food kitchens and six food vouchers, each entitling them to three and a half pints of milk, a quarter-pound of butter, and a loaf of bread per week. They substituted extra bread for some milk. They cooked dinner at home only on Sunday. On other days their hot meal came from a food centre—stew with milk pudding or bread and jam. The school-going children ate at the centre; the mother collected food for the rest of the family in two cans. Meals cost 1s each, but 'the women who run it are not sticklers for payment' so they often ate free. In winter they survived on one candle a week. Four stone of turf in summer and eight stone in winter were supplemented by scraps of turf and turf dust which the children collected from lorries parked at a depot nearby. The family's greatest problem was clothes. In the early years of the war, and before the war, second-hand and charity clothing was available from better-off families, but wartime clothes rationing meant that they were now recycled within the family or altered for their own use.

8. *Report of the Commission on Youth Unemployment*, 1961 R. 82, para 10, p. 4.

9. 'Other people's incomes,' *The Bell*, vii, no. 1 (October 1943), pp. 57-8.

Paving Yard. 1955.

This story captures many of the features of Dublin working-class life during the Emergency. Rising prices and static wages meant that many households with a regular wage also fell into poverty and they did not qualify for food vouchers. Many of the 'new poor' lived in suburbs such as Crumlin where rents and food prices were higher than in the city centre and they had less access to markets, pawnbrokers, or credit from local shops.[10] Communal food centres became a critical part of the charitable network. In 1941 the newly-enthroned Dr John Charles McQuaid set up a programme of charity meals for pregnant women and mothers of young children; St John's Ambulance already operated a similar programme. The Society of St Vincent de Paul and the Marrowbone Lane Fund also provided communal meals.[11] The Irish Housewives Association (founded 1942) campaigned for an extension of the school meals programme, but the Secretary of the Department of Local Government objected to this growing trend of communal feeding, because 'there are strong moral and social reasons for refraining as far as possible from interfering even in very difficult circumstances with the normal family regime of the people.'[12] In Britain, despite wartime shortages, the diet and health of the working class improved, thanks to a dedicated government food policy. The more laissez-faire attitude in neutral Ireland—bread was not rationed until 1947—had a serious impact on the health of the Dublin working class.

During the nineteenth century life expectancy in cities was much lower than in the countryside, but in the United States, Britain, and many countries in northern Europe, the disadvantages of city life were disappearing by the turn of the century; not in Dublin. In 1941 an actuary estimated that a baby boy born in Connacht would live almost ten years longer than a Dublin boy; for girls the gap was seven years. Mortality for Dublin men aged fifty-five was one-quarter higher than for those in Connacht; for women it was one-sixth higher.[13] The incidence of death and disease rose during the war, nationally but most especially in Dublin. Wheat was scarce, so bread was made from high extraction flour, which included almost the entire wheat grain; while we might regard this as healthy, high-fibre bread, the high level of phytic acid in this bread reduced people's capacity to absorb calcium, resulting in a higher incidence of rickets. Britain prevented this by adding calcium to bread. Ireland did not do so, and the incidence of rickets in Dublin children more than doubled.[14] Tuberculosis cases had been falling in the 1930s, but the decline was reversed and the number of deaths and cases notified increased, partly because of a deteriorating diet, including the lack of calcium. Infant mortality in Dublin rose from 90 per 1,000 in 1939 to 126 in 1943, against an increase from 66 per thousand to 83 in Ireland as a whole; 310 children died in the latter year from diphtheria. In 1941 an epidemic of enteritis and diarrhoea killed 506 Dublin children.[15]

Dublin's public health crisis attracted unprecedented attention from doctors and social scientists, prompting a series of studies, which highlighted the low incomes and poor living conditions of the city's working class.[16] The National Nutrition Survey (1946-48) showed that in Dublin 'Among the poorer and larger families, a high proportion of the meals consisted simply of "bread and spread"'; the proportion was less in smaller families and in more prosperous households. A clinical study carried out in association with the Survey showed that seventeen-year-old Dublin boys and girls in larger families were smaller and of lower weight than their peers: there was 'a definite tendency for

10. Fee, 'The effects of World War II,' p. 64.

11. Lindsey Earner-Byrne, *Mother and child: maternity and child welfare in Dublin, 1922-60* (Manchester, 2007), pp. 89-108.

12. Hilda Tweedy, *A link in the chain: the story of the Irish Housewives Association 1942-1992* (Dublin, 1992), p. 17; Daly, *The buffer state*, p. 256.

13. Colm Barry, 'Irish regional life tables,' *Statistical and Social Inquiry Society of Ireland Journal* xvi (1941-2), pp. 10-12.

14. Fee, 'The effects of World War II,' p. 69.

15. Department of Local Government, *Annual Report*, 1941-2, p. 46.

16. Mary E. Daly, *The spirit of earnest inquiry: The Statistical and Social Inquiry Society of Ireland, 1847-1997* (Dublin, 1997), pp. 120-22.

heights and weights to decrease as family size increases.'[17] Social investigation was driven also by the publication of Britain's Beveridge Report setting out plans for a postwar welfare state 'from cradle to grave' and a National Health Service. In 1943 Seán Lemass introduced legislation providing for children's allowances for the third and subsequent children, a measure designed to reduce poverty in large families. Children's allowances (2s.6d.) were first paid in 1944; in 1952 they were extended to the second child and to first children in 1963. One of the controversies in Ireland was that they were paid to the father, not the mother.

'Ireland is Building'—the postwar years

The impact of the Emergency did not end in the summer of 1945. Shortages of food, goods and raw materials persisted until 1947-48; disastrous weather in 1946-47 meant that bread rationing was introduced for the first time, and supplies of raw material did not return to normal until 1948.[18]

The years 1948-58 are a paradoxical decade. Ireland was out of step with western Europe where a booming economy brought full employment and a very substantial rise in living standards. After a postwar growth spurt from 1948 until 1952, Ireland experienced a succession of economic crises; with rising unemployment leading inevitably to soaring emigration. Yet the years also brought a significant improvement in life expectancy for Dubliners, as the health gap between Dublin and rural Ireland began to disappear. Tuberculosis was conquered, and there was a sharp fall in infant and child deaths. We are still uncertain precisely why this happened: part of the explanation lies in the discovery of antibiotics: penicillin saved the lives of countless children who would otherwise have died from pneumonia or dysentery, the major causes of infant deaths; streptomycin conquered TB; BCG—Bacillus Calmet-Guérin vaccine—provided immunity against TB, as did polio immunisation, which was introduced in the 1950s. By the 1950s most Dublin babies were born in the city's maternity hospitals; antenatal care was more common than in the past. Mothers remained in hospital for approximately a week after giving birth, giving midwives time to educate them in infant care and hygiene, and they were encouraged to bring their infants back for checkups. Maternity hospitals passed their details to the Dublin public health service, which continued to monitor child and maternal health. Although Noel Browne's Mother and Child scheme was abandoned by the Inter-Party Government,[19] under pressure from the Catholic church and the medical profession, the 1953 Health Act provided a reduced version of this scheme. The 1953 Act also extended free hospital treatment to everybody who paid social insurance (most working families), and for the first time those who were eligible for medical cards—the poorest households—were entitled to specialist treatments. By the mid-1950s an estimated 85 per cent of the population had free or heavily subsidised hospital treatment. Dubliners traditionally relied on the city's voluntary hospitals to treat their illnesses free of charge, which may explain why the proportion of the population with medical cards was substantially lower than elsewhere. Until 1953 the voluntary hospitals were not paid for treating the city's poor; from that time Dublin Corporation paid the proceeds of one shilling in the pound in rates—approximately £120,000—which was divided among the voluntary hospitals, in return for their treating the city's sick poor. The impact of these changes is evident in the increasing numbers visiting the city's out-patient departments.[20] This meant that chronic illnesses were more likely to be treated than in the past.

Improved housing and sanitation also helped to reduce deaths and disease. In 1946 one-third of Dublin families relied on a shared water supply;

17. Mary E. Daly, *The slow failure: population decline and independent Ireland, 1920-1973* (Madison, Wisconsin, 2006), p. 107.

18. For details see Mary E. Daly, *The first department: a history of the Department of Agriculture* (Dublin, 2002), pp. 264-74; Daly, *The buffer state*, p. 325.

19. The first Inter-Party Government, whose members were drawn from all political parties with seats in Dáil Éireann except Fianna Fail, held office from 1948 to 1951. Noel Browne was Minister for Health.

20. Ruth Barrington, *Health, medicine and politics in Ireland 1900-1970* (Dublin, 1987), p. 253.

a similar number had to share sanitary facilities, and 40 per cent of toilets were outdoors. It was impossible to maintain a high standard of hygiene in these conditions, and disease flourished as a consequence. Dublin remained a city of tenements. Dublin and Cork Corporations were forced to finance local authority housing schemes through stock issues, whereas the other local authorities could borrow money from the Government's Local Loans Fund. Difficulties in raising funds meant that in 1938 Dublin was further behind in its housing programme than any other local authority; the city urgently needed an additional 21,000 dwellings. As part of its 1948 general election campaign Clann na Poblachta—a new left-wing republican party—commissioned a documentary film, *Our Country*, which included graphic pictures of urban tenements and barefoot children; the film was shown on gable walls and other outdoor spaces. In 1948 Alfie Byrne, Dublin's long-serving lord mayor, and an independent TD who supported the Inter-Party Government, demanded the appointment of a separate Minister for Housing. Although this did not happen, T. J. Murphy, a Labour TD who became Minister for Local Government, made housing a priority: he met local authorities, employers, and unions in his efforts to speed up construction. A full-time director of housing was appointed, with responsibility for the city, county, and Dún Laoghaire.

In 1950 the Departments of Health and Local Government published a glossy brochure called *Ireland is building*, where images of Dublin tenements were contrasted with gleaming new houses in Sallynoggin. Photographs of new houses under construction in Inchicore and Crumlin appeared under the heading 'Dublin "splendid among cities"'—a quotation from the poet and revolutionary P. H. Pearse. The text expressed the hope that Dublin, once regarded as one of Europe's finest cities, would regain that position under a native government. The brochure was widely distributed in England in an attempt to encourage building workers, especially craftsmen, to return home; many had emigrated during the war or the years immediately afterwards. They were promised plenty of jobs, higher wages, and better living conditions if they returned.[21]

The new housing provided was concentrated on the outskirts of the city where and was cheap. They were mainly three-bedroom houses, with a bathroom and indoor toilet—a major advance on the specifications of the 1930s. One civil servant specified that houses for tradesmen should have modern kitchens, a small refrigerator, a gas or electric cooker, a boiler for washing clothes, and built-in cupboards in living rooms and bedrooms. Labourers' houses should have a smaller bathroom, and built-in presses but no boiler or refrigerator, with cooking on a solid-fuel range. Dublin Corporation initially planned to include the cost of electricity with the rent. Each house would be limited to a maximum current of 140 watts, enough to power two or three lights; if the family wanted to listen to the radio, it would be necessary to switch off all lights except one. The Department of Local Government vetoed this proposal, instructing the corporation to install coin meters and provide sufficient voltage to make it possible to plug in an electric iron, kettle, or radio, without having to switch off the lights.

The new houses gave women an opportunity to show off their housekeeping skills, but the absence of sheds or workshops where tradesmen could carry on business, and where traders could store produce or carts, was a major drawback. Dublin Corporation was keen to provide workshops in Cabra West, but the planners in the Department of Local Government insisted on strict residential zoning. Priority on the housing list went to families living in condemned properties or those suffering from TB, but higher rents meant that those in greatest need of rehousing could not always afford to move. Cork had introduced differential rents to deal with this issue, but Dublin held out against doing so until the late 1960s. One popular feature of the postwar housing drive was the decision to reserve a small number of houses for newlyweds. The annual newlyweds' housing draw attracted hundreds of applications.

Despite a genuine commitment to solving Dublin's housing problem, by 1952 Dublin was yet again lagging behind all other local authorities in meeting its target. Almost 90 per cent of the postwar target was either completed or

21. Department of Local Government, *Ireland is building*, K. 1950.

Francis Street. 1959.

Courtesy of Dublin City Libraries

underway in rural areas; other urban centres had two-thirds of their target complete or underway. Dublin had built only one-quarter of its target; work was underway on a further 29 per cent. Once again finance was the problem. Construction costs soared in the early 1950s. Lack of sewerage capacity delayed planned housing schemes to the north and northwest. Dublin Corporation was finding it very difficult to raise capital for housing, because it was in direct competition with the National Loans. Lack of capital forced the corporation to slow down the pace of housing construction. Dublin Corporation was also under acute pressure from middle-class families trying to buy their homes, because local authority mortgages were often the only source of finance. Despite these difficulties, in 1955-56 the corporation built a record 5,000 houses.

The year 1956 marked the end of Dublin's and Ireland's postwar housing drive. Government finances were in crisis; there were severe cuts in public capital spending, and the Irish economy went into a serious recession. The crisis of the mid-1950s hit every part of Ireland; emigration soared to levels not experienced since the 1880s. Dublin city and county were the only areas to record a rise in population in the 1956 census—8,500 in the city and 12,700 in city and county combined—the smallest increase in the century. The waiting list for corporation houses fell sharply, because many tenants emigrated to England, Canada, South Africa, or Australia (often after a short stay in England so that they could qualify for the £5 assisted passages) where skilled workers were much in demand.[22]

The age of economic development

The publication in November 1958 of T. K. Whitaker's *Economic development* and the government's first *Programme for economic expansion* are generally seen as marking the beginnings of economic growth and steadily rising living standards.[23]

22. Daly, *Slow Failure*, pp. 188-90.

23. Department of Finance, (T.K. Whitaker), *Economic development* (1958), F. 58; Department of Finance, *Programme for economic expansion* (1958), F. 57.

The story is somewhat more complicated; while Seán Lemass began to boast that the economy was thriving as early as 1959, it was only in 1962-63 that national income was higher than in the mid-1950s. Economic growth brought significant changes to Dublin—some good, some less so. Ireland moved from economic protection to free trade with the signing of the 1965 Anglo-Irish Free Trade Area Agreement and EEC membership in 1973. This had major significance for Dublin. The city was home to many industries that had developed under the tariffs imposed from the 1930s. Significant numbers of men and women were employed in car assembly, light engineering, clothing and textiles, chemicals, and toiletries; making sweets, biscuits, and confectionery; or packing goods made elsewhere but imported in bulk. Many Dublin families found steady work in these factories. Most women workers were young and single, in their teens and twenties; they gave up work on marriage, sometimes because the factory operated a marriage bar (like the civil service), but more commonly because it was the custom at the time. Free trade threatened these jobs.

By the late 1960s many long-established Dublin firms were being taken over by outsiders; factories were rationalised—employment fell, and some factories closed. While the Industrial Development Authority was recruiting new foreign-owned industries, which would concentrate on manufacturing goods for export, government policy and the grants system encouraged these factories to locate in the west of Ireland; large American firms were directed to the Shannon Airport Customs Zone. Although the prohibition on new, foreign-owned firms locating in the Dublin area was removed in the 1960s, firms were only permitted to set up business in Dublin if no other location was acceptable. By the early 1970s the Dublin area, with almost half of total manufacturing employment, had less than one-quarter of jobs in new industries,[24] yet Dublin was at greatest risk of losing manufacturing jobs. Dublin port, which had employed thousands of men, albeit often in casual

---

24. Dermot McAleese, *A profile of grant-aided industry in Ireland* (Dublin, 1977), p. 23; N. O'Farrell, *Regional industrial development trends in Ireland, 1960-1973* (Dublin, 1975), pp. 52-5.

Wolfe Tone Street. 1960s.

O'Connell Street. 1960s.

Courtesy of Dublin City Libraries

Macken Street, close to Lower Mount Street. 1962.

Courtesy of Dublin City Libraries

jobs, was also undergoing a revolution. The volume of trade was rising, but with containerisation and roll-on-roll-off ferries the number of labourers required was seriously reduced. Indeed, the emergence of forklift trucks and other mechanical aids reduced the number of heavy labouring jobs in service industries throughout the city. Bus conductors were also under threat, as CIÉ, the national transport service, tried to introduce one-man buses; this change was prevented for many years by a series of strikes, but the writing was on the wall. Many dead-end jobs taken by teenagers—as messenger boys, delivering groceries, and counter staff in shops—were also under threat.

Yet the city was undoubtedly prospering. But the additional jobs were mainly in the civil service, state companies, banks, advertising, insurance, or other services—jobs requiring a good secondary education. Many Dublin working-class teenagers lacked the education to fill these positions. Dublin schools were very much divided by social class. Half the pupils in Dublin national schools in the early 1960s were in classes of over 50, and there was a shortage of places in vocational schools.[25] Family circumstances often meant that children had to earn money as early as possible, and were discouraged from remaining in school.

Lifestyles were also changing. By the 1960s supermarkets and modern department stores like Dunne's Stores were offering a different style of shopping. The decline in small local shops and the emergence of supermarkets had a wider significance for many families: local shops often provided credit; supermarkets did not. The 1960s and 1970s brought increased advertising, and new consumer demands for fashion items and electrical goods; a new teen market emerged for clothes, records, and magazines. Incomes were rising, but consumer demands were probably rising at a faster rate. Families rented a television so that they could enjoy the programmes on Telefís Éireann, which

25. *Investment in education*, Report of the survey team appointed by the Minister for Education in October 1962 (Dublin, 1965), pp. 70, 234.

opened on New Year's Eve 1961. Between the programmes they watched advertisements for foods, snacks, toiletries, clothes, tobacco and alcohol, electrical goods, and motor cars. Families were buying fridges and record players on hire-purchase; the single plug-in radio was replaced by personal transistors. As spending rose, many families fell into financial difficulties. In 1969 a controversial Telefís Éireann documentary showed that moneylenders had a serious hold on some Dublin families.[26]

As ever in Dublin there was a housing crisis. Modern office blocks were under construction in the city centre and Ballsbridge. Dublin Corporation actively encouraged modern commercial developments, despite the fact that they often resulted in the demolition of cheap flats and tenements at a time when there was already a growing housing shortage. The car was king, and with worsening traffic congestion Dublin Corporation drew up plans for an inner city ring road. Many city-centre communities were destroyed. Families who had left Dublin during the recession of the 1950s had returned and were demanding to be housed. A marriage boom added to the housing list. By 1963 over 4,000 families were awaiting housing. The list soon became much longer; in the very wet summer of 1963 three tenement houses collapsed in Bolton Street and Fenian Street, killing four people. An emergency survey of older tenements led to 367 buildings being evacuated and 1,200 homeless families. Dublin Corporation bought 100 chalet caravans for emergency housing, but many families had to be split up; some were housed in the former Richmond Barracks. In 1966 the American journalist Jimmy Breslin caused severe annoyance to Irish diplomats when his description of Sheriff Street tenements, a short distance from the GPO with no baths and overflowing garbage cans in the doorway, was widely syndicated throughout North America. Breslin suggested that little had changed since 1916.[27] The Dublin Housing Action Committee, which was largely controlled by Sinn Féin, organised protests and squats to highlight the housing shortage and the destruction of the city's Georgian heritage; in the late 1960s a new alliance emerged between some working-class communities and student radicals. The housing list remained at a crisis level well into the 1970s. When young couples asked what they could do to improve their chances of being housed, they were advised to have another child.

The seven tower blocks in Ballymun, which opened in 1966 and were named after the seven signatories to the 1916 Proclamation—Pearse Tower, Connolly Tower, Ceannt Tower, Clarke Tower, McDermott Tower, McDonagh Tower, Plunkett Tower—were a response to Dublin's housing emergency. Over 3,000 houses and flats were built by the National Building Agency, a government agency established to meet urgent housing needs. This was the first Irish high-rise housing development, and the first constructed with prefabricated sections. These were seen as modern solutions that would provide cheap, quality housing for all. Minister for Local Government Neil Blaney promised that Ballymun would provide 'a high standard of planning, including play spaces, car parking and landscaping…shops, schools and other amenities.' The original plan included 36 acres of open space, but the money was not available and so homes were built but the other essentials were postponed. Complaints were soon heard about lifts that did not work, or windows that would not open. Although Dublin families had lived in tenements for generations, the majority wanted a house with a garden. Ballymun flats became a place of transit; those who could move elsewhere departed as soon as possible; those who remained were often unable to move. The 1960s and 1970s saw large housing developments at Coolock, Kilmore, and Kilbarrack and in the new satellite towns to the west of the city around the villages of Tallaght and Clondalkin, where thousands of local authority and private homes were occupied by young families, again without adequate shops, health centres, schools, or social facilities. In time these areas developed into communities with strong local networks. By the 1970s a

26. *Inquiry into the programme on illegal moneylending broadcast on television by Radio Teilfís Éireann on 11th November 1969*. Report of tribunal appointed by An Taoiseach on 22nd December 1969, 1970 R 110.

27. Mary E. Daly, 'Commemorating the hopes of the men of 1916' in Mary E. Daly and Margaret O'Callaghan, ed., *1916 in 1966: commemorating the Easter Rising* (Dublin, 2007), p. 69.

more affluent Ireland regarded owner-occupancy as the norm, and many local
authority tenants in older housing schemes began to buy their homes at very
favourable prices. The new owners added their personal touches, painting the
exteriors, changing the door, adding an extension or a conservatory. The 1960s
also saw the first developments of housing for senior citizens.

A more prosperous economy brought a steady improvement in benefits. The
relationship between economic growth and social improvements was spelled out
in the *Third Programme for Economic and Social Development, 1969-72*, which
was committed to sharing economic progress equitably, and caring for the
underprivileged.[28] Between 1958 and 1968 old-age pensions doubled in value,
and unemployment assistance trebled, while prices rose by one-third. In 1967
old-age pensioners were given free travel on public transport and an electricity
allowance; free television licences came the following year. Occupational
injuries pensions, contributory retirement pensions, and invalidity pensions for
people with long-term illnesses filled major gaps in social welfare provisions.[29]
The new Department of Labour, established in 1966, introduced a new
scheme of pay-related insurance benefits to make redundancy less painful for
those whose jobs disappeared because of free trade, and they established a
new government agency, ANCO (later FÁS) to retrain workers who had lost
their jobs. New benefit schemes were introduced for widows, deserted wives,
and single mothers. The National Association of Widows was one of the first
effective lobby groups campaigning for welfare improvements. In the 1960s
and earlier decades the incidence of premature deaths was much higher than
it is in the twenty-first century, so many women found themselves widowed in
middle age with a family to support, no entitlement to a pension other than
the heavily means-tested widows' pension, and little prospect of finding a job.
In 1970 Irish society finally acknowledged the existence of deserted wives,

---

28. *Third Programme for Economic and Social Development 1969-72*, Laid by the Government before each House of
the Oireachtas, March 1969, p. 16.

29. *Third Programme*, pp. 206-7.

Grand Canal. 1967.

Courtesy of Dublin City Libraries

whose husbands no longer provided them with support; many of these men had emigrated, and while British and Irish authorities worked to ensure that they contributed to their families, in many instances deserted wives had been forced to rely on home assistance. The introduction of an unmarried mothers' allowance in 1973 is yet another example of a more sympathetic state; until that time most single mothers had either to give up their children for adoption or place them in an institution, because they found it impossible to provide for them. The 1970 Health Act gave those entitled to a medical card because of the low income a choice of doctor for the first time, and the right to free medication and dressings.

Ireland in the EEC from 1973

Ireland's membership of the EEC threatened many jobs in protected industries, but it also brought the promise of improved social benefits because the large sums spent on farm subsidies would now be paid by Brussels. During the 1972 referendum on membership, voters were promised that the money saved would be used to improve and extend social welfare. This commitment was honoured. Home assistance—the last remnant of the ninteenth-century poor law—was abolished in 1975 and replaced by a less demeaning supplementary welfare scheme. The qualifying age for old age pensions fell from seventy to sixty-seven. The real value (allowing for inflation) of all welfare payments increased by a minimum of 50 per cent between 1971 and 1981; the real value of some benefits doubled, and a more generous attitude was taken to means-tested benefits.[30]

Working patterns were changing. Until the 1960s many men and some women remained in paid employment into their seventies, mainly because they had no retirement pensions; and it was quite common for fourteen- or fifteen-year-olds from working-class families to hold a job. Only a minority of women in middle age were in paid employment, and most of these were single or widowed. From the 1970s onwards the profile of the Irish workforce changed: teenagers were more likely to be in full-time education (from 1975 children's allowances were paid to all under eighteen in apprenticeship or full-time education), men were more likely to retire in their sixties with a pension, and there was a sharp rise in the numbers of women remaining in paid employment. The global economic recession after 1973—which was caused by a sharp rise in the price of oil—resulted in a significant increase in unemployment throughout the western world. Britain was in recession, so emigration was not really an option. There was a sharp rise in the numbers claiming benefit, partly because of the recession, but also because the extended range of benefits and gender equality had increased the numbers who qualified. Unemployment fell back in the late 1970s, when the Fianna Fáil government initiated a spending and borrowing boom; it rose again with the second oil crisis of 1979 and remained at a very high level throughout the 1980s, as the economy stagnated. While the number of men at work fell during that decade, there was a rise in the numbers of women at work. The economic boom that started in the mid-1990s and continued for over a decade saw numbers in work rise from 1.1 million in 1994 to 1.9 million in 2005, but long-term unemployment did not vanish.

Changes in working patterns and second-wave feminism had an impact on the welfare system. The convention that men were breadwinners and women were dependants, which had been at the core of the welfare system in Ireland and elsewhere, was challenged. The welfare system had to provide pensions and benefits for dependent children and spouses or widowers of insured women workers. These changes were complex; some were introduced as the result of legal challenges in the European Court. By the early 1980s there was evidence that the more generous approach to those in long-term unemployment, especially large families, had created a poverty trap, where unskilled workers might be better off on benefit than at work. Family income supplement, which paid benefits to low-paid workers with children, was designed to remove this disincentive.

30. Tony Mc Cashin, 'Social policy, 1957-82,' in Frank Litton, ed., *Unequal achievement: the Irish experience 1957–1982* (Dublin, 1982), pp. 203-23.

Rutland Street. 1967.

Courtesy of Dublin City Libraries

One of the most significant changes since the 1990s has been the erosion of the gap between social insurance payments and social assistance, which had traditionally been paid at a lower rate. This marks a reversal of policy from the 1960s which sought to have more payments covered by insurance. By 2000 those receiving supplementary benefits or social assistance were on a par with those who had qualified for benefits or pensions under social insurance. Child benefits were substantially increased in 2001; for many decades they had lagged well behind other benefits. Economic prosperity in the 'Celtic Tiger' period which roughly dated from the mid-1990s until the onset of a global recession in 2008, saw pensions and benefits rise to levels that were substantially higher than in Britain or Northern Ireland—the gap in benefits between the two Irelands had been monitored closely from the 1960s because this was seen as a potential barrier to a united Ireland.[31] Despite the current recession benefits remain significantly higher than north of the Border.

Other changes worthy of note are the greater emphasis on rights and a more professional attitude to welfare. Since the 1970s Ireland has seen a massive expansion in social research, which provides evidence to support demands for improved or extended benefits. The report of the 1986 Commission on Social Welfare resulted in the establishment of the Combat Poverty Agency as a state advisory agency to develop and promote evidence-based proposals. In 1997 the government adopted official measurements of poverty, most significantly the definition that anybody whose income was below 60 per cent of the median income was in relative poverty—social assistance and supplementary benefits fell significantly below that threshold. The Combat Poverty Agency and the development of clear measurable targets have kept governments under pressure, as have comparative data from other EEC or

---

31. Jim Walsh, 'Monitoring poverty and welfare policy 1987-2007' in Mel Cousins, ed., *Welfare policy and poverty* (Dublin, 2007), pp. 13-59. Brian Nolan, Richard Layte, and Christopher Whelan, 'Cumulative disadvantage and polarisation' in Brian Nolan, Philip O'Connell, and Christopher Whelan, ed., *Bust to boom? The Irish experience of growth and inequality* (Dublin, 2000), pp. 163-78.

OECD countries.[32] There has also been a remarkable growth in the number of organisations catering for various disadvantaged groups and lobbying on their behalf. The talks on 'social partnership' between government, employers, trade unions, and social organisations, that were a core feature of Irish politics from the 1990s until the recent recession, provided a forum for negotiating additional resources. These NGOs (non-governmental organisations) provide services to specific groups—such as the elderly or the physically and mentally handicapped and their families—and they act as lobbyists or advocates on their behalf. NGOs deploy modern research, highly professional staff, and equally professional skills to do this.

Families are less willing to care quietly and without support for a child or adult needing long-term assistance than in the past. Yet Irish society no longer tolerates institutions such as St Kevin's Hospital, which provided long-term 'care' for thousands of elderly and chronically ill Dubliners in the past, or the institutional care of large numbers of children in need. There is a similar unwillingness to tolerate long-term stays in psychiatric hospitals unless absolutely necessary. The corollary is a growing demand for care in the community, supported by state and state-funded voluntary organisations. The introduction of a carers allowance in the early 1990s reflects changing attitudes. Meals on Wheels, a well-established service catering for the elderly and those with disabilities, is run with the aid of voluntary and community groups, with financial assistance from the health service; similar services offer respite care, hospice home-care, and other supports unimaginable in the past.

National income rose by 216 per cent in real terms between 1987 and 2005; the numbers at work rose by 70 per cent; unemployment fell from almost 17 per cent in 1987 to 4.4 per cent in 2005. Average incomes more than doubled, as did welfare rates; the numbers in absolute poverty fell sharply. Despite the recent recession—the longest and most severe global recession for a century—living standards for the Dublin working class remain unbelievably better than they were in the 1940s. Life expectancy and health have also improved significantly; there have been major health gains since the year 2000. But poverty remains a feature of life, even in boom-time, partly because poverty and an acceptable standard of living are not fixed concepts: the living standard acceptable in the 1940s would be dismissed as abject poverty today. There is growing evidence that some families and some communities face a cumulative risk of poverty: those with poor standards of education, those in long-term unemployment, and those living in local authority housing. The rapid spread of owner-occupancy turned some local authority estates into communities dominated by families living on welfare, where there was little contact with the world of work. Education is now increasingly important in finding jobs, but some young people lack role models for educational achievement in their family or the community.[33] It is noticeable that during the 'Celtic Tiger' boom, employers often preferred to recruit young immigrants rather than older, long-term unemployed Irish workers. Some communities are blighted by social problems such as drugs or antisocial behaviour; employers may also discriminate against certain addresses: this is not new. For several decades lone-parent households have had consistently the highest rates of poverty; single-person households are also at high risk, as are those with disabilities.

Conclusion

The Dublin working community has changed significantly over the period that we have examined. In geographical terms it is now spread much more widely, with thousands living in areas such as Tallaght, Finglas, or Clondalkin—places that were small, sleepy villages in the 1940s. Many parts of the city centre are now home to affluent, highly educated young people, who are often not of Irish birth; other areas in the north city are now populated by recent arrivals from Poland or Nigeria, and shops that traditionally sold Dublin produce now offer much more exotic fare. Life expectancy has been transformed; the

32. Walsh, 'Monitoring poverty and welfare policy 1987-2007,' pp. 13-59.

33. Nolan et al., 'Cumulative disadvantage and polarisation'; Tony Fahey and James Williams, 'The spatial distribution of disadvantage in Ireland' in Nolan et al., *Bust to boom*, pp. 223-43.

diseases of concern are no longer TB (though it occasionally pops up among new immigrants), but diseases associated with greater affluence—obesity, heart disease, and cancers linked to tobacco, drink, and perhaps drugs. Disadvantages in health and life expectancy persist, though they are now based on social class and not on urban-rural distinctions. While the working class of the past was dominated by families consisting of two parents plus children—though widows were common, as were resident grandparents—today there are more one-person households, and many more children who are raised in single-parent families, or in a home where one adult is not their parent. Employment prospects have also changed; while the construction boom of the millennium offered jobs that were not dramatically different from the jobs available back in the 1950s or the 1960s, in many other respects the jobs now on offer are radically different, working with technologies and in media that were unknown even twenty years ago. One of the greatest challenges is to increase the number of Dubliners from working-class backgrounds going on to higher or further education. The children of farmers and other rural families have been extremely efficient in taking advantage of educational opportunities, and the west of Ireland has the highest rate of participation in higher education. In Dublin, however, perhaps because of high pupil-teacher ratios, schools segregated by class, and residential segregation which means that some teenagers may not have many friends, family, or neighbours who have gone to college, the participation remains low. This is important given that education has become a key determinant of income and life expectancy. The range of welfare supports available today (even in recessionary times) would have been unimaginable to the mother of six described at the beginning of this paper. She might also be surprised to see that poverty and disadvantage persists despite significantly higher incomes. But the contemporary understanding of welfare and poverty suggests that while money is important, tackling long-term deprivation extends well beyond financial matters to include the fundamental values and attitudes of a society.

Bride Street. 1970.

Sheriff Street. 1970.

NEW INITIATIVES AND FENIAN STREET
VII
Sarah Perrem

It is a tribute to [the founders'] generosity and wisdom that the Club still survives today in an era of real unemployment, albeit with necessary changes in operations necessitated by the Social Welfare State.[1]

Changes in the 1950s and 1960s

In 1972 the farm at Clondalkin and the premises at 81-82 Mount Street had been sold. The Mount Street Club would never exist in its previous form. There were no more allotments, farm shop, or tallies. The club orchestra, boxing club, and drama shows were long over. Membership was at an all-time low and would continue to dwindle until it finally ended in 1984.

The lead-up to this change and the years that the Mount Street Club spent in 62-64 Fenian Street is not simply a story of slow decline. The governors made plans throughout this time and continued to work and to adopt innovative means to utilise their funds and property to benefit the disadvantaged.

The 1930s and 1940s were the years in which the club grew and thrived. During the 1950s the membership was still healthy and the farm was busy and productive. The economic climate was changing, however, and men with young families to raise, previously a large portion of members, had emigrated to England for work. The profile of the club, its membership, and its ability to raise funds declined in this decade.

The internal correspondence and minutes from these years are, sadly, lost. Newspapers from the time illustrate that the club remained alive and of public interest.

This year [1950] over 200 men have left the club to take up jobs for which they had demonstrated their fitness in the club's workrooms...The number of people who apply to the club for men to do temporary work is increasing every year.[2]

A visit to the club premises was featured in 'An Irishman's Diary' in December 1951.[3] In 1956 an article reported that the membership numbers of the club had swelled. The club was also still attracting the notice of politicians at this time. The deputy lord mayor of Dublin attended the annual Christmas party of the Mount Street Club in 1951.[4] Erskine Childers, then a cabinet minister, attended the annual harvest dinner of the Mount Street Club in 1952 and spoke about the continuing problem of unemployment. 'I would like to tear off the public platform of this country the glib politicians who say they end unemployment, when we know how difficult it is to solve this problem.'[5] The club's profile was high enough to attract attention from politicians, and events at the club were noted by the press. A comment in a speech given at the annual harvest dinner held at the club farm at Larkfield on 28 November 1951 was given column space in the *Irish Independent*, *Evening Mail*, and *Evening Herald* the next day. One of the governors, Stephen Kirwan, warned members against subversive communist groups 'which would gladly entice men like those in the club farm into their ranks and use them for their own ends.'[6] The *Evening Herald* went somewhat further and speculated that:

The authorities are well aware that Moscow trained agents have

1. Peter Perrem to Bill Somerville-Large, 5 June 1991, Dublin City Library Archive (DCLA Ar/add/81/087).

2. *Irish Times*, 4 November 1950.

3. *Irish Times*, 17 December 1951.

4. *Evening Mail*, 19 December 1951.

5. *Irish Press*, 21 November 1952.

6. *Evening Mail*, 29 November 1950.

been employed here, but their operations have been strictly limited, and have met with barely perceptible success. Nevertheless the warning…issued at the harvest dinner of the MSC at Clondalkin last night was timely. Communist methods are very insidious, and the agents are very prompt to seize every opportunity of misleading honest trade unionists.[7]

Finances, social welfare and 1970s

By the end of the 1950s the club was in decline. This was due to the availability of employment both in Ireland and in the United Kindgom, and to substantial increases in social welfare. The club was also having difficulty raising funds. A letter sent to the editor of the *Irish Times* by P. T. Somerville-Large, trustee and founder, and J. J. Newcome, honorary secretary, stated that the Mount Street Club 'may have to close its doors due to lack of funds.'[8] An appeal for fundraising from the 1960s illustrates how much the demographic of the club members had changed.

> This is an earnest appeal to save a home. A farm home from which many of the young and skilled have departed, leaving men, for the most part elderly and less active to work the farm and maintain the household…Today, almost all young workers have found employment…[it is understandable that] the Club should be left with the care of a number of men, many advanced in years, who know no other home but the Club's hostel at Larkfield Farm…In co-operation with a Convention of the St Vincent de Paul Society, the premises at Lower Mount Street now provides entertainment as well as shelter and comfort for elderly men and women.[9]

The farm and club premises no longer functioned as dynamic centres enabling young unemployed men to learn skills and provide food and clothes for themselves and their families through their own labour. This new reality explains why, once the farm was sold, the governors were so eager to build a hostel. Once the sale of the farm finally went through, the remaining residents of the farm would be homeless. It was arranged that these men, of whom there were fifteen, would live in the Iveagh Hostel in Dublin at the expense of the Mount Street Club until the hostel could be built.

The issue of unemployment had become a political one. According to government statistics, the national debt rose substantially during the 1970s due to large increases in public spending by the government. This included substantial increases in social welfare payments. A review of Dáil debates shows that unemployment had become a major political issue. TD David Andrews (Fianna Fáil) criticised the coalition government in a debate in 1976 saying, 'Citizens who are entitled to it and who are looking for it are being denied a basic human right to work.'[10] He criticised the amount that was being received, which he believed was only 20 per cent of a person's reckonable earnings and that 'there is a continual reduction on the amount they are being paid.'[11] The continual increases in payments could not match increases in the cost of living. The government set up a Commission on Social Welfare which published a report in 1986 that was to greatly influence welfare policy between 1987 and 1994. The idea that unemployment assistance provided by the government should not only be a minimum payment, but that the government had a responsibility to ensure that it was adequate to provide a standard of living that would prevent poverty, was established during these years.

Changes in social welfare payments had a direct impact on both the club and the farm activities. In 1971 a letter was sent to the Minister for Social

7. *Evening Herald*, 29 November 1950.

8. *Irish Times*, 6 April 1959.

9. Flyer (DCLA, Ar/add/81/016).

10. *Dáil Éireann deb.*, cclxxxix, col. 168 (24 March 1976).

11. Ibid., col. 176.

THE MOUNT STREET CLUB.

NOTICE.

If the Mount Street Club is to maintain a reputation for reliability, in connection with the provision of casual workers, and thus continue to be able to help provide work for men registering, the following essential points must be kept in mind:-

1. Men agreeing to call on an employer who has enquired for a worker must be careful to be sure to make the visit, or, if for some reason find that they are not going to call to see the employer, must remember to notify the Club, so that other arrangements may be made, and the employer is not left in doubt about the situation.

2. The Club, in talking to the employer, always settles a time and day for the visit of the man who is to arrange about starting work. This time is settled to suit worker and employer.
    Disappointment and subsequent loss of future jobs occur because men sometimes turn up late, or do not turn up at all.
    Men are earnestly requested to think carefully before giving a time, allowing of course for the length of the journey to work. Late arrival can naturally lead to the employer having left home, by the time of the late arrival of the worker.

3. Men who wish to use the services of the Club must never send a substitute to a job without first consulting the Club.

4. Men going out from the Club to jobs must always carry the open letter of introduction. All would-be employers are informed of this arrangement.

THE MANAGER.

This notice was enlarged and framed and on the wall of the club in Fenian Street. 1979.

Welfare as the unemployment benefit of members of the Mount Street Club who resided at the farm was suspended. The letter, sent by the club manager Guy Perrem, states that 'by a long standing arrangment' the unemployed members of the MSC had always received their unemployment benefit over many years. It goes on to add that MSC farm workers should not be classified as rural workers but as urban workers as they are registered members of the club at 81 Lower Mount Street. It states that 'without exception' they lived in 'night shelters' in the city prior to their membership, that their residence at Larkfield farm is 'incidental,' and that should the payments continue to be unpaid 'it is quite certain that they would return to the city and become "city drifters."'[12]

The manager claimed that the work of the MSC was designed to rehabilitate men who were out of work through no fault of their own and stressed that the men were not paid but awarded with tallies for their work in producing food for their maintenance. The activity of the club and farm was no longer filling a gap in the social welfare system as it had in the 1940s and 1950s when the payments were too small to keep a family out of extreme poverty. The men who were resident in Larkfield Farm in 1971 were not merely unemployed but also, according to this letter, previously homeless. This incident shows that the charitable actions of the club were beginning to clash with current social welfare policy which began to differentiate between rural and urban unemployed. In 1984 a change in rules regarding casual work finally put an end to the labour exchange the club had run from the Fenian Street premises because this work would become taxable and interfere with the men's social welfare benefits.

From 1970 to 2006 the Mount Street Club was constantly changing. It was struggling to remain relevant and useful and to stay true to its objectives. Limited funds, a changing economic climate, radical changes in social welfare, and state intervention in unemployment and training all created challenges for the ever-diminishing board of governors. The years that the Mount

---

12. Guy Perrem to the Minister for Social Welfare, 19 April 1971 (DCLA, Ar/add/81/088).

Street Club occupied the Fenian Street premises illustrate how, despite these obstacles, the club managed to make a contribution to the area and to consider alternative and sometimes radical options, in the spirit of the original founders in the establishment of the Mount Street Club in 1934.

The sale of the farm

By 1970 the downturn in activity, membership, and fundraising had continued unchecked. Dublin Corporation's purchase of the club farm at Larkfield by compulsory purchase order marks a major change in the activity of the Mount Street Club. A lack of funds would plague the governors both before and after the sale of the farm. The accounts for 1958 have survived, but otherwise few of the Mount Street Club private files from the period from 1950 to 1970 are available. These show that in 1957 the club issued 147,198 tallies, while in 1958 this number was 146,729. As each tally represents one hour's work, this figure represents roughly seventy men working a forty-hour week for one year. Even if some members were only earning ten or twelve tallies a week, the membership number must have been less than 200 at this point. In 1943 there had been 653 members.[13] The accounts show that the club and farm were both struggling to break even. The capital account as at 31 December 1958 shows that the year ended with an excess of expenditure over income of £1,577 15s. 2d. This is a high figure when we consider that total income was only £7,580 1s. 6d. In addition, weekly membership subscriptions, donations, and income from special appeals were all lower in 1959 than in 1958.[14]

The accounts of 1969 and 1971, just before the sale of the farm, show how few funds the club had. In 1969 the club managed to raise only £860 in bequests and subscriptions and had a deficit of £881. In 1971 there were no bequests and no longer any income earned from allotments. In 1972, with the sale of the farm, the governors had additional income from investments. The excess of income over expenditure, between £10,000 and £15,000, continued throughout the 1970s as the governors struggled and failed to convert either 81-82 Lower Mount Street or 62-64 Fenian Street into the planned hostel. Of this income, in 1979, only £213 came from subscriptions and donations, while over £25,000 came from deposit interest and investment dividends.[15]

The loss of the farm did not prompt the governors to seek an alternative farm site. A lack of vibrancy in other club activities led them to consider using funds from the farm to create a hostel rather than converting the Mount Street Club premises or upgrading it solely for use as a club with workshops for the unemployed.

The hostel plans

A great deal of time was spent during the 1970s trying to turn the Mount Street Club premises and later the Fenian Street premises into a hostel. Letters at this time illustrate some of the complications arising from the sale of the farm. The governors initially thought that they would have access to the money from the sale. However, a ruling at the meeting of the Commissioners of Charitable Donations and Bequests for Ireland (CCDBI) of 28 July 1970 stated that all monies from the sale, less £3,600 interest, be held by the commissioners. It took an affidavit for the governors to get a building fund, and some years for them to gain permanent access to the interest for the running of the club. The governors applied to the commissioners in April 1970 to use £100,000 of the monies from the sale of the farm to build a hostel. This application was granted by the High Court on 17 April 1972.[16]

The sale of the farm went through on 4 January 1972, and the governors rented the farm, at a rate of £10,000 per year, from the corporation until the end of 1973.[17]

The Mount Street hostel plans were continuing. A letter sent to Arthur

---

13. Minutes of the Accounts Committee 31 April 1943 (DCLA, Ar/add/81/001).

14. Income and Expenditure account for Year ended 31 December 1958 (DCLA, Ar/add/81/023).

15. Financial Accounts 1961-1979 (DCLA, Ar/add/81/020).

16. File on the MSC held at the CCDBI.

17. Ibid.

Ganly, governor and secretary of the club, from an unnamed Belfast architect suggested that the dining room and sitting and reading space were over-provided for the planned 38 residents.[18] The dimensions of the rooms suggest that the governors were still hoping to use the premises for other club activities.

According to a report from the manager Guy Perrem, there was no expectation of the club or hostel being used by young men or families, who had once made up the bulk of the club's membership. He specifies that: 'as young active married and unmarried men are generally no longer available...the Hostel inmates will be almost without exception, men of 50 years or more.'[19]

They planned that the residents would include eighteen out of the twenty club members currently living on the farm and an additional twenty 'newly brought in and carefully selected men.' The residents would either do cleaning, kitchen work, or other light internal work or, if they were physically capable, go out on casual work in gardens. Residents of the hostel would be fed and other club members could also eat at a subsidised rate. Members would be able to drop in to enquire about the availability of casual labour and all work would be offered first to residents. All residents and club members would be able to relax and enjoy whatever amenities would be provided. It was envisaged that two or three men drawn from among the club members would take responsibility, in co-operation with the house steward, which would probably have been a paid position, to answer the telephone in relation to requests for men to work.[20]

The club signed a new ninety-nine-year lease with Pembroke Estates for the Mount Street premises in 1972, and bought the freehold for the site in February 1973 for £6,800, a sum that would include all rent arrears. The application for planning permission submitted was refused officially in March 1973. The planning application for Mount Street is what led to the move of the club to its new home at 62-63-64 Fenian Street.

18. Belfast architect to Arthur Ganly, undated (DCLA, Ar/add/81/093).

19. Report of Guy Perrem, 1973 (DCLA, Ar/add/81/087).

20. Report of Guy Perrem to governors, 1973 (DCLA, Ar/add/81/084).

MEMBERS RULES.

1. Membership of the Club is at the discretion of the Governors and may be terminated by them.

2. Upon being made a Member a man will receive a Membership Card and this card should be retained, to be produced on request.

3. Membership of the Club does not follow automatically upon registration for work. Each person wishing to become a Member must first become known to the Manager and the Labour Organiser. The period of delay before Membership will generally be one month from the proposal, but will depend upon the number of times that the man concerned attends the Club for casual work, and the number of times that he goes out for work to an employer satisfactorily.

4. No intoxicating liquor may be brought into the Club by a Member for any reason whatsoever.

5. No person will be permitted to enter the premises who is under the influence of intoxicating liquor.

6. All apparatus and games provided as amenities for Club members will be under the control of the Manager and the Labour Organiser, or his Deputy.

7. The order in which Members may play the various games will be governed by the rule of "First Come First Served". The Labour Organiser will be in general control and may be referred to in the case of any difficulty.

8. The hours of opening and closing of the Club will be decided by the Governors.

9. In the case of any quarrel or dispute arising between Members, the persons concerned may be asked to leave the Club by the Labour Organiser or his Deputy, but may return upon the following day on which the Club is open.

10. These Rules may be amended from time to time at the discretion of the Governors.

11. Members must be prepared to help in keeping the Club rooms and Kitchen clean and tidy, and help with serving from the kitchen where necessary.

12. Membership Cards must bear the name and signature of the Member. On no account are membership cards transferable.

List of rules for members. 1979.

In 1972 the governors received a planning objection to building by Mssrs Hainault who owned a building to the rear of 81-82 Mount Street.[21] They claimed that the development of a hostel at this address would inhibit further development of the property. This led to an agreement to exchange the Mount Street property with 62-63-64 Fenian Street, with an additional £10,000 given to the Club and all legal expenses of the transaction being paid by Mssrs Hainault. The property exchange went through in October 1974.[22]

The plans for the hostel at Fenian Street continued from its purchase until July 1975. In 1972 the governors were still intent on maintaining the activity of the club despite the changes in the economic climate and the sale of the farm. A memo dated in June of this year records a visit from the chairman, P. T. Somerville-Large, to the proposed new Fenian Street premises and gives a glimpse at what was intended for the premises and the club.

The chairman proposed renting plots of land for the raising of food by club members and that they be used on the 'tally system' and that availability of plots should be investigated at the earliest possible moment. Regarding new club rules, the chairman is noted as wishing a draft to be made, based on the old rules, which will give men a definite say in the running of the club of which they are members. The memo states that 'The Chairman stressed this last point a great deal.' He believed that the idea of workshops in which socks and shoes could be made should not be ruled out and that 'the Chairman has in mind workshops... in the new premises.' In addition it is noted that objections and difficulties from certain members, and possibly from unions, should be expected.

These notes are interesting as they show that the chairman, at least, did not see the sale of the farm and the Mount Street premises as the end of the club and its old way of operating. He envisaged the new premises taking over the residential part that the farm had played and new allotments and additional facilities at the premises keeping up the old work of the club. His only concession to change was that 'it is not young men generally, that require the aid of the Club...Changing conditions, however, are increasing the range of ages at which men become most vulnerable to unemployment.'[23]

On 4 July 1975 Arthur Ganly, the club secretary, wrote to the architect to say that the governors 'have decided not to proceed with the scheme to build a residential hostel with ancilliary services…our reasons are that the cost is well beyond the power of the Club to finance.' The cost of the project had originally been estimated at £76,000 which included provision for inflation and professional fees. This sum is described by Arthur Ganly as 'only barely within our capabilities.' The new estimate had reached £118,885. He added that 'it is a great disappointment to us and, in particular, to the Chairman Mr Delap and myself, that we are not able to proceed with the original project, but we had no alternative but to pull back.'[24] In an ironic twist of fate, the planning permission to build the proposed hostel at Fenian Street, which had been applied for in February 1975, had been granted on 27 March 1975.

The club reopens, 1977

In 1975 the premises in Fenian Street was refurbished and central heating was installed at a cost of £49,290.[25] The property had a large recreation room, a reading room, a television room, a kitchen with tables for meals, and a basement with lockers, toilet facilities, and space for workshops. In addition the property consisted of a suite of offices on the first floor and a self-contained flat for the caretaker and his wife. Parking was available due to the demolition, in May 1974, of a derelict public house at 64 Fenian Street that had been included in the property sale.

The club manager, Guy Perrem, circulated the new rules of the club to the governors in 1975. The open hours would be from 9 a.m. to 4 p.m. in the waiting room for those seeking employment; these men would be considered

21. DCLA, Ar/add/81/087.

22. Correspondence from files held by the CCDBI.

23. Internal memo, unsigned, 19 June 1972 (DCLA, Ar/add/81/087).

24. Arthur Ganly to Hope, Cuffe and Associates Architects, 4 April 1975 (DCLA, Ar/add/81/1/096).

25. Guy Perrem to the CCDBI, 13 July 1977 (DCLA, Ar/add/81/087).

Mount St. Club Day Centre
62-64 Fenian Street,
Dublin 2.

The Chairman and Committee
cordially invite

MRS B O'BROLCHAIN

to the official opening of the Centre by
Alderman Alexis Fitzgerald
Chairman of the Eastern Health Board
at 4 p.m. on Wed December 12th 1979

R.S.V.P.

phone 603980

Invitation to the official opening of Fenian Street. 1979.

probationary members and would be eligible for full membership, after their probationary period, with the consent of the governors. Previous workers at the club farm at Larkfield would be automatically members of the club. Full members would have use of club recreation rooms, which would be open from 9 a.m. to 10 p.m., and use of the canteen facilities. Members were allowed to bring their own food but all cooking would be done by the canteen staff who would be on duty from 9 a.m. to 5 p.m. or by the caretaker who would be on duty from 4 p.m. to 10 p.m. Any member under the influence of drink or attempting to bring in drink would lose his membership immediately. 'Men seeking work should turn up in a clean and tidy state.'[26] The rules on alcohol remained unchanged from the earlier club rules. Women were not specifically prohibited, but it seems clear that they were not expected as they are not mentioned.

The club premises officially opened in September 1977 as both a facility for unemployed men to seek casual labour and as a club for recreational use of its members. A membership card was necessary for club members to gain admission. The manager, Guy Perrem, recommended that someone be employed, preferably a former army man or garda, to man the door of the club in the evenings. He believed that members who had consumed alcohol might need to be turned away. He was also concerned that the presence of the pool table, available to members for free, could draw men from the area who were not members. The game, it was noted, was popular in the city and was available elsewhere, but at a charge of 50 pence a game.[27] It seems that these fears were unfounded. Guy Perrem sent a letter to Brian Hogan of Women's Aid asking if he knew of any charity that might wish to purchase the pool table 'which has never been used.'[28] The manager had an expectation of the premises and membership of the club being highly sought after but there is no

26. Rules of Mount Street Club, dated 1975 (DCLA, Ar/add/81/084).

27. Guy Perrem to governors, 1977, Ibid.

28. Ibid.

evidence of this, a radical change from the waiting list for new members that had existed in the 1940s.

The old spirit of the club, in which the members themselves both proposed and approved new members, and took responsibility for the upkeep of the facilities, had changed radically.[29] Now the governors approved new members and a paid caretaker took responsibility for the building. There was no longer a sense of the club belonging to the members.

Even in 1976, a year prior to the official opening, the governors were already seeking additional uses for Fenian Street. In July Guy Perrem wrote a letter to Eugene O'Keeffe of the Eastern Heath Board (EHB) proposing that the Mount Street Club 'take on some useful additional charitable activity which would fit in with our other arrangements, and…be of good use to the work of the Eastern Health Board.' The letter explained that the club was 'now in a position where our newly created premises is capable of supplying facilities for recreation, social activities or rehabilitation work, beyond that required for our present circumstances.'

Guy Perrem explained that the men who had been living and working on the farm were being looked after by the club in the Iveagh Hostel and York House in Dublin and that the club also ran a 'small labour exchange to try to help men get daily work.'[30] This letter gives a clear picture of how limited the work of the club was by 1976.

The scale and activity of the club during the late 1970s and early 1980s was continually decreasing. In 1980 Guy Perrem presented a graph to the governors at the board meeting which clearly showed a downward trend in jobs found for unemployed men. 850 jobs were secured in 1975 but by 1981 only 88 jobs were recorded for the whole year.[31]

The day activity centre and Fenian Street

With the plans for a hostel finally shelved the governors sought other means to make a contribution. In 1977 Guy Perrem sought permission of the CCDBI to use the premises in Fenian Street as a shelter for 'battered wives and their

·hildren.'[32] Since the club had been granted permission to use funds to build
ι hostel, Mr Perrem suggested that erecting prefabricated buildings in the
·acant area of land created with the demolition of 64 Fenian Street could
ιouse '23 wives and their children.' This plan would not end the other work
ɔf the club which would also continue to pay for the former farm residents in
·ity hostels. 'We would stress that there is no question of giving up the work
ve do of finding employment for casual workers.'[33] The governors wished to
·espond to what they considered to be an urgent need in the city of Dublin.

The commissioners finally gave their consent that the Mount Street Club
ιse part of their new building in Fenian Street, as a Centre for Battered Wives
ιnd their children.'[34] In October the governors had approved the idea in
ɔrinciple, although details and funding had yet to be finalised.[35] By November,
ιowever, Women's Aid had found more suitable premises. The sale of the farm,
:he plans to convert Mount Streetand subsequently Fenian Street, and now
:heir plans to partner with Women's Aid had all faltered due to delays. Legal
ιssues and the required permissions that were needed from the CCDBI played
ι part, as did economics. The governors all gave of their time voluntarily and
met less than once a month. Although they employed a manager, all decisions
ιvere deferred to meetings and all correspondence had to be forwarded to all
the governors; this circumstance made quick, decisive action difficult.

The idea of using Fenian Street to accommodate battered wives led to
the club and its manager corresponding with the EHB. This ultimately led
to the idea of the EHB, and from 1979 the Irish Wheelchair Association,

29. Rules of the Mount Street Club, 1934 (DCLA, Ar/add/81/224).

30. Guy Perrem to Eugene O'Keeffe, 27 July 1976 (DCLA, Ar/add/81/117).

31. Internal memo, undated (DCLA, Ar/add/81/210).

32. Correspondence relating to redevelopment of the Fenian Street premises, 1975-1978 (DCLA, Ar/add/81/117).

33. Ibid.

34. The CCDBI to governors of MSC, 12 September 1977 (DCLA, Ar/add/81/117).

35. Correspondence relating to redevelopment of the Fenian Street premises, 1975-1978 (DCLA, Ar/add/81/117).

using Fenian Street as a day activity centre. The shift from catering for the unemployed to working with the EHB was to direct the actions of the club for the next five years.

By July 1979 a letter from Guy Perrem to Dr Val Barry, director of Community Care, states that 'in referring to the Mount Street Club it is meant to include both the activities of the Centre for the Disabled, and the earlier organisation for finding work for the unemployed.' The governors wanted this change to be proposed to the CCDBI through their solicitors and that the list of trustees expand to include Dr Val Barry and one other person from the EHB, and that Dr Barry would also act as a governor. While not all of these changes took place, it is clear that the intent of the governors was to alter the objectives of the club to include their association with the day activity centre. In 1980 it was proposed to change the name of the club to the Mount Street Centre; this new title was placed on letterheads and used in all correspondence until it was formally changed back in 1982.

The list of governors and trustees was to change in 1979 and 1980 to reflect these changes in the club's activities. The trustees of the club were men who were active members on the board of governors. In July 1979 the governors included P. T. Somerville-Large, Hugh Delap, and Arthur Ganly, these three men also being the trustees of the MSC. Guy Perrem was manager, Dr Val Barry was listed in minutes as Director, Community Care, and Medical Officer of the EHB and Blánaid O'Brolcháin as legal advisor. In the meeting of 15 April 1980 the existing trustees resigned, but remained on as governors. Hugh Delap and Arthur Ganly resigned as governors in January 1981. Their positions as trustees were taken up by their sons, Dr Charles Delap and Dr Michael James Ganly. P. T. Somerville-Large remained on the board of governors but his son Bill Somerville-Large took over as trustee. Three new governors, Dr Ciaran Barry, Dr Harry O'Flanagan, and Dr Henry Purcell, were proposed by Dr Val Barry, now a governor himself. These new governors reflect the changing direction of the club and its new focus on helping those with mental or physical

MOUNT STREET CLUB

Chairman: Day Activity Centre for the Physically Handicapped
Dr. Val Barry.
                   62-64 Fenian Street, Dublin 2.   Telephone: 603980

Treasurer:
Henry Dunne.

Senior Occupational Therapist:
Helen A Lee.

Headed notepaper of Day Activity Centre. 1979.

GOOD O GANLY

DIRECTORS: ARTHUR GANLY, M I A.A. DAVID GANLY, M.I.A.A.

AUCTIONEERS · HOUSE AGENTS AND VALUERS
20·LINCOLN PLACE
DUBLIN 2
TELEPHONE: 62468

14th December, 1973

CERTIFICATE AS TO RELATIVE VALUE:

MOUNT STREET CLUB SITE, LOWER MOUNT STREET, DUBLIN.

AND

SITE AT 62/63/64 FENIAN STREET.

We have been instructed to advise as to the relative value of the site at present occupied by Mount Street Club at Lower Mount Street, Dublin and a proposed alternative site at 62/63/64 Fenian Street, Dublin.

The Club occupies a site at Lower Mount Street (comprising in the area of slightly over 8,000 sq.ft.) under an expired lease. Pembroke Estates who are the head landlords have agreed to grant the Club a new 99 year building lease at a rent of £250 per annum with rent reviews on the basis that the site will be used for the erection of a hostel for the Mount Street Club, and for no other purpose.

Messrs. Hainault who have purchased adjoining properties and are desirous of developing the Mount Street area as a single unit have approached the Club and have made them an offer of an alternative site at 62/63/64 Fenian Street comprising an area similar to that in Mount Street. Hainault have offered to make this site over to the Club on the terms as set out in the attached memorandum. We have consulted the Club's architect, Mr. Cuffe of Messrs. Hope Cuffe & Associates, who has already drawn up provisional plans for the Mount Street site and who has inspected Fenian Street site. Mr. Cuffe has indicated that in his view the Fenian Street site is preferable to the Mount Street site for the proposed hostel.

We certify that in our opinion the exchange as indicated is to the advantage of the Club and have no hesitation in firmly re-commending that the Commissioners of Charitable Donations and Bequests for Ireland should approve of the arrangement.

Arthur Ganly.

Sale of Mount Street. 1973.

disability.[36] Guy Perrem resigned from his post as manager in 1980 and became a governor, and upon his death in 1981, was replaced in the latter capacity by his son Peter Perrem. P. T. Somerville-Large had stepped down as chairman by 1986. All of these changes in the board led to a new and fresh outlook on the work of the MSC, which would continue until the mid-1980s.

During the years 1980 to 1984 the governors were focused on expanding and extending the activities of the day centre. In June 1981 Henry Dunne, the new manager of the club, suggested that the day centre be extended to take in some of the vacant lot at the rear of the premises or to sell Fenian Street and build or rent a larger premises. The aim was to enable all patients of the day centre to attend three days, instead of only two, and to enable 'heavier' occupational therapies such as woodwork.[37] The day centre was a success. At a meeting of the governors in September 1981, Dr Val Barry noted that the day centre was now at full capacity with a weekly attendance of eighty patients.

Governor Dr Ciaran Barry made further suggestions for the expansion of the club's activities to tackle needs were not being met in the local area. These included child-minding facilities, recreation for elderly people living alone, and a trust fund to help families in need. He added that 'he hesitated to suggest too much of a breakaway from the old and well known traditions of the MSC.' Co-founder P. T. Somerville-Large responded that 'breaking new ground has a lot to be said for it.'[38] There were no objections noted in the minutes to this change of direction, or any suggestions for a renewed focus on the unemployed. In January 1982 Dr Val Barry suggested that the club could extend its activities by tackling the problems of the elderly.

The issue of finance and a lack of funds was to continue. The accounts of 1981 list the substantial investments from the sale of the farm, but also show

36. Minutes of the MSC (DCLA, Ar/add/81/016).

37. Minutes of the MSC, June 1981 (DCLA, Ar/add/81/016).

38. Minutes of the MSC, September 1981 (DCLA, Ar/add/81/016).

that a limited fund of £25,000 was available annually to the governors.[39]

In 1983 the governors prepared to alter the objectives of the Mount Street Club charity by a *cy-près* scheme application to the courts.[40] The objects that were proposed would include maintaining the old farm residents in city hostels and the continuation of providing opportunities for unemployed men to gain casual work. The idea of using the Fenian Street building as some form of hostel had not been completely ruled out in the future as they included an objective which specified the possibility of creating accommodation or buildings to cater for the objects of the charity. They also added that the charity had an objective to develop and maintain services in the community 'with particular reference to the physically and/or mentally handicapped, the elderly and the socially deprived or mal-adjusted'. This final object was a radical departure from the official aims of the club as it was established in 1934. It reflected one of the main activities and preoccupations of the club since 1979 in its work with the EHB.[41]

This application never proceeded as unemployment figures were high at the time and it was considered by the governors that it would be refused on these grounds. This decision marked the end of the club's close association with the EHB. Dr Val Barry fell ill and left the board, and the governors took a less active role in the day centre. From 1985 no governors served on the day centre committee. The day centre, however, continued to operate until all tenants left the building in 2000.

Between 1985 and 1995 the day centre continued to be active. In 1994 they received a £15,000 grant from the EHB and Mr O'Byrne of the day centre committee brought proposals for new activities to the board of governors. His list included provision of instruction in domestic economy to mothers (married, unmarried, or separated) in the locality, the provision of crèche facilities, a social entitlements information centre, a literacy programme, a club for retired or redundant men and women in the locality, and helping start-up or small businesses.[42] The board of governors did not choose to support any of these plans. In 1997 the running of the day centre was taken over by the Irish

Wheelchair Association. The governors were involved only by charging the day centre rent of £1 a year.

In minutes from May 1994 the activities of the MSC are summarised as facilitating the day centre and its Community Employment Development Programme (CEDP) scheme[43] which employed twenty-four people, utilising the premises to house three start-up businesses, and setting up the Nautical Trust to generate local employment and training.

A new search for purpose

Although the day centre would continue to operate in Fenian Street the focus of the governors now moved away from working with the Eastern Health Board and instead turned to the local area and how, with their limited resources, they could alleviate the problem of unemployment. In the 1980s reports were commissioned by the governors in an attempt to gain some new direction for the club now that it was clear that it would remain true to its original objects in relieving poverty due to unemployment. Professor John Jackson of Trinity College Dublin joined the board of governors and helped move them in this new direction. He had a sociology student named Jim Lynch complete a study which concluded that the club should get involved in a local project and link with local community groups.

As a result of this study, Peter Perrem, a governor, presented a report to the board meeting of October 1985 in which he promoted the idea of working

39. Unaudited accounts of the MSC, year ending 31 December 1981 (DCLA, Ar/add/81/016).

40. A *cy-près* scheme is the means by which a charitable fund whose original object has ceased to exist, with the approval of the CCDBI or the Courts, is given new objects as near as possible to the original object. See Brian Hunt, ed., *Murdoch's dictionary of Irish law* (5th ed., Dublin, 2008), p. 308.

41. Minutes of the MSC, 11 May 1983 (DCLA, Ar/add/81/016).

42. Minutes of the MSC, 25 February 1994 (DCLA, Ar/add/81/454).

43. The Community Employment Development Programme is funded by the government and is directed at the long-term unemployed.

with the Grand Canal Basin project in Ringsend. He stated that the Outer Grand Canal Basin could be developed as a viable leisure and recreational centre and that the MSC could be involved in a co-ordinated approach to student placements and community work in the area. From 1985 until the mid-1990s the governors' work focused on the establishment and support of the Dublin Nautical Trust and on their involvement in the Basin project. Mr Peter Perrem and Prof. John Jackson alternately held the position of chairman from 1985 until 1989.

In 1994 the governors commissioned a report prepared by Judith Kiernan and Brian Harvey.[44] This report summarised the history of the club, discussed its current operations, and gave recommendations for the future. The governors hoped that the report might guide them as to how best to proceed and whether it would be best to wind down the activities of the charity. The report had not been favourable regarding the recent activities of the club. In discussing the years following the sale of the farm the report concluded that the club 'had failed to change with the times, starting in the 1950s.' It stated that the involvement of the club in the day centre and its work with the Eastern Health Board 'was not strictly or directly compatible with the original charitable objectives of the club.'[45] The report concluded that the limited resources of the club meant that expansion was not viable. It suggested that the club either continue as a funder of projects that met a clear criteria and application process or wind up operations. It recommended that the Fenian Street premises be sold as part of the wind up or to create an asset to enable the club to become a funder. The governors only had £3,000 per annum at their disposal at this time.[46]

In response to the Kiernan and Harvey report the governors decided to 'evolve a new programme for action.'[47] Each governor would put in writing any ideas for objectives or activities. They also decided that the 'option to wind up the club should be very seriously considered.'[48] Some governors were getting frustrated with the lack of direction and activity of the club. Bob Carroll stated that 'he did not want to continue as a governor unless the club became active within the coming few months.'[49]

These discussions led the governors to consider the best future use of Fenian
Street, their major asset. The idea of using the premises exclusively as a club
for unemployed men was discounted as there were already two community
centres in the area. 'It was noted that the club is essentially an enabling body.'[50]
Some of the suggestions for using the premises were not feasible as they would
require the hiring of a full-time manager, which they were not in a position to
finance. One suggestion was to contact the Irish National Organisation for the
Unemployed (INOU) to see if they would be interested in the building as they
had no permanent headquarters. Other ideas included using the building as a
training centre for the unemployed, funding and giving space to Community
Technical Aid (who occupied one of the serviced offices within the building
and give advice and expertise to community groups to develop their plans), or
to work with the Training and Employment Authority (FÁS) and the EHB to
provide training for carers of the elderly. The governors felt that the club 'needs
to re-establish its identity' and 'needs to change the way in which it achieves it
objectives; the traditional means are no longer economical or feasible.'[51]

The possibility of redeveloping the building was now being discussed
in 1995.[52] Community Technical Aid was in need of more space and the
building needed updating as it was not complying with fire regulations. The
day centre and Community Technical Aid were both interested in remaining
in the building, within the new development. The original plans to develop

44. Judith Kiernan and Brian Harvey, 'The Mount Street Club: past present and future,' November 1994 (DCLA, Ar/add/81/130).
45. Ibid, p. 15.
46. Ibid.
47. Ibid.
48. Ibid.
49. Minutes of the MSC, 26 January 1994 (DCLA, Ar/add/81/010. Closed until 2025).
50. Minutes of the MSC, 25 January 1995 (DCLA, Ar/add/81/010. Closed until 2025).
51. Minutes of the MSC, 26 January 1994 (DCLA, Ar/add/81/010. Closed until 2025).

Jobs Secured by Men

MONTHLY ~~INQUIRIES RECEIVED FOR WORKERS~~

1972 and onwards.

	1972	1973	1974	1975	1976	1977	1978	19~
January	15	17	27	45	30	20	28	12
February	15	21	37	81	35	32	22	12
March	30	95	98	71	70	57	59	26
April	66	58	130	88	53	69	66	30
May	53	55	65	101	60	93	66	49
June	45	80	75	101	68	62	50	38
July	65	42	63	84	42	35	50	40
August	43	51	73	61	40	31	52	28
September	32	55	69	76	45	39	46	25
October	30	65	81	68	40	48	42	25
November	36	26	53	45	45	30	28	21
December	14	24	46	29	20	20	14	12
	443	589	817	850	548	536	523	318

	1980	1981	1982	1983	1984	1985	1986
January	7	8	5				
February	12	12	4				
March	7	11	10				
April	28	17	14				
May	31	8	8				
June	26	9	2				
July	26	1					
August	23	8					
September	16	7					
October	15	4					
November	6	2					
December	4	1					
	201	88					

Jobs secured by members. 1972-82.

MOUNT St. CLUB.

MEN MAY REGISTER FOR
CASUAL OR PERMANENT EMPLOYMENT
AS
LABOURERS DRIVERS HANDYMEN.

GARDENERS. HOTEL OR KITCHEN.

PORTERS — OR ANY TRADE

NO. CHARGES

EMPLOYERS. PLEASE PHONE
761838

Sign taped to the window of Fenian Street. c. 1980.

Fenian Street in 1998 involved bringing a developer on board who would build approximately fifteen apartments, that would finance the rest of the development. They hoped to create a space which would include office spaces, training spaces, and a community centre. In May 1998 a letter from Pat Buckley, the architect, stated that there would be a difficulty in getting permission for the community centre as the site was zoned residential, despite its current use.[53] In October 1998 Community Technical Aid moved out of Fenian Street into different premises. The governors once again shelved plans to redevelop Fenian Street and began to look around again for new possibilities.[54]

In September 1999 Peter Perrem produced a document for the other governors which he presented to the meeting, entitled 'the Future of the premises at Fenian Street.' In it he proposed a project that would provide social housing, education, and training for the young homeless unemployed. The governors discussed donating the Fenian Street building as a legacy to this project. The idea of winding up the club and creating a legacy project led the governors to consider creating a Foyer.

The Foyer project

The interest that the governors took in working with Focus Ireland to build a Foyer hostel in the Fenian Street premises was in keeping with both the original aims of the club and their interest in innovation. Their lack of funds had hindered them, since the sale of the farm, in undertaking any large-scale projects. They did, however, own their premises, which was their major asset. The idea was that Focus Ireland would secure funding and the Mount Street Club would provide the building to create a Foyer in Dublin which would bear the name of the Mount Street Club, thereby providing a legacy for the club.

Foyer was a French idea. It was a hostel aiming to provide cheap urban accommodation to young people moving from rural areas to gain employment, as these people made up a large proportion of the homeless in cities. Training and safe accommodation were provided for six months to enable them to get a job and become independent. The idea was taken up in the United Kingdom in 1992 with the establishment of five Foyers under the leadership of Sheila McKechnie. Her aim in setting up Foyers was to 'meet the challenge of rising youth unemployment and homelessness.'[55] She wished to break the cycle of no home therefore no job therefore no home. The Foyer Federation describes itself as 'a not-for-profit organisation that helps to transform the circumstances of young people who have faced barriers in their lives.'[56]

Focus Ireland was looking for a partner for this project, that was immediately attractive to the governors who had considered converting Fenian Street into a hostel themselves in the 1970s after the sale of the farm. The Foyer contained a training and re-skilling element which harked back to the days of the club farm at Larkfield and the workshops in Mount Street run by the club. Tom Nolan recalls the first meeting with Sister Stanislaus Kennedy, a member of the Sisters of Charity and co-founder of Focus Ireland, and how impressed all of the governors were with the high standards that Focus Ireland had insisted on in their project for the homeless and unemployed in Stanhope Street. In addition, Des Byrne, chairman of the Focus board, had assured Tom Nolan of the commitment of Focus to the Foyer project.[57]

In April 2000 the governors met to view the architectural plans and a meeting between the architect Gerry Cahill and the local area planning officer was held. Dublin Corporation's Housing Department was informed of the proposed project and was keen to support it, and Focus Ireland had also submitted an application for funding to the National Children's Hour Millennium Fund. The governors estimated the cost of the project at £3.8 million.[58] They seemed

52. Minutes of the MSC, December 1997 (DCLA, Ar/add/81/011. Closed until 2029).

53. Pat Buckley to Governors, May 1998 (DCLA, Ar/add/81/011. Closed until 2029).

54. Minutes of the MSC, October 1998 (DCLA, Ar/add/81/011. Closed until 2029).

55. The Foyer Federation website, http://foyer.net. Accessed 14 November 2013.

56. Ibid.

57. Tom Nolan, interview with the author, 9 September 2013.

58. Minutes of the MSC, 6 April 2000 (DCLA, Ar/add/81/017).

eager to go ahead with the planning approval process. An application to the High Court for a *cy-près* scheme to enable the governors to use the assets and funds of the club in a way that might not exactly fit its original aims and objectives would be necessary before full planning permission could be sought. Meanwhile, Focus Ireland was incurring all costs in relation to the architect's fees and planning applications. In August 2000 governors Pat Morgan and Jimmy Tinkler went on a site visit to Belfast Foyer, which was run by the Simon Community. This hostel catered for seventeen- to twenty-six-year-olds for up to two years and had forty-two bed-sits. Pat Morgan concluded, in his report to the governors,

> We were left in no doubt that the Foyer was a highly desirable project and…would fit the charitable aims of the MSC and recommend that we facilitate the establishment of a Foyer in our premises at 62/64 Fenian Street.[59]

By April 2001 it was decided that Focus would pay slightly less than market value for the Fenian Street premises and that, with the agreement of the CCDBI, this money would be used to build the Foyer on the site. Focus had obtained funding but had a shortfall of €500,000 which they hoped could be met in part by the MSC. The governors agreed in principle to allow three years for Focus to undertake this project, with some provision to extend this time should there be building delays. The governors considered that a convenant should be included so that the site would always be used for charity in the future.

The project faced local objections, and a meeting to answer questions of nearby residents was held. At the end of 2002, Justin O'Brien of Focus was hopeful that, in the worse case, building would start in September of 2003.[60] At the end of 2003 it was clear that the project had stalled despite being granted planning permission in January of that year. Dublin City Council withdrew its funding, having decided to support another Foyer built in Marrowbone Lane. The governors were frustrated. It was suggested that Focus be given a deadline of February 2004 to give an update presentation 'and if the MSC is not satisfied at that stage they can pull out of the Focus arrangement.'[61] By mid-2004, however, the project was finally shelved. Focus had been unable to find another funding partner, partly due to the high cost over-run of the Marrowbone Lane Foyer. David Burke of Focus attended a meeting of the MSC and told the governors: 'Focus is making efforts to re-assess the situation since the Foyer project cannot go ahead.'

A certain momentum had been achieved, however, and the governors remained determined to realise the potential of Fenian Street and move the club forward in its aim of 'getting people into the workforce.'[62] This determination would lead to the sale of the Fenian Street premises in 2006 and the establishment of the Mount Street Club Trust in 2007. The history of the Mount Street Club during its years in the Fenian Street premises shows an organisation struggling to redefine itself in the face of change, to maximise its assets and its impact with little funds, and to rebound from disappointment and embrace innovation and new possibilities. The inspiration of the original founders and governors, some of whom continued their involvement into the 1980s, resulted in a constant stream of new energetic governors who believed that this charity was worth donating their time and efforts to. This loyalty and perseverance to the spirit of the Mount Street Club is the reason that it survived and that it was able to reinvent itself once more, upon the sale of Fenian Street, into a philanthropic trust.

59. Report of Pat Morgan and Jimmy Tinkler, August 2000 (DCLA, Ar/add/81/454).

60. Minutes of MSC, 4 December 2002 (DCLA, Ar/add/81/018).

61. Minutes of MSC, 2 December 2003, Ibid.

62. Minutes of MSC, 9 April 2004, Ibid.

THE IRISH NAUTICAL TRUST
VIII
Colin Murphy

One day in 1987 a group of men and women arrived at a locked gate in Ringsend, at the end of South Dock Road, carrying a pair of steel cutters. There was an old lock on the gate; they cut it and swung the gate open. They walked into a vast, derelict industrial site, bordered on two sides by the water of the Grand Canal Basin and on the others by walls. There was nobody about. They walked the site slowly, wandering into buildings, remembering. When they were young, this place had been at the heart of their community, a source of employment and camaraderie across generations. Hundreds worked in the industries on the quayside; still more found daily employment servicing the regular shipping traffic. But now, it was quiet. And it was scarred: the walls falling down; the cobblestones upturned; the warehouses weather-beaten; the remnants of industry discarded across the site. 'We could put together a training programme to clean it up,' thought one of the group. Another emerged from a warehouse and proclaimed, 'This would make a great office!'[1]

Almost 25 years later, the surrounding area has undergone an extraordinary transformation. And yet, much of that site, on Charlotte Quay, remains undeveloped. The youth unemployment that blighted the area in the 1980s is back. And some of the same people are still there, fighting it again.

This area, and Charlotte Quay in particular, was the focus for much of the work of the Mount Street Club in the 1980s and 1990s. Much energy and money was spent here; and yet that work remains unresolved. The complexity of community development and the extraordinary changes in the Irish economy in the time since (for better, and then for worse) conspired to compromise the impact of the club's work. And yet it retains a legacy in the Grand Canal Basin

1. Charlie Murphy, interview with the author, 26 April 2013.

IRISH NAUTICAL TRUST

NAOMH EANNA
The Naomh Eanna was built in Dublin in 1958 for service as a ferry between Galway and the Aran Islands. Flagship of the Irish Nautical Trust, she will accommodate a cafe and shop within the Maritime Heritage Centre. Throughout the ship, there will be exhibits and displays embracing every aspect of life afloat from merchant shipping, fishing and weather forecasting, to sail training, scuba diving and inland waterways. The Naomh Eanna will be a window to the maritime world - past and present.

© Pat Sweeney

Irish Nautical Trust brochure. 1989.

and, as the local community faces into the same challenges as before, that legacy is being invoked again.

The establishment of the trust

In the 1930s, when the Mount Street Club sought occupation for the men of the inner city, it looked west, to the land. Fifty years later, when the club sought to revitalise itself, it looked east, to the sea.

The Grand Canal Basin lies at the meeting point of three waterways, the Liffey, the Grand Canal, and the Dodder, roughly a mile upriver from the sea. The community around it, that of Ringsend, has a deep connection to those waterways and to the sea. Ringsend's nickname is Raytown, from the local staple, the ray fish, and the area was known as the 'home of Irish rowing' for the prowess of its local teams. There is a history of service in the merchant navy; many worked in the industries that grew up around the docks; and still more worked as casual labour on the docks, loading and unloading vessels. On the basin alone, ships brought coal for the many coal yards and for the Dublin Gas Company on Grand Canal Quay, sand for the Bottle House (as the Irish Glass Bottle Company on Charlotte Quay was known), and grain for the flour mills, particularly Boland's Mill. Every ship required linesmen to tie it up and stevedores and dockers to unload it. Other businesses on the basin included the International Meat Company, Hammond Lane Metal, and Joe Behan's log yard. And there was a long history of boat building; 'the last of the great Ringsend boat builders,' Joe Murphy, closed his yard in 1957.[2]

There was so much work that there was relatively little premium placed locally on schooling. Local businessman Jimmy Murray left school at 14; he explains: 'you didn't have to have an education because there was so much industry locally. And everybody in Ringsend had big families, so as soon as you were able to contribute and bring something in to the family, that's what you did.'[3]

By the 1980s, however, much of this industry had collapsed or moved elsewhere, and the demand for casual labour had been decimated by the introduction of containerisation and roll-on-roll-off shipping in the port. With an established pattern of early school leaving, the community was particularly vulnerable to unemployment: one study recorded a 39 per cent unemployment rate (compared to a rate in the city as a whole of 17 per cent), and a Leaving Certificate completion rate of less than 5 per cent.[4]

In the meantime the Mount Street Club too had lost its *raison d'être*. The farm had been acquired by compulsory purchase order; the Mount Street building had been sold; the generation who had founded it had stepped aside. The social and political approaches to unemployment, as well as the needs of the unemployed, in the 1980s, were vastly different to those of the 1930s. The club needed to refocus, and a new generation of governors wrestled with this challenge.

Peter Perrem was chairman at the time, having followed his father, a former Guinness employee, onto the board of the club. On Perrem's initiative, the club approached a leading sociologist, Professor John Jackson of Trinity College, seeking advice on a new direction for the club. Jackson recommended a postgraduate student, Jim Lynch, and the club duly commissioned Lynch to carry out a study on the club's options.[5] Lynch identified a particular problem of chronic unemployment in nearby Ringsend, and saw a potential resource for fighting it in the Grand Canal Basin, which some in the local community were suggesting could be a focus for leisure activities and regeneration.[6]

2. A.P. (Tony) Behan, 'Ringsend memories,' *Dublin Historical Record*, lxi (Spring 2008), pp. 50-61.

3. Jimmy Murray, interview with the author, 4 May 2013. According to a local study by St Andrew's Resource Centre, *A Community response to unemployment* (1993), 'local residents had little difficulty in securing unskilled or semi-skilled employment in manufacturing or port related activities'; as a result, there was a 'well-established pattern' of early school-leaving, which left the local population all the more vulnerable when changes to the industries on the docks led to 'the virtual disappearance of full time unskilled manual occupations.' Cited in Grand Canal Docks Trust and Irish Nautical Trust, 'Grand Canal Basin Area Action Plan,' July 1995 (DCLA, Ar/add/81/368).

4. St Andrew's Resource Centre, *St Andrew's Community Survey* (1990), cited in Grand Canal Docks Trust and Irish Nautical Trust, 'Grand Canal Basin Area Action Plan'.

5. Peter Perrem, interview with the author, 15 January 2013.

6. Jim Lynch, 'Report on the possible developments of the Mount Street Club,' April 1985 (DCLA, Ar/add/81/151).

The club seized upon this idea and moved quickly. In March 1987 the governors of the Mount Street Club established the Dublin Nautical Trust as a separate company to drive regeneration in the Grand Canal Basin area; its flagship project was to be the development of a Nautical Heritage Centre, a floating museum of seafaring, located in the basin itself; this, it was hoped, would ultimately create jobs, while providing for training opportunities as it was developed. (The trust was soon renamed the Irish Nautical Trust.) The project, however, had a deeper objective, albeit one that was not quite so tangible. As with the Mount Street Club's original ventures, on Mount Street and at the farm, the governors hoped that their project would be the seed of an idea. By celebrating Ringsend's maritime heritage and opening it up to new investment, they hoped to be a catalyst for a wider revitalisation of the area, one that would be characterised by culture as much as commerce. They hoped to help give the people of the area something to be proud of.

The Nautical Trust was set up as an independent company but, especially from the perspective of those on the ground in Ringsend, it was almost inextricable from the Mount Street Club. Two of the club's governors, Peter Perrem and John Jackson, joined the trust's board, and the club provided crucial funding through the 1980s and 1990s, although this, as we shall see, would become a source of some tension.[7] John de Courcy Ireland, the famous maritime historian and activist, became president of the new trust, and the trust forged a connection with the newly-opened Ringsend Community Training Workshop in order to strengthen its local roots and develop ideas.

Meanwhile, the Mount Street Club's interest and investment in the area led to parallel connections with other groups, and it became involved in the Grand Canal Basin Working Group, an initiative led by Pauline Geoghegan of St Andrew's Resource Centre on Pearse Street, which brought together some of the key local actors in an attempt to drive the regeneration of the basin. The club commissioned Deirdre McDermott of the architectural firm McDermott Parker to research regeneration possibilities; amongst the ideas considered was a museum of local heritage which would commemorate the area's connections with the 1916 Rising. It is clear from the archives that great energy and imagination was invested in the project to regenerate the Basin, but the environment was bleak, as captured in a simple reference in the minutes from September 1987: 'The economic circumstances prevailing in Ireland are austere. The only available government funding source for research work in relation to the inner city has been axed within the last week.'[8]

Still, the Mount Street Club and Nautical Trust ploughed ahead with ambitious ideas for the regeneration of the area. It was that energy, shared with other active community groups,[9] that drove Charlie Murphy and some other local activists to break into the Charlotte Quay site in 1987.

The *Mary Stanford*

Charlie Murphy had been to sea himself, in the merchant navy. He returned home to Ringsend in the late 1970s, got a job at Dublin Port, and started to involve himself in community activities. 'I wanted to give something back,' he says.[10] Like other local activists, he felt a strong association with the Grand Canal Basin and saw potential in it:

Unemployment was rampant. Grand Canal Basin was a derelict site with locked gates and sunken boats. Someone said, 'let's see what's down there.' 'If the State's not going to help us, we'll help ourselves,' we thought. We were all a bit radical. 'If you're not with us, you're against us'—that kind of thing.

7. Judith Kiernan and Brian Harvey, 'The Mount Street Club: past, present and future,' 1994 (DCLA, Ar/add/81/130).

8. Minutes of the Grand Canal Basin Working Group, 18 September 1987 (DCLA, Ar/add/81/355).

9. According to one local report, there were thirty-eight local voluntary and community organisations, with the Mount Street Club being the oldest. (Grand Canal Basin Working Group, 'Submission to Grand Canal Docks Trust on Area Action Plan,' 1995 (DCLA, Ar/add/81/358).

10. Murphy interview.

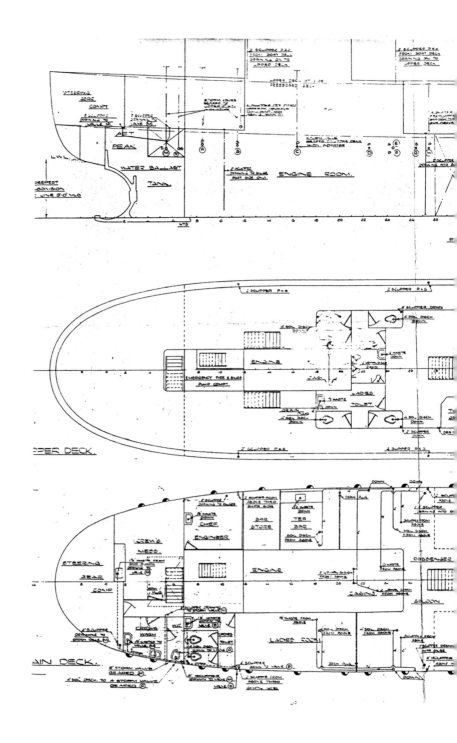

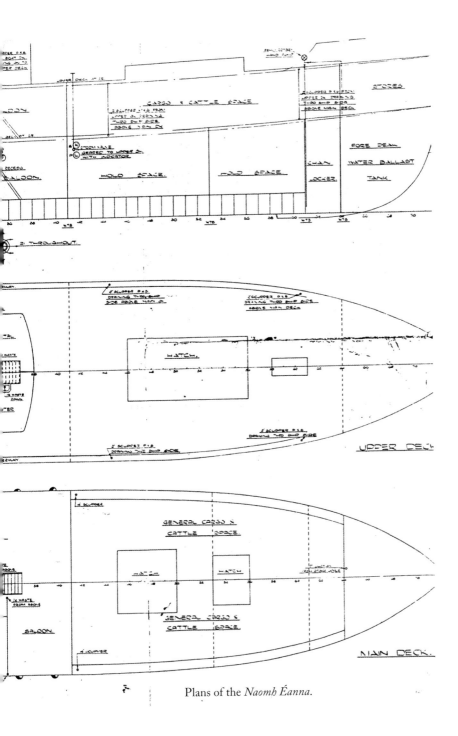

Plans of the *Naomh Éanna*.

We went in and cleaned the place up. We were over two months there before anyone came in and asked us what we were doing. We had cleaned it, put offices in buildings, refurbished toilets. We got unemployed plumbers, electricians, carpenters, bricklayers, stonemasons—grafters, guys who were proud of putting stone on stone. We reset the cobblestones on the quayside and built a slipway. There were old sunken trawlers in the basin and we cut them up and removed them.

For a time, they worked under threat of possible eviction. "Bring it on," we thought. We were squatters. There was never a guarantee of anything, but we felt we were in a win-win situation. If you're long-term unemployed and get a few months of work or training, that's all good.'

It was a question of the 'ownership' of the Basin. It was owned by the community. The local kids swam in the Basin in summer. The men had worked in the factories alongside it, like the Bottle House and Boland's Mill, looking out over it. We were trying to restore and protect that sense of ownership.

Eventually, they regularised their position, obtaining a letter from the Office of Public Works giving permission to them to base themselves on Charlotte Quay. Michael McNamara, who had been employed by FÁS, the national training and employment authority, at the Ringsend Community Training Workshop, became the manager of the Irish Nautical Trust also, and gradually the various interests and institutional distinctions amongst those active in the basin began to blur.

The Nautical Trust set about acquiring vessels for restoration and display, and developing training programmes in boat restoration and building. Ultimately, three training programmes were established under the auspices of various state schemes, targeting teenagers, young adults, and the long-term unemployed. At their peak, there were approximately 150 people occupied on the programmes. A pontoon was acquired from B&I Shipping for £1 and restored so that it could be used by the project and hired out. A retired Aran Islands passenger ferry, the *Naomh Éanna*, was acquired from the national transport company, CIÉ, restored and converted to a micro-enterprise centre, with the intention of ultimately being used as the base for the nautical heritage centre. It became home to a small windsurfing school, Surfdock (which has since established itself as a leading watersports outfit, from the same base on the *Naomh Éanna*), and to a sailmaker, Willie Brennan, and it was used for maritime safety training. A replica was built of one of the first-ever catamarans, the *Simon and Jude*, designed and built by William Petty in Dublin in 1664. An ambitious plan was hatched to build a seaworthy replica of a sixteenth-century Portuguese caravel; the trust held meetings with officials of the Portuguese navy and embassy and eventually acquired a set of plans for the caravel, but it never materialised.

The high point of this phase was the acquisition of an apparently humble lifeboat, the *Mary Stanford*. Built in 1930, the *Mary Stanford* had been the lifeboat in Ballycotton, Co. Cork, where, in 1936, she was involved in an extraordinary rescue. On the morning of 8 February 1936, in the throes of a ferocious storm, the lifeboat station received an SOS from the lightship *LV Comet*. The lightship was normally stationed at Daunt Rock in order to warn ships of the danger there, but she had broken her moorings. Coxswain Patsy Sliney led his crew out to sea in the *Mary Stanford* to attempt to rescue the *Comet*'s crew. They laboured at sea all day, without food, attempting to secure a steel cable to the *Comet*; each time they got it aboard, the waves would separate the boats again, and the cable would snap. The *Mary Stanford* then made for Cobh to get stronger cables, where the crew ate and slept for three hours. Returning to Daunt Rock in the morning, they found it covered by fog. They remained there through the day and night to no avail. After a second brief trip to Cobh, the *Mary Stanford* spent a third day attempting to rescue the crew of the *Comet*. As darkness fell, they realised the *Comet* was drifting towards the rock. Patsy Sliney decided there was no option but to bring the *Mary Stanford* alongside the *Comet* (which was extremely dangerous, because the heavy lightship could easily hole the smaller boat if they crashed together) and to have the crew jump for it. Some of the crew were by then too exhausted to jump; eventually, the *Mary Stanford* went so close that its crew could seize them. After six approaches, all the *Comet*'s crew were rescued, and the *Mary Stanford* made for home. The rescue had taken 63 hours, during which the crew had just three hours' sleep. The coxswain, Patsy Sliney, was awarded the Royal National Lifeboat Institution gold medal and his crew were each awarded silver or bronze medals. And for the first time in history, the boat herself, the *Mary Stanford*, was decorated.[11]

Subsequent to its service in Ballycotton, the *Mary Stanford* had seen service in Bangor, North Wales, and had been spotted there in the early 1960s by the harbour master of Limerick Harbour Commissioners, Capt. E. K. Donnelly. Donnelly acquired her, put her to service as a pilot boat on the Shannon, and contacted Patsy Sliney's family to alert them. Patsy's grandson, Brendan, then acquired the *Mary Stanford* from Limerick Harbour Commissioners for £1, and later agreed to transfer her to the Irish Nautical Trust for restoration. On 6 June 1988, the *Mary Stanford* sailed into Howth, with Brendan Sliney at the helm, to a welcome from the Defence Forces Band of the Curragh Command. 'This is one of the most emotional and important days in the history of the Irish maritime service,' said John de Courcy Ireland, on behalf of the Irish Nautical Trust. 'We are proud to have this magnificent souvenir of this country's maritime tradition.'[12]

The *Mary Stanford* had been extensively refurbished along the way, often unsympathetically, and Michael McNamara set about trying to uncover details of her original design, fittings, and decoration. In the meantime, the Nautical

11. Wikipedia, s.v. 'RNLB Mary Stanford (ON 733),' http://en.wikipedia.org/wiki/RNLB_Mary_Stanford. Accessed 5 May 2013.

12. Lorna Siggins, 'The *Mary Stanford* comes home to a safe berth,' *Irish Times*, 7 June 1988.

Crew of the *Mary Stanford*. 1936.

Trust was preoccupied with ongoing restoration work on the *Naomh Éanna* and with securing its presence on Charlotte Quay. Work on the *Mary Stanford* proceeded slowly—too slowly for Brendan Sliney, who checked on her on a number of visits to Dublin, and wrote to the trust to complain about the lack of progress and lack of information.

Meanwhile, the trust struggled to establish itself financially, and remained dependent on the Mount Street Club. In 1990 John de Courcy Ireland wrote to the then Taoiseach, Charles Haughey, seeking support for the 'Floating Maritime Museum Project,' but to no avail. 'I would like to leave the briefing you suggest over for the moment and in the meantime I wish you every success with the project,' the Taoiseach replied.[13]

Today the *Mary Stanford* is moored alongside the *Naomh Éanna*, still waiting for the day when she will be returned to her former glory and celebrated again for the lives that she saved. After a number of years of neglect, that day may be coming again.

The Grand Canal Basin

In 1994 the governors commissioned a report on the 'past, present and future' of the Mount Street Club from consultants Judith Kiernan and Brian Harvey.[14] By then the club had been involved in various activities in the Grand Canal Basin area, through the Irish Nautical Trust and other initiatives, for seven years. The basin had become something of a hive of maritime activity, not all of it related directly to the trust. There was winter boat storage for 150 boats; a boat security company called Shipwatch; the surfing school, Surfdock; and a number of small businesses housed on the *Naomh Éanna*, including the Surfdock shop, a sail maker, and a miniature ship carver. Looking to the wider basin, the Nautical Trust and the Mount Street Club could derive some satisfaction from having been part of a wider regeneration movement. There was a year-long programme of steel-fabricated hull production at Poolbeg Training; a programme in basic boat-building skills for early school leavers at Ringsend Community Workshop, and a post–Leaving Certificate course in

Marine Studies at Ringsend Technical Institute.[15]
So the various activities in the Basin, in part supported by the club, had made an impact: what had been derelict was now a site of activity and some hope. But the club and the trust had encountered some difficulties, as Kiernan and Harvey reported. Both within the club and to outside observers, it was not always clear where the club ended and the trust began; although they were legally separate entities, they were regularly perceived as the same. And the Trust had remained financially dependent on the Club, failing to attain significant sponsorship. 'The relationship between the Mount Street Club and the Irish Nautical Trust became confused,' wrote Kiernan and Harvey. 'Funding of the Trust deteriorated from initial project marked amounts to clearing overdrafts,' and this 'placed the Mount Street Club in financial difficulties.'

Peter Perrem, who represented the Mount Street Club on the board of the Irish Nautical Trust, recalls that a key problem was that the rules for eligibility for the FÁS training schemes, on which the trust relied to fund its training activities, kept changing, making consistency impossible, and that these funds eventually 'dried up.'[16]

Kiernan and Harvey traced these problems to the inception of the Irish Nautical Trust. The governors, they said, had been 'keen to re-establish the good name of the club' and had seized on Jim Lynch's suggestion of exploring the employment-generating potential of the Grand Canal Basin in order to do this. The governors had taken 'a large step into the dark,' they found; the Irish Nautical Trust and the nautical museum project had been launched without an adequate understanding of the work or resources that would be involved, or of the direct impact these could have on unemployment. From the outside, the laudable energy and initiative being shown by the Mount Street Club was

13. Charles Haughey to John de Courcy Ireland, 4 May 1990 (DCLA, Ar/add/81/407).

14. Kiernan and Harvey, 'The Mount Street Club: past, present and future.'

15. Grand Canal Basin Working Group, 'Submission on Area Action Plan.'

16. Perrem interview.

THE MARY STANFORD

This is the Ballycotton Lifeboat famed for the rescue
of the eight-man crew of the drifting *Daunt Rock
Lightship* in hurricane conditions in February 1936.
For his part in the 63 hour service, Coxswain Patrick
Sliney was awarded the RNLI Gold Medal.
Uniquely, the *Mary Stanford* herself was also
awarded a Gold Medal, the only lifeboat ever to be
so honoured in the history of the RNLI. She was
later converted to serve as a pilot boat in the Shannon
Estuary where she was discovered by Brendan
Sliney, Patrick's grandson. He has entrusted her to us
for refurbishment to her original state. She will take
pride of place in the Maritime Heritage Centre.

LIFFEY FERRY NO. 9

From the granting of a character by Charles II in
1660 until 1984, a ferry has operated across the River
Liffey. One of the last vessels to operate this service
was *'No. 9'* and her presence in the Maritime
Heritage Centre will surely stir nostalgic thoughts for
many Dubliners.

Irish Nautical Trust brochure. 1989.

THE TUG NORAY

The Tug Noray worked in the River Liffey since the early 1930's. During the 'Emergency' she saw service as a port control vessel in Dublin. Having ended her active life, she has come to us for refurbishment and display as a good example of her kind. Like all our other projects, she will have a team of 'friends' drawn from amongst our membership who will carry out research and advise the FAS group working on her on how she would have been in her prime, from fittings and fenders, to paint colours. Friends may also be able to help procure items suitable for the vessels or suggest potential sponsors. We are fortunate to have had the financial support of the Mount Street Club for 'seed funding' to help us initiate most of our schemes.

A PORTUGUESE CARAVEL

The Trust has received, from the Portuguese Navy, the plans and specifications for the building of a replica *15th Century Caravel* in Dublin to commemorate Henry the Navigator and the Portuguese age of discovery. There are invitations to sail the vessel to Lisbon to join in celebrations and to the New World for Columbus's anniversary, as he took two *Caravels* with him on his voyage.

Irish Nautical Trust brochure. 1989.

interpreted as indicating a substantial financial commitment, which the club had not in fact made. The club consulted the community, but did not make them integral to the design of the project: they did not see 'the importance of having the community with the project, as opposed to merely being accepting of it.'

These comments were qualified, however: 'Retrospective clarity of view is notorious. The enormous energy and commitment of individuals can be forgotten or ignored. The sense of being part of a living development is potent and carries all of us along at some stage,' wrote Kiernan and Harvey. The Mount Street Club's investment in the Grand Canal Basin had been 'laudable and enviable' and displayed 'the vibrancy of positive action' and a 'commitment to do something constructive in the face of need', they found.[17]

By now, however, there were seismic forces at work on the landscape of the city. The Irish economy grew at almost 9 per cent in 1995;[18] for the following five years, growth would average 9.4 per cent.[19] The Irish Financial Services Centre had transformed the north quays of the Liffey in the late 1980s and Temple Bar provided another prototype for successful large-scale urban regeneration. There was a growing sense that the Grand Canal Basin could be the site for a major development. By then, there had been nine separate studies done on the development of the Grand Canal Docks and basin area since 1988 (when the Grand Canal Basin Working Group, in which the Mount Street Club was involved, had produced an action plan),[20] and the Nautical Trust and other local groups fought to ensure that their views, and those of the local community, would be reflected in any development plan.

The breakthrough came in 1997, with the establishment of the Dublin Docklands Development Authority by the Fine Gael–Labour government, driven by Brendan Howlin as minister for the environment and local TD Ruairi Quinn as minister for finance. The authority was tasked with prioritising 'sustainable inner city regeneration, one in which the whole community enjoys the highest standards of access to education, employment, housing and social amenity and which delivers a major contribution to the social and economic prosperity of Dublin and the whole of Ireland.'[21] The legislation set up a Docklands Council to oversee the development of a master plan for the Docklands; there were to be a number of community representatives on the council.

For Charlie Murphy and other local activists, this was precisely what they had been seeking. 'The years of hard work came together. The master plan vindicated everything done by the Mount Street Club and Irish Nautical Trust over the years,' he says. Indeed, this was precisely what had been envisaged by Judith Kiernan some years earlier. She wrote: 'The future of the trust…lies within the mainstream of the area development plan. The Irish Nautical Trust is a player in that development and has been assisted to achieve that position by Mount Street Club financing and the commitment of individual Mount Street Club governors.'

Charlie Murphy elaborates: 'The involvement of the local community in the Docklands master plan wouldn't have happened without the backing of the Mount Street Club. It took us about ten years to get credibility. If the Mount Street Club hadn't got involved it would have been taken over by private developers; the local community would have been excluded.'[22]

And his appraisal of the club's approach echoed the club founders' own statements, of fifty years earlier: 'The Mount Street Club never came in and told people what to do. They were very subtle about their contacts, about how

17. Kiernan and Harvey's conclusions were not accepted by the Mount Street Club's board of governors, who felt there was a direct and considerable link between the Nautical Trust and employment, as the graduates of the various courses the trust ran went on to get employment and the trust successfully supported various micro-enterprises based on the *Naomh Éanna* (Perrem interview).

18. Indexmundi, 'Ireland GDP—real growth rate,' http://www.indexmundi.com/ireland/gdp_real_growth_rate. html. Accessed 29 April 2013.

19. Wikipedia, s.v. 'Celtic Tiger,' http://en.wikipedia.org/wiki/Celtic_Tiger#Tiger_Economy. Accessed 29 April 2013.

20. Grand Canal Docks Trust and Irish Nautical Trust, 'Grand Canal Basin Area Action Plan.'

21. Docklands Authority, 'About Us,' http://www.docklands.ie/index.jsp?1nID=93&pID=99&nID=138. Accessed 5 May 2013. For more, see Turtle Bunburry, *Dublin Docklands—an urban voyage* (Dublin, 2008).

22. Murphy interview.

A Presentation of photographic, historic and topical information and local children's impressions of the Grand Canal Basin... An opportunity to comment on and influence the future of the area...

'raising the issues'

VENUE: St Andrew's Community Centre   Ringsend Community Workshop
         Pearse Street   Regal House
         City Quay   Fitzwilliam St
                                           Ringsend

TIME: 10.00AM to 6.00PM   Monday 27 April 1987 for one week.

Grand Canal Basin Working Group brochure. 1987.

they intersected with everyone else. The club empowered the local community to move forward on its own.'[23]

Over the following decade, the Dublin Docklands Development Authority would drive enormous change in the Docklands area, transforming it into a densely-populated, modern urban quarter. The Mount Street Club continued to support the Irish Nautical Trust, in order to help it 'give the local community a viable presence in the basin' in the midst of this development.[24] This process was due to culminate with the implementation of the 2008 master plan,[25] which foresaw the development of a community training and micro-enterprise centre on what was then known as Plot 8, or the site of the old graving docks at the south end of the basin. This was intended to house Ringsend Community Training Workshop and the Irish Nautical Trust and to provide workshop spaces for their skills-training courses, helping to guarantee the survival of the area's heritage of maritime skills into the future. The project was given the name Flagship 21; a steering group was established and a billboard announcing this 'new neighbourhood facility', erected at the entrance to the site.[26] But by the time the master plan was published, in late 2008, the Irish economy was already in recession and heading for a severe and prolonged contraction. Controversy arose around aspects of the Dublin Docklands Development Authority's work, in particular in relation to the Irish Glass Bottle site in Ringsend, which had been purchased in 2006 for €412 million by a consortium that included the authority. (A report by the Comptroller and Auditor General in 2012 was highly critical of the authority's involvement in the deal.[27]) By January 2011 the Glass Bottle site was valued at just €45 million, and the authority was effectively

---

23. Murphy interview.

24. Perrem interview.

25. Dublin Docklands Development Authority, *Dublin Docklands Area Master Plan* (Dublin, 2008).

26. Photo retrieved at http://www.iwai.ie/forum/read.php?1,37656,38145. Accessed 13 May 2013.

27. Comptroller and Auditor General Special Report, Department of the Environment, Community and Local Government, Dublin Docklands Development Authority, February 2012.

insolvent. The Glass Bottle site loan, which had been provided by Anglo Irish Bank, was acquired by the National Asset Management Agency (NAMA) and in November 2011, the authority transferred a number of properties to NAMA in lieu of its debt on the Glass Bottle site. Amongst these sites was Plot 8,[28] leaving the future of the community facility in the hands of NAMA.

'Born on the Liffey'

One of those involved with the Irish Nautical Trust throughout this period was Jimmy Murray. 'Born and reared on the Liffey,' Murray left school in the mid-1970s, aged fourteen, to work in the local dairy, and remembers, when he was even younger, how he and the other local children would watch for the arrival of the coal ships. 'From the flats where we lived, you could see the tops of the cranes on Sir John Rogerson's Quay moving. When we saw that, we'd head straight over to the docks with our box carts. We were told not to steal anything, but we'd catch the coal that was spilled from the cranes and run it home.'[29]

Murray set up a successful engineering business in the early 1980s, but towards the end of the decade, as business slowed down, he sought a new venture, and looked to the water. Realising there was going to be a period of heavy construction along the Liffey, he noticed that there were no facilities for construction companies to use the river. 'There was a gap in the market that I saw and I thought I'd better get set up for it.' He also thought there was advertising potential on the water. He went to talk to the Irish Nautical Trust and the neighbouring organisation, Poolbeg Training, which were based in portacabins on Charlotte Quay. They agreed to back him, and Murray set up Water Borne Productions, specialising in creating floating advertising and in providing industrial pontoons for construction works on the quays. 'The Irish Nautical Trust was a fantastic idea,' he says. 'It saw there was an indigenous maritime people and it sought to restore the pride and passion in what they did. It was a seed of hope. It lifted a lot of spirits.'

Murray remained involved with the Nautical Trust over the years on an ad-hoc basis, and regularly checks on the *Mary Stanford*, baling her out when necessary. In 2012 he joined the board of the trust and is engrossed in plans to revitalise it and renew the vision of its founders. In an interview with this author, he said: 'History is repeating itself, with the recession, but the Irish Nautical Trust is still there. We want to repeat what the founders did and train kids who won't otherwise get opportunities.' He hopes to set up a port cadet course and get accreditation from Dublin Port and support from the shipping companies, which will lead to apprenticeships and possibilities of employment. He is working on plans for a 'marine park' on Charlotte Quay, to be housed in refurbished shipping containers, that will expand on the original hope for a nautical heritage centre, and he intends to finally restore the *Mary Stanford*. They day we met, he had been up till 3 a.m. working on plans with his designer. 'There's a lot of young fellows around here that are on the wrong road. This can provide the incentive for them to turn things around. The port needs a local maritime skills base. I have that passion. A lot of kids around the area have that passion too, but they just need guidance—I know how to give them that guidance. I intend to fight their corner.'

So the Irish Nautical Trust lives on, and the *Mary Stanford* awaits restoration, patiently.

28. Namawinelake, 'NAMA does secret deal with DDDA to erase liability for idiotic property development decisions,' 26 November 2011, http://namawinelake.wordpress.com/2011/11/26/nama-does-secret-deal-with-ddda-to-erase-liability-for-idiotic-property-development-decisions. Accessed 13 May 2013.

29. Murray interview.

THE MOUNT STREET CLUB TRUST, 2006 TO PRESENT

IX

Sarah Perrem

> To me the legacy of the Mount Street Club was its almost unique
> approach to reducing unemployment and that it served its purpose
> so admirably for so long.[1]
>
> —*Bill Somerville-Large*

The Mount Street Club Trust exists today as a private philanthropic trust
with a Board of Trustees that distributes its funds to large projects aimed at
the alleviation of poverty and disadvantage associated with unemployment.
They faced a significant transformation from an active hands-on charity in
the 1930s and 1940s to a funding philanthropy, which does not personally
oversee the day-to-day running of the projects. The decisions and focus of the
governors in the 1990s to create a legacy project and to wind up the activities
of the club led to the sale of the Fenian Street premises in 2006. For the
first time the governors had a large sum of money but they had no obvious
direction or project to fund. From 2006 to 2013 the charity worked hard to
distribute its funds to innovative projects that would have a positive impact on
the community and would also have the potential to influence policy makers.

The sale of the Mount Street Club premises, 62-64 Fenian Street, Dublin
2, was the catalyst for changes in the club. The governors had been working
throughout the late 1990s to get a hostel built and to use the premises to
benefit the local community. The ambitious plans to build a Foyer hostel on
the site, which would have provided a home as well as training and support
for young homeless people, were finally shelved in 2004. The costs of securing
planning for the project, which had been paid by Focus Ireland, had risen to
over £100,000 and had resulted in permission being granted for a multi-storey

building on the site. This planning permission had taken some years and the delay had ultimately cost the project its promised funding from Dublin Corporation. A Foyer had been built in Marrowbone Lane and, as it had overrun on its projected budget, Focus Ireland was unable to secure funding elsewhere. In their decision to build a Foyer the governors intended to wind up the club while creating a legacy project that would be worthy of its original aims. The lack of a suitable use for the property, which would be in keeping with the objectives of the MSC, led the governors to the decision to sell the property, and grant the resulting funds to charities that would alleviate poverty associated with unemployment.

The premises at 62-64 Fenian Street was sold in 2006. The governors and trustees found themselves in a unique position in the history of the Mount Street Club of having an abundance of funds in a city of unprecedented high employment. Tony Crooks of Pobal, a not-for-profit corporation that was established by the government in 1992 to tackle the problem of long-term unemployment, visited the board of trustees in July 2007 to make suggestions of areas in need of funding. The areas highlighted as most in need of funding were refugees and asylum seekers and the integration of non-nationals.[2] There was no pressing problem of short-term unemployment in 2007 in Ireland.

Transition from club to trust

The years 2006 and 2007 saw the transformation of the Mount Street Club through a *cy-près* scheme[3] into a corporate body called the Mount Street Club Trust (MSCT) with new charitable objectives and a set of rules.

1. Bill Somerville-Large, interview with the author, 4 April 2013.

2. Minutes of the Mount Street Club, 9 June 2004. Taken from the private collection of Peter Perrem. The private papers of the Mount Street Trust will be added to the collection of the DCLA by 2018.

3. A *cy-près* scheme is the means by which a charitable fund whose original objective has ceased to exist, with the approval of the CCDBI or the Courts, is given new objectives as near as possible to the original object. See also Brian Hunt, ed., *Murdoch's dictionary of Irish law* (5th ed., Dublin, 2008), p. 308.

In 2006, at the time of the sale of Fenian Street premises, the board of governors numbered six: Peter Perrem, who had joined in 1981 and had been chairman since 1987; Edward Gleeson and Tom Nolan, who had been governors since the late 1980s; Bob Carroll and Pat Morgan, who had all joined during the 1990s; and Michael McNamara, who had been manager of the club in the 1990s and had been actively involved in the Irish Nautical Trust on behalf of the club. The trustees, who had been appointed in 1983 as sons of the outgoing trustees, were Dr Charles Delap, Dr Michael Ganly, and Bill Somerville-Large. The club had always been run by the board of governors, and the trustees had previously also been governors. The trustees at this time had never held positions as governors but, as sons of the original founders and governors, felt an interest and obligation to involve themselves in this new era of the club. They joined with the governors in working towards a decision on the future of the club.

The Mount Street Club had set its objectives and club rules when it was established in 1934 to relieve poverty associated with unemployment. In the years that followed the club evolved in its activities, culminating in the sales of its premises at Mount Street and the farm. By 1983 the Commissioners of Charitable Donations and Bequests for Ireland (CCDBI) considered that the club's objectives had essentially failed and invited the club to apply for a *cy-près* scheme. Consideration was given to the making of such an application to the High Court but the governors decided that it was unnecessary at that time to apply for such a scheme.

In 2005 the objectives for the Mount Street Club were discussed again in the context of plans to sell its premises at Fenian Street. The CCDBI indicated a willingness to approve a *cy-près* scheme in the event of a sale. Between 2006 and 2007 the governors and trustees agreed upon a proposed new main objectives which sought to preserve the values of the club albeit fulfilled through new means. Primarily the club would become a grant-giving trust which would identify and support self-help oriented charities. The main objective would change from 'relieving poverty in the city of Dublin with particular reference to the problem of unemployed men' and would now read:

The main object and purpose of the Mount Street Club Trust… is the relief of the effects of disadvantage and poverty associated primarily with unemployment either through donations and grants to charities in the Republic of Ireland…which provide basic skills and training, rehabilitation, education and other relevant assistance aimed at such relief or by any other direct means that may seem appropriate from time to time.[4]

By order of the CCDBI a *cy-près* scheme[5] with the foregoing objective was approved on 15 May 2007 and the trust was subsequently incorporated pursuant to the Charities Act 1973 on 7 August 2007. Under the scheme of incorporation the positions of governor and trustee were replaced by a board of trustees in which all of the responsibilities of governance and trusteeship became vested. The trustees on this day were Bill Somerville-Large, Dr Charles Delap, Dr Michael Ganly, Peter Perrem, Bob Carroll, Edward Gleeson, Tom Nolan, Pat Morgan, and Michael McNamara.

The trustees could now directly fund charities for the benefit of all those who were disadvantaged in society rather than simply focus on the unemployed man directly. The objectives acknowledged that the great changes in social welfare and involvement of state agencies in job creation over the life of the Mount Street Club had changed the nature of solutions to unemployment. The new response to tackle the problem of unemployment would 'lay emphasis on community responses and initiatives based on Community Development Principles and interaction with statutory and other agencies.'[6] This was very much in keeping with the activities of the club throughout the 1980s and 1990s in Ringsend with the Grand Canal Working Group and the establishment of

---

4. *Cy-près* scheme application, 7 August 2007. Copy held at the Office of the Commission of Charitable Donations and Bequests in Ireland.

5. Ibid.

6. Ibid.

Children attending early numeracy play event at the Early Learning Initiative,
National College of Ireland. 2011.

'Count Me In', Rose Martin Fingal Parenting Initiative. 2011.

Fingal Parent Initiative parents, Balbriggan. 2011.

the Irish Nautical Trust.[7]

They stated their wish to 'explore applying its assets to…charities dedicated to the relief of poverty among the unemployed through self assistance projects geared to meet current-day needs.'[8] They retained their interest in unemployment and poverty and, as part of their rules stated that the target beneficiaries would reside in the greater Dublin area, maintained their identity as a Dublin charity. They also had a rule which stated: 'the donee charity must not be affiliated to any political party'[9] and that 'any eligible charity will be without regard to gender, marital status, family status, sexual orientation, religion, age, disability, race, or membership of the Traveller community'; this was in keeping with the then progressive rules of the club in the 1930s which explicitly did not discriminate on the basis of religion or politics. The new objects simply formalised the way the governors had already been working since the mid-eighties. The *cy-près* scheme and scheme of incorporation would enable the club to become a charitable philanthropic trust with the authority to manage and spend its fund.

Funding decisions

The process of seeking tenders from charities was delayed until late 2007 when all the legal issues related to the scheme of incorporation and *cy-près* scheme were settled. The trustees now faced the challenge of how to distribute their funds. They needed to decide how to choose the charities to fund and how to administer the funded projects. There was a conflict between taking the time to create a thorough and accountable process and making a more immediate response to poverty and unemployment.

By October the trustees identified training towards employment, research, direct aid, service provision, and promotion of good practices as desirable areas of interest for charities applying for their funds.[10] Between November 2007 and February 2008 the trustees discussed their criteria for applicants extensively. Bob Carroll had created a document entitled 'The design, development, management and administration of a scheme for the application of the funds of the Mount Street Club Trust in accordance with its main objects and rules,' which formed the basis of their discussions. The tender document was issued in March 2008 with a closing date for applications of May 2008. It would be a competitive tender and applicants would be assessed on costs and value, on the applicant's ability to understand the subject area, to address and identify risks and problems, its proven experience, and its capacity to complete the project.

The trust received applications and decided to split the main body of their funds between projects which would be administered by Pobal and the Work Research Co-operative (WRC). In September 2010 they committed funding to Community Foundation Ireland (CFI) to administer. They continued to discuss the practicality and problems associated with direct aid or small donations. In 2010 and 2012 they granted one-off small donations to the Taney Employment Centre, Pearse College Allotments, and Protestant Aid.[11] The decision to create an accountable and transparent system to deal with small one-off grants was finally shelved until all of the larger projects were concluded and the amount of the remaining funds could be properly assessed.[12]

The trustees had spent a great deal of time and effort since the sale of the Fenian Street premises in 2006 to reach the point where they were in a position to fund a range of innovative and diverse projects. Bob Carroll recalls that he was eager to see the club achieve something and wanted to make sure that the projects funded would target those in need, have the biggest impact and leverage funds from other sources.[13] Peter Perrem said that in funding decisions 'the challenge is to find areas that are not supported or provided by

7. See chapter 8, 'The Irish Nautical Trust.'

8. *Cy-près* scheme application, 7 August 2007.

9. Ibid.

10. Minutes of the Mount Street Club Trust, 2 October 2007. The private collection of Peter Perrem.

11. Minutes of the Mount Street Club Trust, September 2010, September 2012. The private collection of Peter Perrem.

12. Minutes of the Mount Street Club Trust, 9 May 2011. The private collection of Peter Perrem.

13. Bob Carroll, interview with the author, 23 April 2013.

the government or current social policies while retaining the core principle o
helping people to help themselves.'[14] The trustees had chosen projects that wer
in keeping with its newly stated objectives. They had also striven to remair
true to the original spirit of the club by supporting innovative approaches tc
long-term unemployment. The original club had set up a premises and usec
the allotments, the club workshops, the farm, tallies, and the farm shop tc
help the unemployed man support his family while retaining or updating hi
skills. The new Mount Street Club Trust used its fund of money to suppor
approaches to tackle poverty and unemployment within the community.

The funded projects

The trust divided the main part of its fund between projects administered by
Pobal and the Work Research Co-operative. The original project proposec
by Pobal faltered when the government funding, which matched the trust':
50 per cent stake, fell through in 2009 as the project contracts were about tc
be signed.[15] Pobal returned to the trustees with a new proposal in September
The original project planned to enhance access to third level education. The
new project, entitled the National Early Years Access Initiative (NEYAI
would focus on early years education and services for children up to six year:
old. Atlantic Philanthropies, another private philanthropic trust, would alsc
be funding the project and Pobal gained funding and support from botl
the Department of Education and Skills and the Office of the Minister fo:
Children and Youth Affairs.[16]

The project planning was completed and expressions of interest wer
received in 2010 and the eleven chosen projects were approved in March 2011
six of which were located in Dublin. NEYAI was officially launched by the
minister for children and youth affairs, Frances Fitzgerald, on 20 June 2011
The projects varied in their focus; some involved staff training, others focusec
on child literacy and numeracy, some were concerned with parenting courses
and others dealt with the integration of family services. It was hoped that by
having such variety the projects could be evaluated and the outcomes coulc

ɔe analysed and used to influence best practice in the area of early education. Participation in high-quality early education is a factor in a child's ability to succeed in primary and post-primary education. This increases the likelihood ɔf attaining further education and employment after leaving school. The trustees had chosen to fund NEYAI, as it presented a unique opportunity to be involved in a well-thought-out and structured project with government support that aimed to affect future policy in early-years education.

The thorough evaluation of the NEYAI projects is still ongoing, so the final results and outcomes are not yet known. Interim assessments and feedback from individual projects show that they were making an immediate impact on the local participants and families. Staff from a numeracy project run in Dublin Docklands reported the immediate impact on their work on children's learning. 'Parents told me that the children were scanning everything on their way home looking for circles, squares, triangles and rectangles.'[17] Fingal Parenting Initiative received feedback from its seven-week parenting course:

> I found the course very useful a great confidence boost as a parent to realise that you are not the only one experiencing difficulties. I doubt anyone would do this course and not come away having learnt something.[18]

Tony Crooks, member of the Steering Group, and Chairperson of the Evaluation & Learning Expert Advisory Group (ELEAG) called the evaluation one of the biggest studies in Ireland in this area.[19]

---

14. Peter Perrem, interview with the author, March 2013.

15. Minutes of the Mount Street Club Trust, 10 July 2009. The private collection of Peter Perrem.

16. Minutes of the Mount Street Club Trust, 29 September 2009. The private collection of Peter Perrem.

17. Pobal, 'Project Updates to Steering Committee' (December-May 2012).

18. Fingal Parents' Initiative, PPEY Parent Testimonials attending the course. Courtesy of Pobal.

19. Minutes of the MSCT, 3 December 2012. The private collection of Peter Perrem.

Father and son from Dublin Docklands share a book during the Docklands Early Numeracy Week at the Early Learning Initiative, National College of Ireland. 2011.

Dr Carmel Duggan of the Work Research Co-operative (WRC) helped the trustees identify organisations that could be considered for funding. The Trustees, in their meeting of April 2009, chose to fund the Ballymun Job Centre, the Irish National Organisation of the Unemployed (INOU), and OPEN.[20] The three projects within the Mount Street Training and Employment Initiative (MSTEI) were quite diverse. Although all three groups had expertise in working at community level, all three strove to use innovative approaches, and all three had links to the labour market.

The MSTEI projects were based on up-to-date research on the best interventions to tackle long-term unemployment. They not only achieved extremely high participation rates from the targeted groups but had a significant impact on the individuals and their families. OPEN ran a FETAC (Further Education and Training Awards Council) horticulture course called Grow Your Own Future for lone parents which included mentoring and career guidance. One participant was said to be 'very conscious of her lack of education when she started' but 'after a negative experience of formal education, [she] discovered a hunger and enthusiasm for education as an adult.'[21] In addition, OPEN created a community garden next to the Finglas Addiction Support Team (FAST) project which was very successful and is now being kept running by FAST. Freda Keeshan of OPEN described the project as an enriching and grounding experience for all the staff and participants.[22]

The focus of the Ballymun Job Centre (BJC) is to enable people to find a long-term route out of poverty by accessing long-term well-paid employment. The centre had already developed a programme called eMerge, which was part of their pilot system to target an individual's interest, aptitudes, and needs, and then refer them into employment or relevant training. The MSTEI project enabled them to implement their new system with over a third of all

---

20. OPEN is the national network of one-parent families. www.oneparent.ie.

21. GYOF participant case study, February 2013, courtesy of Dr Carmel Duggan of WRC.

22. Freda Keeshan, interview with the author, 29 May 2013.

people using the centre. According to the initial findings of the social return on investment report (SROI), for every €1 spent on this project €3 in social return was gained and there was a significant, positive effect on the families of participants also. Mick Creedon of the BJC described working on this project as a 'terrific, positive experience' and said that it was 'embraced' by the staff. He praised Carmel Duggan of the WRC for the supportive framework she created for them, and the MSCT for the risk they took in funding them.[23]

The INOU, Irish National Organisation of the Unemployed, delivered a one-year FETAC-accredited training course and internships aimed to enable participants become trainers, mentors or peer educators. The course was called 'Building Futures.' By 2011 two of the participants from the first course had already gained employment and to date twenty-five of the thirty graduates have progressed to employment. The participants, carefully chosen to ensure that they were interested in the course, were met with individually and supported throughout the programme. Tutors allowed the participants to hand up draft copies of assignments, and extra help was given to participants with literacy issues and to those who were struggling with the course. This led to a high retention rate, with only one person dropping out in the first year for personal reasons.

John Farrell of the INOU said that the flexibility and support for the project, from Carmel Duggan and the MSCT funding, enabled the participants to be supported when it was needed. For example, the INOU were able to purchase software for one participant who is dyslexic. He added that the figures for retention and completion of the course and the move to further education and employment were very good but that the 'Building Futures' programme had had an additional impact. Participants had said that it had 'transformed their relationships with their children and [had transformed] their own children's attitude to education.'[24] Lorraine Hennessey of the INOU said that

23. Mick Creedon of the Ballymun Job Centre, interview with the author, 19 May 2013.

24. John Farrell of INOU, interview with the author, May 2013.

Grow Your Own Future course participants at work. 2011.

Grow Your Own Future plots in Finglas. 2011.

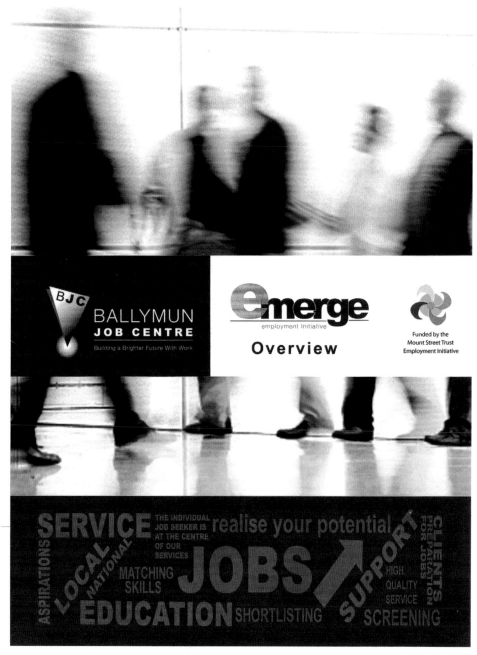

Ballymun Job Centre Emerge brochure. 2011.

participants had shown a new engagement with society and the world around them. They began watching and reading the news and taking an interest in current affairs and developing confidence in expressing their own opinions.[25]

Carmel Duggan said that her understanding of the history of the Mount Street Club was that they had always intervened to help the unemployed in a way that was appropriate to the time. The MSTEI project followed in this tradition as it was appropriate to the reality of today and the real experiences of those who were far from the labour market. She added that the MSCT differed as funders: they did not overly regulate and so allowed for scope, flexibility, and personal support that enabled the organisations to work and support the participants as individuals. Carmel Duggan described the MSTEI project as 'one of the most satisfying experiences of my professional life' because it was so well delivered by the three organisations and so well supported by the subgroup of trustees, Charles Delap, Pat Morgan, and Margaret Barry.[26]

The trustees considered the MSTEI project a great success. Trustee Margaret Barry added there was significant pressure to divert activity to the huge numbers of newly unemployed accessing social welfare, at the risk again of neglecting long-term unemployed people whose opportunities to gain access to work were already very limited. Policy interest in this group has continued to be minimal, reflecting the overwhelmed nature of public policy and interest at present.[27]

Carmel Duggan is continuing to work in creating reports and research to maximise the impact of the projects and disseminate the learning from MSTEI. The immediate benefit to the participants and their families is already evident. It is hoped that when the outcomes of MSTEI are fully reported upon they will have a lasting impact on policy in addressing poverty linked to unemployment.

25. Lorraine Hennessey of INOU, interview with the author, June 2013.

26. Carmel Duggan, interview with the author, May 2013.

27. Margaret Barry, interview with the author, April 2013.

In September 2010 the trustees funded two new projects through Community Foundation of Ireland (CFI), First Step, and the Community Growers Fund. First Step was a micro-finance company providing loans of up to €25,000 to new start-up businesses who had been refused bank finance. MSCT provided funding for one part-time staff member to promote First Step and help mentor applicants. At the conclusion of the project eight new businesses had been established, creating fourteen full-time and nine part-time jobs with the potential of creating eight additional positions in the following two years.[28] The trustees were happy with such a positive outcome from their small amount of funding.

The Community Growers Fund project, which was run by Grow It Yourself (GIY), was created with the aim of assisting the unemployed by encouraging them to become involved in community gardens. GIY is a registered charity founded in 2009 which encourages, supports, and promotes people's growing their own food. Four separate rounds of applications were received over three years with a mixture of new and existing community gardens being given grants from €500 to €10,000. Ciaran Walsh of GIY estimated that there were now over double the 240 unemployed people involved in the gardens in 2011.[29] The gardens provide a resource for the community and a meeting place for mothers, children, the unemployed and retired persons.[30] Ciaran Walsh said that it was wonderful to see 'the enthusiasm the participants have for the betterment of their community.'[31] One of the project organisers said, 'Overall the garden gives a new opportunity and dimension to life in Fettercairn.'[32] Gilbert Strouts of Fettercairn reported on some of the participants:

28. Minutes of the MSCT, January 2013. The private collection of Peter Perrem.

29. Ibid.

30. Ibid.

31. Ciaran Walsh, 'Community Grower's Fund,' *Grow: The GIY Magazine* (2012).

32. Communicated by Ciaran Walsh, project manager of the Community Growers Fund, to the author, 15 April 2013.

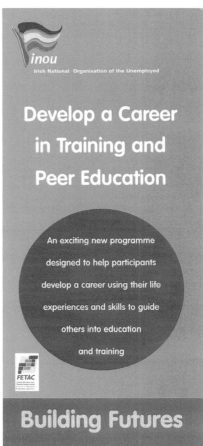

(left) Andrew Montague, Lord Major of Dublin, and INOU graduate
Michelle Seymour. 2011.
(right) INOU Building Futures brochure. 2011.

Community Growers Fund, Mud Island. 2011.

Community Growers Fund, Fettercairn. 2011.

Lena comes from Latvia and lives in Fettercairn...Lena sees the garden as a place where she can come if she is feeling down, a place where she feels included in the community.

Sean is the mainstay of the garden, the 'head gardener'... The local Fettercairn kids and youth call into the garden and help out. Often Sean finds the kids calling to his house at weekends asking when he is next going over to the garden.[33]

Some of the gardens had a particular community focus. For example, the Clondalkin Global Gardening Club in Corkagh Park was established to enable the resident asylum-seekers to grow their own food. This was particularly positive as asylum-seekers are prohibited from seeking employment and some may have experience in growing their own food in the past.

According to Ciaran Walsh of GIY, community gardens 'help unemployed people learn something new and it empowers them because they are making a contribution to a bigger project.' Charlie Delap added, 'those people might have the confidence to go across the city to volunteer for something else.'[34]

Bill Somerville-Large, a trustee and son of a founder has said:

I am sure that he [P. T. Somerville-Large] would be most pleased particularly by the allotments schemes which are being funded by the Trust in the Dublin area.[35]

Conclusion

The Mount Street Club Trust had spent the years 2006 to 2008 transforming itself into a philanthropic trust which would remain true to the principles and objectives of the original club. They spent a great deal of time considering the

33. Ibid.

34. Gabriell Monaghan, 'Dig your way out of the dole queue,' *Sunday Times*, 10 October 2010.

35. Bill Somerville-Large, interview with the author, 4 April 2013.

best way to spend their fund, generated from the sale of their Fenian Street premises. During these years Ireland's prosperity and unprecedented high employment rates ended abruptly and unemployment figures soared. The trustees responded by searching out innovative projects that targeted those most likely to suffer from long-term unemployment and poverty. Many of these projects are still ongoing and their final assessments and evaluations are incomplete at this time. The common theme for all of their projects is the desire to target those at risk of poverty and unemployment within the communities, either through training towards employment, education, mentoring and career guidance, funding of community gardens, or improvement of childcare, education, and community supports. In accordance with their objectives they funded 'projects geared to meet current day needs' and 'which provide basic skills and training, rehabilitation, [and] education.'[36]

> I think my father would be pleased that the Mount Street Club, which he and Jim Waller founded in 1934, is still benefiting the unemployed in 2013.[37]

36. *Cy-près* scheme, 7 August 2007, copy held at the office of the Commission of Charitable Donations and Bequests in Ireland.

37. Bill Somerville-Large, interview with the author, 4 April 2013.

Grow Your Own Future course participants at work. 2011.

THE MOUNT STREET CLUB EXPERIENCE: PERSONAL STORIES
X
Colin Murphy

'One of the last that's still in it': Patrick Cummins

'What age do you think I am?' challenges Patrick Cummins, sitting in the living room of a Salvation Army accommodation centre in Dublin. 'I'm gone 90 since the first of December. Born in 1922. I'm gone 90.' In case I don't believe it, he offers proof: 'I have a passport up there.'

His walk is slow but steady and his mind is sharp, though his memory is erratic. 'Things that happened a year ago, you don't remember at all.'

I ask about his childhood. 'I'll tell you what I remember. I was born with a club foot. I was here two years in Clontarf General Hospital.' Were either of his parents with him? 'No, I was left there. I was born down in the west of Ireland. They put you in and left you there. I was two years there. But the strange thing was, I remember my father calling for me to take me home. I was only four years of age. I didn't want to go. I think the nurses had to persuade me. At four years of age. The hospital was my home. I didn't know who my father was.'

His parents were from Sligo; he knew one of his grandparents, who was from Mayo originally. He had two younger brothers, now dead, and has six sisters living abroad, four in London and two in Canada. The family lived on a farm in Curry, Co. Sligo, near the Mayo border. 'Well, they called it a farm but it was only a few acres.' What was on it? 'Cows. And a horse to work there. That's all.' It was fourteen acres, he says.

He left school at fourteen, then worked on the farm. Was it a good school? 'Ah, sure they're all the same. There was some subjects you would like and there were others, you weren't as keen on them. Everybody'd be like that.'

Does he remember the war breaking out? 'I do. There was a lot pro-Germany. It was either that or the Black and Tans—they were only a few years [past].' In other words, people saw the choice as being between supporting Germany or supporting the British, whose 'Black and Tans' forces were notorious for their attacks on civilians during the War of Independence, just twenty years earlier. He clarifies: 'I wouldn't say the majority was pro-Germany, but it was some.'

In 1942 he left for England. Why? 'Sure they were all going to England that time. There was no work in Ireland. And the West of Ireland was worse; Dublin was bad too. There was no work for people in Ireland.'

He spent three years there, working at the Colwick sugar factory in Nottingham from 'the back end of September or October' to February, and then on farms in the neighbouring county of Lincolnshire in the summers. In Nottingham he shared accommodation with other Irish men; on the farms the labourers would be Irish and English. Did he enjoy living there? 'It was all right. Sure, lookit here: there's not much difference between this place and that place, once you settle in with the people.'

Was it hard to make a living? 'The money that time was different to the money now. You'd be getting a great wage if you were getting £20 a week.' Did he send wages home? 'Some of it.'

What about the war—was there any danger of conscription into the British army? 'You had an exemption for two years. De Valera was in power at that time and he had made some agreement: they couldn't call up the Irish. You had to be there two years [to be called up].' So how did he manage to stay for three years? 'You could come back and break the three years. That's what I did.'

He knew some men who signed up and 'went abroad' with the British army. Others 'did their term in the army and their training and then before they were sent out abroad, they got leave of absence and they could come back to Ireland—and some of them didn't go back. And when they went back, they got a passport under a different name.'

He came home, and then went back to England for another three years, finally returning to Ireland in 1949, even though there was 'plenty of work...

They had to rebuild England.' So why did he come back? He laughs: 'Ha, ha You're asking all the questions…' He won't say.

The family farm has since been sold. Does he miss Sligo? 'Ah no. You see, lived there after my parents died. You live in a house on your own, it's very— How shall I put it? If you stayed there, the next year, you'd be talking to the walls.' Did he have good neighbours? 'They're all doing their own stuff. And let you do your own. They're not going to carry you on their back.'

His comments recall an observation in the Senate debate on the Mount Street Club in 1939, when the proposer of the debate, Professor Joseph Johnston, commented on 'the isolation which is part and parcel of the small farmer mentality.'[1]

Patrick Cummins left Sligo in the 1960s, but didn't come straight to Dublin. 'Well, now I did a bit of travelling, here and there.' He is deliberately enigmatic. 'My story and somebody else's story is different. There might be something solid to my story and not something solid to another story.'

He came to Dublin in 1972, and heard about the Mount Street Club farm at Larkfield. 'I heard a rumour going around: there was good work…The condition there was you worked for your food. They didn't pay you.' There was then 'fourteeen or fifteen' men living on the farm, of different ages, from Dublin and around the country.

He worked in the dairy. Milking? 'No,' he laughs, 'I wasn't milking. All I had to do was separate the cream from the milk. Sure, I'd do my job in an hour or an hour and a half.'

They lived in the 'big house.' 'We were in a big room; the beds were all one after the other…The big house was a bit rough.' He clarifies: 'I don't mean the behaviour. It was a rough house: very old; big thick walls. Vermin running around on the floor: mice and rats. That's why they knocked it down. It must have been infested with rats.'

For diversion the men went into nearby Clondalkin. They were allowed

1. *Seanad Éireann deb.*, xxiv, col. 303 (13 December 1939).

Mount Street Club Farm. 1941.

drink ('There was no control over you and that way you can do what you like', but that wasn't a particular feature of life there. 'It was a quiet place—the general way people goes on.' Would he go to the pub? 'No pints. I usen't to go into any pubs. I used to buy cans, maybe five or six cans and have one a night. But I had to give it up.' Were he and the other men at the farm friends? 'You'd be doing your own things. At the end of the day, you'd have a bit of a chat. We had a television.'

He knew of the club's facilities on Mount Street. 'It was a club where the men used come in and they used send them out to anyone who wanted a few hours' work gardening or whatever. I never did that. I used go into the club. They used make you a cup of tea and a few biscuits. You'd put in an hour's time; bit of a chat.'

When the farm closed, he and the other men moved into the Iveagh Hostel and later he moved to the Back Lane Hostel, before moving in to the Salvation Army's centre in the early 1990s. Did he stay in touch with the other men? 'I used meet them now and again but they died off...I'd say that I'm one of the last that's still in it.'

He never got married nor had children. Did he like his independence? 'It happened that way anyway.'

Since he returned to Ireland from England, he has been back to London on holidays, and has also travelled in Italy and to Fátima in Portugal. Is he a man of faith? 'I just go to church, but I'm not very avid....I do my duties. I look at it like this: when I go, if there's anything in it, I'll be right for it...if there's any such thing as the afterworld.' He was last abroad in October 2012 (aged 89), on a group tour to Italy.

He keeps busy: he has a well-practiced daily routine. He gets himself breakfast in his apartment at the centre (which provides supported accommodation), then goes out into the city. 'You want a little bit of exercise.' He takes the bus and the Luas rail line, using 'the free travel,' and visits the main stations, Connolly, Busaras, and Heuston, where he finds newspapers. He does the Simplex crossword in the *Irish Times* and follows Gaelic sports and the Irish occer team. He thinks manager Giovanni Trapattoni 'doesn't have the players ight'; although, like the rest of the country, he enjoys Trapattoni's Italian nannerisms and 'little gestures with the hands.' He returns from town for linner at half past four, skipping lunch. 'Two meals is enough for you.'

He has been interviewed about the Mount Street Club before and is politely)emused at my interest in his life. My gentle prodding fails to provoke any urther stories: the memories are there, but he is discreet. Meanwhile, the norning is moving on. 'I've to go over and get cleaned up and go out.' He walks me to the door, and heads on to his apartment.

'The Mount Street Club saved us': Peter Geraghty

Peter Geraghty was born on Cumberland Street, Dublin, in 1908, into a 10use that was home to seven families totalling thirty-nine people. The other families lived in one room each; the Geraghtys managed to have two. Peter's father, Thomas, was a labourer and volunteered as a verger in St Andrew's Church on Westland Row. At the time of the 1911 census, Thomas and his wife, Mary, had eight children, of whom Peter was the youngest. His eldest)rother, Jack, fought in the First World War.

According to family lore, the house on Cumberland Street collapsed at some)oint after that, and the family moved to a derelict house on Lower Mount Street, number 74, which had been boarded up.

Lower Mount Street had been well-to-do—at the time of the 1911 census, there were just two families living in number 74 and next door was a hotel. But that side of the street then fell into decline. By the 1930s number 74 was occupied by fourteen families.

After moving to Mount Street, Peter met a girl from Ballybay in Monaghan, Annie Markey, who was working as a servant in a nearby house. According to the 1911 census return, Annie had grown up in a three-room, single-family house. Annie got pregnant and they married. They would have nine further children; all but one survived childhood.

Initially Peter and Annie reared their family in one room at the top of

Peter Geraghty and his wife, Annie, on their wedding day.

number 74; later they acquired the room next door as well. A number of Peter's siblings also lived in the same house with their families.

Peter first joined the Mount Street Club after a time in the National Army, in the 1930s. (An elder brother, Jack, had served in the Royal Dublin Fusiliers in the First World War.) He went to England to work during the Second World War and resumed his membership of the club when he returned. In the 1950s the family moved to a new Dublin Corporation house in Milltown but Peter continued to come to the club, cycling in daily and tying any goods he acquired to the bicycle frame for the cycle home. He died after a stroke in 1967.

Anna Geraghty, his daughter born in 1937, left for England in 1958 and stayed; she lived in Birmingham until her death in 2012. Peter's son, Peadar, born in 1944, lives in Clondalkin, coincidentally very near the location of the Mount Street Club farm, which later became Rowlagh housing estate. Both Anna and Peadar were active in the children's activities at the Mount Street Club and have clear memories of growing up in the tenement. This story is based on their account, augmented by that of their younger brother, Victor.

There was one toilet, a wooden one, and one sink in number 74, located in the basement. The toilet 'stank to high heaven,' recalled Anna, but it was grim for another reason too: one of the residents had hanged himself from the cistern. A family story tells how the Geraghtys' aunt, who lived in the basement, took the dead man's shoes off his feet and pawned them. The story may be apocryphal, but that it was told at all illustrates the extent of the poverty.

The Geraghtys kept a bucket for a toilet in their room, behind a curtain; this would be carried down to the basement to be emptied a number of times a day. Anna remembered having to carry it by night, in the dark. They filled a white enamel bucket from the basement sink to have water for washing and cooking in their room. They used jam jars for cups. The hall door didn't lock: 'You'd come down in the morning and there'd be a few lads sleeping in the hall, down and outs,' remembered Peadar; Anna added, 'If you had a front door that closed, you were posh.'

When the family acquired a second room, Anna and her sister went to sleep in it. But the room was rat-infested, and Anna's sister woke one night to feel rat running across her neck. 'Every room in the house had a cat. There was no cat food. It was, "catch it or do without."'

Tuberculosis was rife: Anna lost a friend to it in her early teens and contracted it herself. She spent 'a year in bed,' she recalled, and recovered. Peadar survived scarlet fever.

Breakfast consisted of tea with bread and jam; the evening meal was much the same. After school, the children went to the Penny Dinners on Holles Row (now St Brigid's Food Centre, run by the Catholic diocesan social care agency Crosscare). Peadar remembers 'a big bench with about three hundred kids sitting on it.'

'Every day it was stew. And you had to eat everything. If you didn't eat it—There was a guy walking around to keep an eye on it. You'd have to eat the rashers with the hairs and all on it.' As they were leaving, they got 'a slice of Swiss roll' as 'a treat.' Anna remembered the dinners as 'every kind of gristle in a stew.'

Still, 'the Penny Dinner in Holles Row kept us going,' says Peadar. 'That was our main meal of the day. If you hadn't got the penny, they still fed you.'²

Their father, Peter, went regularly to the Mount Street Club, though he wasn't a social type and apparently suffered from depression after the death of his son, Pearse, who drowned in the nearby canal in 1946, aged seven. Two weeks later, when his body was found, Peter had to identify him. He never recovered. Anna recalled that he had violent rages at times.

Nonetheless, their younger brother, Victor, recalls his father talking fondly, in later years, about the club and the camaraderie there. As well as work at the club, he would earn cash for gardening and occasional odd jobs, such as window cleaning, which were organised through the club.

The children got involved in activities at the club. Peadar joined the boxing club, which had a proper ring in the basement. Anna went to sewing classes there, and she and her sisters joined a children's band; they gave concerts in the

1all in the club and played at the annual performing arts festival, the Father Matthew Feis. She recalls playing 'Blaze Away,' the song made famous by Josef Locke. There was a 'cracking' Christmas party every year and the children would be taken carol singing around Dublin, on the back of a truck, to raise money for the club.

Peter brought home his tallies earned at the club and they would gather in a pile on the mantlepiece. (Anna kept one until her death.) Often, he bought food with them: fresh vegetables and milk from the farm, or sometimes meat. 'Once, he brought home a complete cow's head,' recalled Anna. 'He got the chopper and chopped it up in pieces to make a broth and a stew.' Other times, he saved up the tallies to exchange for a piece of furniture from the club's warehouse on the back lane, which had been donated by 'well-to-do people' from the likes of Mount Merrion and Foxrock, remembers Peadar. He was thrilled when, one day in the early 1960s, Peter came home with a present of some golf clubs.

'Without the Mount Street Club we would have starved,' said Anna. 'They put food in our bellies.' The family relied on other organisations too: the Society of Saint Vincent de Paul provided clothes and sometimes 'a few bob'; the Herald Boot Fund gave footwear. Both, though, had their donations branded: the boots were stamped with 'HB' on the sole and the jumpers and coats provided by 'the Vinny man' had a blue stripe, 'so you couldn't pawn them or sell them.'

The Mount Street Club was both part of this charitable infrastructure and apart from it. As Peadar recalls it: 'The Geraghtys weren't the only ones that used the Mount Street Club [and other charities]. The whole street used it. But people were kind of ashamed to say they were using it—that they were

2. A quarter of a million 'penny dinners' (or other meals) per month were being provided in Dublin in the early 1940s by various religious organisations, coordinated by the Catholic Social Service Conference, which had been set up in 1941 by the Archbishop, John Charles McQuaid. In 1946, McQuaid would claim, 'In this city no one need suffer the dread of hunger.' (J. H. Whyte, *Church and state in modern Ireland 1923-1979* (2nd ed., Dublin, 1980), pp. 77-8.

lowering their standards. But the Mount Street Club were different, totally [to the others]. They gave men somewhere to go. To me, there's no stigma about the Mount Street Club; I didn't see it as a stigma.' Other sources of support included the Sick and Indigent Roomkeepers' Society (which had been founded 'for the relief of the poor' in 1790) and the local Catholic church St Andrew's, on Westland Row.

The pawn shop was another vital institution: the local shop was on Grattan Street. Peadar remembers the routine: 'You'd go in the front door and do your business and go out by the side door into the lane, so people wouldn't see you coming out the pawn shop.

'My mother pawned my father's shoes every week—they were pure leather— and the suit. She'd bring them in on a Monday and they'd give her a couple of pence, not a fortune; on Friday, when she had the money, she'd take the stuff out again, and my father'd wear them for mass on Sunday; and then they'd go back in again Monday.'

'The street was our playground,' said Anna. Play involved 'skipping on lampposts and scutting on carts,' but also 'streetfighting': 'it was very rough, you had to stick up for yourself.' They didn't play in the nearby Merrion Square. 'You'd go up to the railings and they'd say, "Shoo! Get out of there,"' recalls Peadar. 'The archbishop of Dublin owned the square and the residents had a key, but the lower classes weren't allowed in.'

Growing up on Mount Street 'was a great education,' says Peadar. Hardship taught him the virtue of hard work: 'I've never been unemployed in my life. I left school at fourteen and started working on the Monday.' And there was solidarity amidst that hardship: 'People were different then. People looked out for one another. Everybody was in the same boat.' 'They were rough times but they were good,' said Anna. 'We didn't consider ourselves poor.'

Seamus O'Flanagan

Rev. Seamus O'Flanagan was a member of the Mount Street Club in the 1950s. Here he tells his story:

I was brought up in inner city Dublin, in Dorset Street, in the early 1930s, during the depression. They were very hard times. In school I was one of few boys with a pair of boots: I remember many children in their bare feet, suffering with rickets and often hungry. I went to Saint Joseph's School on Dorset Street from 1934 to 1943. I left with a basic education to become an apprentice in ladies' tailoring as a hand presser and learned some sewing skills. But by the late 1940s, trade was rather bad in the high-class trade; I was made part time and then was unemployed for some time. I was now almost homeless as both my parents were deceased. I made contact with the Mount Street Club and went and had an interview. They suggested I join them on their farm in Cherry Orchard until a vacancy occurred in their tailoring section.

In early 1950 I was collected in the club and taken to the farm by horse and cart. I thought this would be just for a few weeks, but I spent over twelve happy and productive months in the farm house. They also had a cottage accommodating a further six farm workers. I spent all my time on the farm helping with the growing and reaping of crops. I also looked after the feeding and cleaning out the cattle sheds. I spent a period of time in the greenhouse learning to grow tomatoes and summer fruits. The head gardener was a very experienced man. He taught me a lot about market gardening, which came in handy in later life, bringing up a family. The farm was well run by a supervisor who detailed your jobs for that day. We had our own laundry man, cooks, cleaners, tractor drivers, farm horse, donkeys, and a horse and cart delivering milk and food to the club in Dublin and bringing back any items needed on the farm.

We had a lot of young men from England and Wales who were evading the call-up staying on the farm doing different jobs, some skilled tradesmen amongst them. Our head chef had worked in one of the top hotels in London. He laid on a couple of banquets when we had some special visitors, and then he wore his chef's hat. We earned our tallies by the hours we worked and used them to buy clothing and other items. If we worked out of hours the foreman paid us in cigarettes or sweets or chocolate bars. The farm was run by a manager who (I think) was Mr Brophy, and his assistant.

Christmas and Harvest Suppers were great occasions with plenty of food and entertainment, mostly amongst ourselves. We had some great natural comedians. We were very self-sufficient and economical in our living. We had fires made from sawdust packed in old oil drums; they gave out great heat. We even cooked on them outside; inside, they were better than our modern central heating. Turf was very scarce after the war, and rationed. We also had a small wood, a copse, where we felled our own timber. We had an extensive piggery with two men employed boiling potatoes and mixing grains for the pigs. We had a bull and a number of cattle, all Herefords, both for milk and stock cattle for beef. I remember two men milked by hand, twice daily!

We finished work at 4 p.m., summer and winter. After tea we had our radio and papers—there was no television in those days. We had a snooker table and a tennis table. Most of us read a lot from the library or went for walks on Sunday, or our day off, to Clondalkin or Lucan. Sometimes we had a drink. No alcohol was allowed in the house. During the season, on my day off, which was Monday, I went cutting sugar beet or mangels for local farmers who were glad of our help: it paid for little extras or else I saved a little for when I left the farm.

In 1951 a vacancy became available for me to go to the tailoring section in Mount Street where I had a suit made to measure for me, which I paid for with my tallies: it was a good quality, bespoke (hand made) suit; you would not get that type of suit in your city shops today. I did some of the sewing and all the under pressing and top pressing. The tailor was a qualified man.

By the end of that year, 1951, passports were no longer needed to go to England, so in February 1952 I emigrated, aged 22. I worked for many years in the ladies' fashion trade as a top presser using hand irons. I became very well known amongst some well-known designers for my quality of work. When I lived in London, I worked for two years in Savile Row, in a world-famous gents' outfitters. I did not return home for over twenty years.

I studied and trained for the ministry at the age of 48 and was ordained as a non-conformist pastor. During this time, I got married to a lady pastor, had a family of six children, and travelled throughout the UK. I retired from the ministry at 65 and went into business for myself, in dry cleaning. I won an award for my quality of work and customer service. I finally retired at age 72. My period on the Mount Street Club farm and in the club taught me a lot as a young man. I am now 83, and still involved in community work locally. I am still a regular choir member and active in church affairs.

Work to do

An essay in *Work to do*, a book published by the Mount Street Club in 1945,[3] gives further insight into the roles of charity and state assistance in providing for the living expenses of families such as the Geraghtys. The author, an unnamed governor of the club, described a typical family and estimated their weekly income and expenditure. His model family lived in a two-room flat on the top floor of a tenement; the father was an unemployed builder's labourer; they had three children. This family received an income of roughly thirty-nine shillings per week, comprising the 'dole' (unemployment assistance), children's allowance, local authority food vouchers, and additional support known as home assistance (or able-bodied relief). Using other studies, the author calculated that, after other necessary expenses, this family would spend 18s. 8½d. per week on food. This was far less than what they needed to spend, however: he cited a contemporary study which found that such a family would need to spend forty-three shillings per week on food in order to meet its nutritional requirements.

In a comment revealing of the tenor of some of the debates around social assistance at the time, the author observed: 'Even if allowance is made for the fact that an unemployed man lives a less active life and may be expected to eat less than one fully employed—and this appears to us to be arguing in a particularly vicious circle—the gap between what John's family should spend on food and the eighteen to twenty shillings per week that they do in fact spend is sufficiently startling.'

The author did not argue that this gap was of no concern to public policy makers: 'The state has never claimed that national or public assistance alone can enable a man to live, even in "frugal comfort." The state assumes, and has never been disappointed, that voluntary organisations will always be at hand to supplement its allowances.'

So who were these voluntary organisations? 'The various food centres, supplying hot meals for children and adults...the activities of the Society of St Vincent de Paul, of the Sick and Indigent Roomkeepers' Society, of the St John's Ambulance Brigade, with its work for mothers and babies; the Mansion House Coal Fund, the Herald Boot Fund, the Guild of Goodwill, the Catholic Social Service Conference.'

He concluded: 'The inescapable fact remains that large numbers of able-bodied men must at present rely to some extent on charity to keep themselves and their families from want.'

3. *Work to do: a survey of the unemployment problem* (Dublin, 1945).

With the Compliments
of the
Mount Street Club

62/64 Fenian Street,
Dublin 2.   *Telephone 761838.*

Fenian Street Stationery. 1980.

THE MOUNT STREET CLUB IN A CHANGING IRELAND

XI

Mary E. Daly

The Mount Street Club forms part of a long-established tradition of philanthropy and voluntary service in Irish civic society. Throughout the nineteenth century many leading Dublin businesses made annual donations to hospitals, orphanages, and other good causes. Business and professional men served as trustees or on fund-raising committees for voluntary bodies. Their wives and daughters organised the elaborate bazaars, pageants, and concerts, which combined philanthropic giving with glittering social occasions—an experience beautifully captured in James Joyce's story 'Araby,' a fantasy bazaar in the Royal Dublin Society's showgrounds in Ballsbridge to raise money for Jervis Street Hospital.[1] The fundraising activities of the Mount Street Club Society, such as Lilac Day, and the special performances of *The Mikado* and other musicals followed a familiar pattern; likewise the contributions in kind or in money given to the club by leading city businesses.

While Dublin in the 1930s did not lack voluntary institutions, the decision to establish the club was prompted by the economic crisis of the 1930s. The Wall Street crash of October 1929 brought to an end the fevered economic speculation of the 1920s—a speculation that had little direct impact on Ireland. The Great Depression that followed resulted in falling prices, mass unemployment, and increased poverty across large sections of the globe. Governments, economists, intellectuals, and voluntary organisations searched for new ways to address mass unemployment and its social and personal consequences: some of the debates and ideas of the 1930s bear an uncanny echo of more recent discussions about the post-2008 international crisis. When the Depression began, it was seen as mainly affecting the more industrialised economies. In his radio addresses to the Irish in the United States and Britain to mark St Patrick's Day in 1931, W. T. Cosgrave, President of the Executive Council of the Irish Free State,[2] claimed that Ireland was 'one of the few countries relatively unaffected by the present crisis'; 'exports consisting principally of agricultural products, had escaped to an appreciable extent the adversity which has overtaken world prices in the commodities of other industries'; the adverse trade balance continued to fall; average unemployment in October 1930 was 50 per cent lower than in 1922.[3] These statements were misleading; the volume and value of Ireland's trade was falling; the prices paid for agricultural produce were plummeting, businesses were closing; government revenue was declining, remittances from Irish emigrants in the United States and Britain were dwindling, and emigration was no longer an option for Ireland's poor and unemployed. Indeed some emigrants were returning to Ireland in the belief that they would be better off at home than among the millions of unemployed in the United States.

Chronic unemployment and under-employment in Dublin did not begin with the 1930s depression; it was a feature of city life throughout the nineteenth century, and probably for centuries before. Many Dublin working men were casual labourers, who might get two or three days' work in a week as dock labourers; and perhaps a spell of work on building sites, punctuated by periods with no work because of bad weather or a slump in the building cycle. Men who were sick or injured often went for long periods without employment, and as men became older the spells without work became longer. In the early 1930s the volume of trade passing through Dublin port fell, partly as a consequence

1. For a description of the spectacle which attracted almost 100,000 visitors, see Stephanie Rains, 'Joyce's "Araby" and the historical Araby Bazaar, 1894,' in *Dublin James Joyce Journal*, no. 1 (2008), pp. 17-29.

2. The term 'Taoiseach' only came into use following the adoption of the 1937 Constitution.

3. NAI Taois/ S5111/7 and 8, Broadcast messages by the President. The proportion of the workforce making social insurance contributions was small, and entitlement to unemployment insurance benefit was limited to six months, so the numbers registered as unemployed fell because of the rise in long-term unemployment.

of the international depression, but also because trade between Britain and Ireland was disrupted by the Economic War.[4] This dispute meant less work for Dublin's dockworkers. At the same time an ambitious government housing programme created additional jobs in the building industry, and many new factories opened around the city to take advantage of the protective tariffs introduced by the Fianna Fáil government, though these factories tended to hire young and often female workers, rather than adult men. In 1934 the government introduced unemployment assistance, which was paid to those who were unemployed, yet did not qualify for unemployment insurance. So it is not entirely clear whether unemployment and poverty in Dublin was actually worse in 1934 than ten years earlier. Nevertheless the Mount Street Club is very much a product of the 1930s depression.

While the club was unique in Ireland, many similar clubs were established in Britain around the same time. They were concentrated in South Wales, Lancashire, and the North-East of England—the areas that were most seriously affected by long-term unemployment. The clubs that opened in more prosperous regions appear to have been less successful, because there were fewer long-term unemployed and therefore greater turnover of members. By the late 1930s there were so many clubs for the unemployed in Britain, that *Men without work*, an investigation of the impact of long-term unemployment, devoted a long section of its report to 'the club movement.'[5] Jim Waller may well have suggested the name Mount Street Club as an amusing reference to the Kildare Street Club (see p. 30), but the concept of a club for the unemployed was well-established in Britain by 1934.

All the clubs described in *Men without work* share common features with

---

4. This trade dispute between Britain and Ireland began in August 1932 when the Irish government refused to pay back money owed to Britain as part of the financial settlement relating to independence. This was at a time when Britain had renegotiated its repayments of debts incurred to the United States because of the First World War. In retaliation Britain imposed tariffs on Irish goods entering Britain. The dispute ended in 1938.

5. Pilgrim Trust, *Men without work* (Cambridge, 1938), p. 298.

THE

MOUNT STREET CLUB

JOURNAL

Vol. 2. No. 1.   May, 1940.

"Digging for Victory" against unemployment.

the Mount Street Club. Membership was confined to unemployed men—a small number of women's clubs also existed—but there were no mixed clubs. Members had to leave the club when they found a job. Members paid for all services through some form of tally system. Most clubs offered meals, newspapers, gymnastics or some form of physical exercise, card games, darts and billiards, a wireless, and often a choir, music lessons, and amateur theatricals. All the clubs described in this book gave members the opportunity to do carpentry, boot repair, and occasionally other tasks. All the clubs had gardens or allotments where members grew vegetables and fruit. Poultry keeping, which featured in the Mount Street Club, was also common; a number of clubs had a farm or some residential space in a rural area where members could go for a period of more intensive physical exercise or education and training. Peter Somerville-Large has found evidence that the Mount Street Club was aware of the Brynmawr Experiment, a voluntary programme in South Wales which was initiated by the Society of Friends, but it is very possible that the founders were aware of other clubs, perhaps in Liverpool, a city that had close commercial links with Dublin.

The English and Welsh clubs had a variety of financial and governance arrangements. In the Rhondda Valley of South Wales, for example, the unemployed clubs grew out of an established tradition of workingmen's clubs, and the Rhondda clubs jealously guarded their independence—they were wholly controlled by an elected committee of members, and they tolerated no oversight or advice from outsiders. Clubs in other areas were closer to the Mount Street Club model, with a committee of members determining who should be admitted and overseeing the day-to-day running of the club, a committee of patrons, and a paid warden responsible for finances and more strategic decisions. In England, clubs were often adopted by companies or professional organisations, which provided money or goods, and were represented on the board of governors. The underlying motivation for all clubs was similar: the recognition that unemployment did not simply mean a shortage of money; unemployment also brought with it serious psychological, physical, and social consequences. Men who had worked in physically strenuous jobs became physically unfit; depression and social isolation were common features of life for unemployed men. (There would appear to have been an implicit belief that unemployed women were less affected because they had domestic and family duties.) For men who suffered long-term unemployment, membership of a club restored their sense of belonging to a community and helped them to retain their dignity and a modicum of personal independence.[6] The club atmosphere—empowering members to accept or reject applicants—strengthened this sense of community. This model probably worked well in the tight-knit communities of Dublin's working class tenements, where families often survived personal and financial crises through the support of their neighbours, and where most people married a near neighbour and often spent their life in the community where they were born. The club also offered men an alternative to going to the pub. Sir Charles Cameron, who was Medical Officer of Health for Dublin for many decades, once described the pub as 'the working man's club.' The restriction of membership to men—with women and children only admitted for special occasions—reflected social life in 1930s Ireland, irrespective of geography or social class: there were no women members of the Kildare Street Club either.

Many of the guiding principles behind the Mount Street Club were in tune with contemporary thinking in the Ireland of the 1930s, most especially the belief that the unemployed should be provided with work; that providing work was morally superior to giving them a dole. The general election of 1932 brought a change of government—with a minority Fianna Fáil government kept in office by the support of Labour TDs. By the early summer of 1932 that government was determined to provide work for the unemployed.[7] The government remained committed to that principle until the mid to late 1930s;

6. The information relating to British clubs is based on Pilgrim Trust, *Men without work*, pp. 272-386.

7. Mary E. Daly, 'The Irish Free State and the Great Depression of the 1930s: the interaction of the global and the local,' *Irish Economic and Social History*, xxviii, pp. 19-36.

Harrowing with Ferguson tractor. 1941.

PRODUCTION
3 MONTHS ENDING DEC. 31st 1939

BAKERY : 4½ lb. loaves	2,436	
MEALS	38,071	
SOCKS : pairs	127	
BOOTSHOP : Boots (pairs)	45	
TAILORING : Boys knickers	31	
Repair jobs	652	
Overalls	46	
Girls' Coats	2	
Boys' Overcoats	9	
Boys' Suits	6	
Men's Suits	14	
Skirts	2	
Shirts	3	
Men's Overcoats	42	
Men's Trousers	4	
Patchwork Quilt	2	
Rugs covered	4	
Girls' Frocks	33	
Girls' Overcoats	2	
Towels hemmed	57	
Pillow Cases	60	
Repair jobs	59	
WILLOW WORK : Baskets	79	
WEAVING : Mats	8	
Tweed (yards)	5½½	
WOODWORK : Seedboxes	25	
Tables	4	
Forms	10	
Dressers	12	
One hand loom		

Table legs	4
Wardrobes	7
Bookcase	1
Window Frame	1
Presses	2
Drying Rack	1
Chest of Drawers	1
Meat Safe	1
Doors and Frames	3
Child's Dresser	1
Repair jobs	32
FARM : Milk (gals.)	1,190
Butter (lbs)	36¾
Lettuce (doz.)	5
Potatoes (st.)	1,255¾
Cabbage (doz.)	571½
Celery (doz.)	42¾
Turnips (st.)	254
Beans (lbs.)	20
Eggs (doz.)	46
Brussel Sprouts (lbs.)	123
Onions (lbs.)	72
Cauliflowers (doz.)	14¾
Carrots (lbs.)	96
Apples (lbs.)	524
Parsnips (st.)	3
Beef (lbs.)	60
Ducks (heads)	19
Poultry (heads)	5

TALLIES ISSUED		
C. & F.	Kitchens	6,510¼
„	Bakery	1,128½
C.	Tailoring	4,868¼

TALLIES RECOVERED		
C. & F.	Meals	23,796¼
	Wearing Apparel	7,560
	Footwear and Repairs	4,091

Mount Street Club Journal. 1940.

the introduction of unemployment assistance was seen as an interim measure. In his 1934 budget speech Minister for Finance Seán MacEntee announced that the government planned to replace spending on unemployment maintenance with spending on 'socially remunerative work,' including clearing litter, providing public gardens, and similar schemes. An interdepartmental committee of civil servants was established to devise a mechanism for placing as many unemployed men as possible on rotational public works schemes—perhaps three days a week or week on, week off—and then be replaced by another group. A pilot programme was introduced in Limerick, but the plans went no further because the Department of Finance determined that it was actually cheaper to pay unemployment assistance.[8]

There is no indication that the government or the civil service considered asking voluntary organisations to take responsibility for these work schemes for the unemployed, although this might have made them economically feasible. It is interesting to contrast the apparent success of the turf-harvesting camp established by the Mount Street Club during the Emergency years with the difficulties experienced by similar government-run camps. In 1940 over 1,000 unemployed Dublin men aged 18-25 were selected to work on Clonsast Bog in Co. Laois. Only 173 actually turned up at the camp, and half of these abandoned the work—most within a week of arriving; sixteen of the small number remaining were dismissed as slackers.[9] There were of course some key differences between the two groups: the Mount Street Club vetted everybody before they were admitted to the club; the club's turf camp was small in size, and was probably well managed and supervised, by somebody with an interest in the men. Above all, the thirty or forty members of the club who spent several months living on Lullymore bog were there of their own free will.[10] By contrast

8. Mary E. Daly, *The buffer state: the historical roots of the Department of the Environment* (Dublin, 1997), pp, 187-96.

9. Gerry Fee, 'The effects of World War II on Dublin's low-income families 1939-1945,' Ph.D. diss., University College Dublin, 1996, pp. 30-2.

10. See above, chapter 3, p. 98.

the young men assigned to work on the bogs by a Dublin labour exchange were there under duress, and some may have been totally unsuited to this work.

The question arises, why was the Mount Street Club model not copied elsewhere in Ireland? Colin Murphy (p. 122) mentions the Waterford Unemployed Men's Club—were there similar clubs in other towns? By the late 1930s most British clubs were regarded as part of the network of local voluntary services. Many were getting funds or support in kind (such as a premises) from the local authority, and their work was being co-ordinated with other voluntary services through the local branch of the National Social Service Council, which acted as a collaborative forum for voluntary organisations. There was little prospect of a similar organisation in Ireland at this time; many voluntary services were designed to cater for one religious denomination, and competition rather than co-operation was occasionally the dominant motivation. In addition the new Irish state saw itself as rural and agrarian, and the main focus of socio-economic programmes tended to be on improving life in the countryside, not in the city. Cities were regarded as alien to Ireland's culture and heritage; they were viewed as unhealthy places whose growth should be discouraged. This mindset gained additional currency—not just in Ireland—from the belief that the 1930s depression signalled the failure of industrial capitalism, and that governments and voluntary agencies should attempt to move people back to the land. (In the case of Mount Street Club, one may ask whether this idea featured in the decision to buy Larkfield Farm.) In the late 1930s the Irish government came under pressure to provide funds for village halls, which would function as local community centres. There was also a strong drive on the part of the rural development organisation Muintir na Tíre to develop parish guilds or parish councils which would organise a range of community programmes: a local employment exchange, feeding schoolchildren, providing allotments, communal turf-cutting, and other programmes that would foster self-sufficiency in local communities. While these ideas share some common features with the Mount Street Club, their primary aim was the revival of rural Ireland and discouraging emigration or migration to Dublin. Furthermore this movement was strongly associated with Catholic Action and activist priests such as Fr Michael Hayes, the founder of Muintir na Tíre.[11] So despite some evident similarities with the Mount Street Club, any potential alliance would have faced the insurmountable barriers of an anti-urban philosophy and the determination shown by many Catholic clergy to control voluntary services.

The Mount Street Club was a nondenominational organisation, with Protestant and Catholic patrons and governors. It successfully avoided becoming involved in a serious clash with the Catholic hierarchy at a time when denominational divisions were deeply entrenched in Irish philanthropy. The fact that the club membership was confined to adult men, with women and children relegated to attending occasional social events, or using their husband's tallies to purchase food and household goods, was important. Women and children were regarded as vulnerable creatures, whose religious and moral well-being needed protection. In the early 1940s the nondenominational St John's Ambulance Brigade, which had established maternity kitchens to feed undernourished expectant Dublin mothers, found itself facing direct competition with a similar feeding programme established by the formidable Dr John Charles McQuaid, archbishop of Dublin.[12] The nondenominational Civics Institute, which provided playgrounds for the poor children of the inner city, was also a target of criticism from Archbishop's House. But there is no indication that the Catholic Social Services Council, which McQuaid established in the early 1940s to implement a range of welfare programmes—including a maternity feeding programme—gave any consideration to creating an organisation similar to the Mount Street Club. Unlike its counterparts in England and Wales, the club does not appear to have offered lectures to its

11. Maurice Curtis, *The splendid cause: the Catholic Action Movement in Ireland in the twentieth century* (Dublin, 2008), pp. 172, 187-8; Daly, *The buffer state*, pp. 305-11.

12. Lindsey Earner-Byrne, *Mother and child: maternity and child welfare in Dublin*, 1922-60 (Manchester, 2007), pp. 65-4, 96-9.

members on contemporary social questions; this omission may also reflect a wish not to become embroiled in any dispute with the Catholic hierarchy.

Peter Somerville-Large's account suggests that the war years had a significant impact on the club. In the autumn of 1939 there were widespread and justifiable fears that unemployment would soar, especially in Dublin, but these fears were not realised. Many members of the club joined the British and Irish armies; others emigrated to take work in England. Emigration, or rather its absence, was a critical element in the success and popularity of the club during the 1930s. When the club was founded in 1934, emigration was not a realistic option because of the high level of unemployment in Britain. But wartime labour shortages and Irish government restrictions on emigration by men from rural Ireland and small towns—because they were needed for the national tillage programme and for turf-cutting—encouraged emigration from Dublin, Cork, and other Irish cities. This had a major impact on the club. Turnover increased, and it is highly probable that those who left were the most dynamic and active members. By 1940 only one-third of the club's 241 members had been members for longer than three months. According to a contemporary report, 'The young men who are now members of the club are of a different type from those who joined before the war. They are principally young men who could obtain some sort of employment but who would have to leave home to do so, or men who for some reason or other are incapacitated from obtaining ordinary competitive employment. Young men with initiative seldom now appear in the membership.'[13]

The decline in membership which began during the war continued in later years. While the Dublin economy did not experience any long-term prosperity until the 1960s, and indeed suffered a serious recession in the mid and late 1950s, Britain enjoyed almost full employment. Work was plentiful for labourers and skilled construction workers. Dublin building craftsmen and labourers moved to England when times were slack, especially during the winter, returning when jobs became more readily available. The 'young men with initiative' did not stay around long enough to have a serious impact on the club. The practices of self-sufficiency, boot repair, and growing food in allotments, which had been central to the club (and to similar clubs in England and Wales) were no longer in tune with contemporary attitudes. By the 1950s, especially with the introduction of the Beveridge Plan in the United Kingdom, unemployment benefit was increasingly regarded as a right, and the belief that work could or should form part of programmes for the unemployed was no longer fashionable. But while there was a view that the welfare state meant that voluntary organisations were no longer necessary and that philanthropy was redundant, this was not the case, especially in Ireland where the level of welfare payments and the range of state-funded services remained modest, even parsimonious, until the 1970s. Indeed William Beveridge in his book *Voluntary action*, explicitly stated that there would be a continuing need for voluntary services in the welfare state, particularly services that money alone could not buy—such as care for the elderly, the handicapped, or needy children. 'Voluntary action is required to do the things the state should not do.' He was also insistent that voluntary services needed to change continually, to reflect the changing circumstances of society.[14]

The sale of the club's farm and Mount Street premises in the early 1970s prompted a review of the club's work. During the 1960s Dublin city and suburbs expanded much more rapidly and extensively than at any time in the city's history. A rising population, thousands of newly-wed couples in search of modern houses, the boom in office construction, and the creation of new industrial estates transformed the physical environment. The development plan for the Dublin region published in 1967 identified Clondalkin, which was close to Larkfield Farm, as one of the projected new towns that would accommodate the rising population.[15] By 1971 Clondalkin was home to over

13. 'Survey of young male adult members of Mount Street Club,' NAI/Taois, S 11952 , Mount Street Club General File 1944, reproduced in Appendix I of Fee, 'The effects of World War II,' pp. 255-6.

14. William Beveridge, *Voluntary action: a report on methods of social advance* (London, 1948), p. 302.

15. Myles Wright, *The Dublin region: advisory regional plan and final report* (2 vols., Dublin, 1967).

7,000 people, more than double the population in 1961. Mount Street was also prime development land—in the south city, close to Ballsbridge, which changed almost overnight from being an elite residential suburb to become the most sought-after area for office developers, lured there by the opening of the new United States Embassy.

The sale of the farm appears to have been a critical moment for the club. When Larkfield Farm was purchased on the eve of the Second World War, the main objective was to increase the opportunities for members to become more self-sufficient in food and to improve family diets. By the 1970s the farm had assumed a new, initially unintended function, as a long-term home for men who would otherwise have been homeless and lonely; the farm also provided them with useful occupations that gave meaning to their lives. The later years of Larkfield Farm reinforced the message that poverty is not simply a matter of employment versus unemployment, and it pointed the way towards a new mission for the club—providing a hostel and home for elderly men. This idea was in tune with the times: it was only in the 1960s that the Irish state began to identify the elderly as a group with specific needs that went beyond a pension; the first dedicated sheltered housing for the elderly was provided by local authorities, following principles and funding set out in a 1964 White Paper.[16]

In many respects the early 1970s was an ideal time for the club to review and update its mission. A growing economy during the 1960s had resulted in higher tax yields and a significant expansion of social spending. The government's *Third programme: economic and social development 1969-72* emphasised that economic growth must be accompanied by an expansion in social services.[17] With Ireland on the brink of joining the EEC (now the EU), there were expectations that more state money would be available for social spending. The Eastern Health Board (one of a network of regional health boards) was given charge of medical and social services in the Dublin region, and it began to develop a new range of community-based services, often in partnership with local voluntary agencies. The 'mixed economy of welfare,'[18] ith the state providing financial support for services provided by voluntary rganisations, was both a challenge and an opportunity. The 1970s was narked by a shift from institutional care towards care in the community, for ne elderly, those with mental health problems and disabilities, and children n need. This emphasis on community-based services, without any distinction ased on religious denomination, reflected two principles that had informed ne Mount Street Club from its foundation. These changes appeared to offer real opportunity for the club and its hostel to work in collaboration with ne state services. But these were also years of rampant inflation, with prices ising by more than 10 per cent a year, so that it is little surprise that the cost f constructing the planned new hostel proved to be much greater than the apital sum available.

Traditional methods of fundraising were also changing; record inflation ncreased the pressure on all voluntary organisations; higher tax rates educed many people's capacity or willingness to contribute; and many of ne established Dublin firms that had supported the club and other Dublin harities were disappearing. Long-established philanthropic bodies were nerging or closing, and philanthropy was becoming much more professional, ith paid fund-raisers and paid organisers, who spent an increasing amount of heir time negotiating with government agencies, such as the Health Boards, bout programmes and funding or devising original methods of raising money or a good cause.[19] This changing climate of philanthropy proved extremely ifficult for small organisations that lacked the resources to hire professionals.

6. Department of Local Government, *Housing—progress and prospects* (Dublin, 1964), Pr. 7981.

7. Department of Finance, *Third programme: economic and social development 1969-72* (Dublin, 1969), F57/7.

8. Joanna Innes, 'The "mixed economy of welfare" in early modern England: assessment of the options from Hale Malthus (c. 1683-1803)" in Martin Daunton, ed., *Charity, self-interest and welfare in the English past* (London, 996) pp. 139-80.

9. For an analysis of modern voluntary agencies, see Matthew W. Hilton, James McKay, Nicholas Crowther, and ean-François Mouhot, *The politics of expertise: how NGOs shaped modern Britain* (Oxford, 2013).

The focus of voluntary action was also changing, with a greater emphasis on agencies that focused on relieving famine and poverty in developing countries and organisations focusing on women.

The history of the club in the decades since the 1970s reflects the changes that were taking place in Dublin city, and in the wider society. When the club was established in the 1930s, the main focus of organisations targeting the unemployed was on men. Men were regarded as the normal breadwinners—women and children were generally seen as their dependants. Social insurance and welfare systems throughout the western world were based on this principle until the 1980s or later. The second-wave feminism of the 1970s prompted greater consciousness of the specific needs of women and children—and the emergence of a growing number of voluntary organisations run by and for women. The governors of the club offered Fenian Street premises as a possible site for a women's refuge. Further evidence of their wish to meet the changing needs of their local community was their offer to turn the club into a day centre that would meet the needs of the Eastern Health Board, and their support for the Irish Nautical Trust. The mission of the Mount Street Club Trust, which was incorporated in 2006, with its specific references to education and training, reflects a growing awareness of the links between poverty and the lack of education and skills.

Much of the physical and institutional fabric of 1930s Dublin has disappeared. The community where the founding members of the Mount Street Club and their families lived has been transformed; the mills and docks where some members worked are now home to global high-tech companies and a highly educated, cosmopolitan population of young professionals. Most of the voluntary hospitals scattered throughout the city have closed (the National Maternity Hospital—a neighbour of the Mount Street Club—is the obvious exception), as have many of the philanthropic agencies, schools, and church-run institutions that formed a crucial part of Dublin's social fabric. There are fewer men with personal memories of the club in its glory years; no traces survive of Larkfield Farm. Yet there is a continuing need for voluntary ction, for agencies and individuals to work with communities, providing vision and an active response to long-standing and emerging needs. The mphasis that the Mount Street Club placed on community, dignity, and ersonal responsibility remains relevant today.

Between 2007 and 2013 the numbers of unemployed have almost trebled.[20] Against this background it remains a continuing challenge for the trust to se its remaining funds imaginatively and wisely to respond in the spirit of s founders encapsulated in its main objective: "the relief of the effects of isadvantage and poverty associated primarily with unemployment."[21]

One would hope that this relevant and noble objective would be pursued by ther charities when the trust's funds run dry.

GOVERNORS AND TRUSTEES OF THE MOUNT STREET CLUB

* * *

1939

Chairman: P. T. Somerville-Large

Honorary Secretary: J. J. Newcome

Honorary Treasurer: J. McNamara

Governors

J. Harold Aylward

R. W. Archer

Very Rev. W. Burke, Adm.

Dr James Bell

L. V. Bishop

G. N. F. Barry

T. R. Beddy

G. C. H. Crampton

H. A. Delap

Rev. W. T. Grey

G. S. Gamble

G. Harris

R. Hennessy

D. Kellett

J. Lennox

J. T. Mohan

Very Rev. Msgr. Molony, P. P.

W. P. Mulligan

A. O'Donovan-Sheil

A. M. Plumer

Cmdr H. B. Pollock

T. de Vere White

Capt. J. H. Webb

Dr L. B. Somerville-Large

J. H. de W. Waller

* * *

* * *

1964

Chairman: P. T. Somerville-Large
Deputy Chairman: Very Rev. T. O'Neill, Adm.
Honorary Secretary: H. A. Delap
Honorary Treasurer: A. M. Plumer

Governors

J. Harold Aylward

R. W. Archer

G. N. F. Barry

T. R. Beddy

A. C. R. Bewley

L. V. Bishop

A. Ganly

D. Kellett

S. Kirwan

A. Lanigan-O'Keefe

R. Maguire

B. O'Carroll

D. O'Clery

A. O'Donovan-Shiel

D. O'Kelly

G. Shackleton

Capt. J. H. Webb

Dr L. B. Somerville-Large

J. H. de W. Waller

T. de Vere White

A. E. Wilson

* * *

* * *

Trustees of the Mount Street Club Trust from 2007 to present

Chairman: Dr Charles Delap

Honorary Secretary: Tom Nolan

Honorary Treasurer: Pat Morgan

Margaret Barry

Edward Gleeson

Mark Harding

Peter Perrem

Bill Somerville-Large

Bob Carroll	resigned 2009
Prof. Brian Nolan	resigned 2011
Michael McNamara	died April 2008
Dr Michael Ganly	resigned 2009, died 2012

* * *

1975-2006

Managers

G.C. Perrem	Capt. E. Sheehan
Henry Dunne	Denis Murphy
Michael McNamara	

* * *

For every hour a member work
whole, he receives one Mount Stree
not unlike a tram ticket in appe

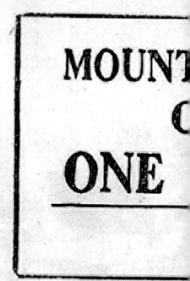

The question at once arises—
be exchangeable for something t
work for one hour to obtain. If it
work will cease and the Club go

LY

is, renders service to the Club as a
This document is a piece of paper,

ET TALLY.

a tally worth ? It must at least
nber considers it worth while to
t command *at least* this par value,
business.

If you do not already s
or one of its

WILL Y

During the year 1940 each shill
Street Club enabled its members t
Workshops, Vegetable Gardens and
food, clothing, footwear and other
families.

Membership during this period
available to provide the necessary ra
number of unemployed men to pa

The unemployment problem is
APPEAL MOST EARNESTLY TO
to make the benefits of this moveme
ployed men *WHO ARE WILLING*

the Mount Street Club,
iated clubs,—

J HELP?

ributed to the funds of the Mount
in return for their work in the Club
Farm) more than 2s. 6d. worth of
ind services for themselves and their

be limited to 250, as funds were not
ials and land to enable a much larger
in this method of self-help.

ng more and more acute, and WE
UBLIC to support us in our efforts
able to the vast numbers of unem-
LP THEMSELVES.